Ecology and Utility

The Philosophical Dilemmas of Planetary Management

Lincoln Allison

Leicester University Press
Leicester and London

© Lincoln Allison, 1991

First published in Great Britain in 1991 by Leicester University Press
(a division of Pinter Publishers Ltd)

Editorial offices
Fielding Johnson Building, University of Leicester,
University Road, Leicester, LE1 7RH

Trade and other enquiries
25 Floral Street, London, WC2E 9DS

British Library Cataloguing in Publication Data
A CIP cataloguing record for this book is available
from the British Library
ISBN 0-7185-1329-0 ✓

Typeset by Witwell Ltd, Southport
Printed and bound in Great Britain

Contents

Foreword

The book started life as an ambition to write a critique of post-socialist or post-industrial radicalism, including feminism, the Green movement and various kinds of rights campaigns. It narrowed to focus only on green thought and became more balanced because some aspects of this tradition and its critique of contemporary society can and must be assimilated into the broad, sceptical utilitarian position from which I write. An important influence was that I went around the world while writing the book, including a period in Australia where the relevant debate is at an advanced stage and where I met 'green' philosophers and trade unionists.

Lincoln Allison

Preface

This is an account of two traditions in human thought, constructed from the point of view of one of them. Utilitarian approaches to policy seek to maximise human well-being. 'Green' or 'ecological' thought reveres nature or it seeks harmony with nature or a balance of nature. There is a fundamental incompatibility between the two, but it is a central theme of this book that utilitarianism has much to learn from 'Green' thought.

The theme is a broad one and, in a general way, I have been working on it for over twenty years. It follows that a bibliography is not an appropriate form of appendage to the argument. Instead I have used the traditional style of notes to present information on sources of quotation, information and argument. Occasionally I have used it to put points which did not fit particularly well into the text. It follows also that it is very difficult to thank people for their help and inspiration in the preparation of the argument. There would be literally hundreds who have informed, stimulated or corrected me and they would include colleagues, in both the broad and narrow senses, students, friends and a variety of professionals.

Thanks are due to two organisations, though. First, the University of Warwick has and maintains a generous system of sabbatical leave which enabled me to take an entire year off to write this book on full pay. Second, the Sir Robert Menzies Centre for Australian Studies offered me a Visiting Fellowship during the year. This enabled me to visit Australia and to travel round the world in doing so. As a result I met many people I would not otherwise have met and saw a wider variety of places than I would otherwise have seen. These experiences were very valuable and I hope they have changed some of my arguments for the better. If it is apparent to the reader that I care more about the English 'environment' than any other, I hope it is also clear that I have heeded Kipling's warning that 'What should they know of England, that only England know?'

Lincoln Allison

1 Two traditions of planetary management

Human beings are animals living on a planet. We are descended from other creatures, we need other creatures, we constantly affect them and are affected by them. We are also 'rational' creatures. This does not mean that we always act rationally or even that we usually act rationally. But it does mean that we have language, that we are capable of stating our wants, perceiving our interests and of forming contracts with one another.

Much of our lives we rely on habit, instinct and tradition as the guides to action. We love and revere each other, but also the things around us. We experience mystery and enchantment, we believe in 'magic'. We treat the earth as if it were a living thing, or a series of living things. But we choose what we do and we are capable of making choices by calculating advantage against disadvantage.

In these two aspects of human 'nature' or being lie the roots of the dichotomy which is at the core of this book. The opposing sides of the dichotomy could be given many different names, but the most useful are 'ecology' and 'utility'. 'Ecology' is a word coined in the nineteenth century, for peculiarly nineteenth century purposes: the same can be argued of 'utility' in respect of its eighteenth century origins. The essence of both as ways of looking at the world vastly pre-dates the concept. The antecedents of utilitarianism can be found in the 'Hedonism' of Aristippus. Arguably they are detectable in Aristotle and a close relation is often alleged to be in the Book of Genesis. Certainly, Shakespeare put utilitarian sentiments into the mouths of his characters. But the precursors of utilitarianism were relatively rare in pre-modern times compared with those of ecology. It has been important to human beings throughout their history (and probably even more important in their pre-history) that they revere nature and conform to Her ways and that they respect the requirements of familiar totems which represent aspects of nature.

In many ways the utilitarian and ecological bases of practical philosophy are in sharp contrast. At the simplest, one tradition says that we revere the planet or at least treat it as if it had rights of its own, irrespective of relation with humans. The opposite tradition says we should use the planet and subject our own activities only to the criteria of efficient use. Jonathan Porritt and Richard Sylvan call these 'grey' and 'green' ways of thinking.[1] The images are complex: 'green' has suggestions of naivety, freshness, spring and the 'celtic' peoples. 'Grey' has usually been a more derogatory word, being used to mean a bore in public school and university slang, but suggestive also of industry, urban life and winter. But, the colours will serve for useful labels, even for me and I intend to argue from an essentially 'grey' perspective.

Much of my case will consist of arguments that 'green' and 'grey' are not necessarily so far apart. Some of the philosophical distinctions between the two traditions are blurred and unclear when examined more closely and often one side or the other is only distinct by being incoherent. But in at least one respect, the philosophical basis of ethics, the two traditions are clearly and irreconcilably opposed. The 'green' tradition is *deontological* ethically; it suggests that people have duties arising out of their condition or nature, irrespective of interests. All deontological morality implies that there are rules to be obeyed, practices to be followed, whether the consequences make us 'better off' or not. But the 'grey' morality of utilitarianism is *teleological*. The word comes from the Greek *telos*, purpose, and 'teleogical' was once associated with God's purposes. But now it refers to moral systems whose ultimate criteria refer to human purposes. 'Grey' morality is based on a calculation of interests: it seeks to do what is 'best', for a relevant *population*. What ought to be done changes with the tests, size and condition of that population. Deontological moralities assume that right and wrong are to be inferred from true propositions, whether about God, Nature, the 'human condition' or the nature of rational thought. Secular teleology allows and assumes a logical 'gap' between truth and values. Facts, even the nature of things, cannot tell us what to do. No argument can generate practical conclusions unless it contains value-judgements, such as the 'fundamental value propositions' that pain is bad and pleasure good.

The distinction between these two philosophies of ethics is irreconcilable and important to the participants in the argument. The 'green' case cannot be fully translated into utilitarian terms: the 'mere environmentalism' which seeks the more efficient protection of human interests in the condition of the planet is formally rejected by all 'green' and 'ecological' thinkers, even where they have to argue in its terms on public platforms. Porritt, for example, says that, 'Though we would never be so foolhardy as to assume that reason alone is sufficient to build a caring, civilised society, the politics of ecology is nonetheless profoundly rational'.[2]

Of course, the discerning reader will have noted that there are important arguments which draw together the opposite sides of this ideological gap. An important one concerns time: the difference between respecting a planet and using it becomes much less as we extend the time-horizon over which use is envisaged. Some of the questions about time are complex and difficult: What sort of time-horizon is it 'rational' to use? How do we evaluate the uncertainties of the future? What sort of evidence might help us estimate the future tastes of human beings? They will have to be discussed later in this book. But the converging effect of a lengthening time-horizon is intuitively obvious: maximising efficient use of the planet in the period to 2100 is likely to look much more like respecting nature than is a policy of maximisation which dismissed any post-2000 consideration as excessively conjectural.

For all the drama, contemporaneity and philosophical lineage of the grey-green argument, it is likely to be regarded by many observers as both new-fangled and peripheral. It has emerged on the fringes of politics in the 1980s. This perception is at odds with the acceptance of the extreme importance of 'green' issues in most 'developed' countries. The reason for this contradictory status is that the green-grey debate has been confused and overlaid by two other historical struggles between ideas: between scientific rationality and orthodox religion and between left and right. I think it is possible to argue from either a utilitarian *or* an ecological stance that these distinctions in themselves are likely to diminish in importance compared with the debates between ecology and economics, between Utility and Nature.

The principles I intend to apply in assessing arguments about policy in the course of this book are ultimately utilitarian, though based on a version of utilitarianism which is, in some respects, deliberately vague and which is reached by a residual, negative logic. In other words, I regard the kind of utilitarianism I will outline as the 'least silly' practical philosophy available, rather than treating it with any fervid enthusiasm or believing that it solves all problems. At the same time, I am sympathetic to expressed 'green' positions. I have strong feelings of respect for land and landscape and of magic and enchantment in relation to nature. The evidence suggests that these feelings are widely shared. But existing forms of deciding things, of calculating what ought to be done and evolving policies, seem to underestimate these sensations. Thus, though I perhaps share something in common philosophically with established, orthodox thought about the purpose and criteria of public policy, I also share 'green' reservations about that orthodoxy. Much of what we do seems too destructive even judged by its own standards.

Part of what I want to defend is 'mere environmentalism' as some 'green' writers call it. Generally, this is the view that certain goods inherent in our surroundings are undervalued by public decision-making compared to 'material' goods. These are typically what economists call 'public goods' because they are indefinitely available to a population: acts of consumption do not diminish the stock of them. They are such things as a complex ecological system, beautiful landscape and pure air. They are different kinds of goods from those which are marketed and individually consumed and sometimes (but not always) the two kinds of goods as aggregates are rivals or alternatives; the supply of one can vary inversely with that of the other.

In practice, such mere environmentalism implies that the state should assume greater powers over economic and social activity. Typically, the state penalises certain kinds of activity (as with hydro-carbon taxes) or takes as regulatory powers what were once the rights of private ownership (the assumption of development control, for instance), or directly manages sectors of the economy for long-term public benefit rather than according to commercial criteria (forests and railways are usually treated in this way). The environmentalism which recommends these practices is far from radical. Unlike much 'green' criticism of existing practice, it does not demand a fundamental change in public philosophy, nor a great change in institutional practices. It requires only a reinterpretation of the philosophy already prevailing and a reform and redirection of practices.

Campaigning for the 'environment' in this sense usually consists of putting pressure on state policymakers to lean towards 'conservation' or 'preservation'. Truly 'green' or 'ecological' critiques are different in kind: they demand re-examination and rejection of much of the way we now think and radically different ways of producing, consuming and relating to one another.

It is not very surprising to claim that utilitarianism can be pointed in a more environmental direction if that is only taken to imply more conservation and preservation. The details of this redirection are important, though, and some of them are surprising. But I want to pull utilitarianism in 'green' directions in ways which go further than this and are likely to prove more controversial. One of these directions involves some degree of scepticism about some of the concepts which tend to be practically equated with utility, such as 'economic growth' and 'free choice'. Another involves the assertion of the utilitarian value of a respect for, deference to and security in, some aspects of the planet which some time ago I named 'environmental totemism'.[3]

Utilitarian philosophy can be taken some distance in a green direction, but there are significant boundaries which it cannot cross. No utilitarian can acknowledge the existence of duties arising out of our ecological role which are not reducible to instruments of human benefit. As a philosophy, it is determinedly secular, while several versions of 'green' and 'ecological' philosophy are philosophically analogous to religious belief and morality; the similarity is noted by proponents as often as by opponents. But the next step must be to outline the range and nature of the two philosophies which I intend to compare and compromise. In the case of utilitarianism, which is relatively familiar, well-defined and orthodox, this outline will consist of a brief recapitaluation. The 'green' tradition of thought must be described at much greater length.

A recapitulation of utilitarianism

Broadly defined as an ethical system, contemporary utilitarianism has three central properties. It is:

- *Consequentialist*: Decisions are made, actions are judged, according to their effects.
- *Aggregative*: Effects are assessed in terms of aggregates of relevant populations.
- *Sensualist*: The only entities which count in the assessment of aggregates are feelings.

This tri-partite definition is intended as a modernisation and clarification of Francis Hutcheson's famous slogan, which Jeremy Bentham described as a 'sacred truth', that 'That action is best which procures the greatest happiness of the greatest number'.[4]

The substantive meaning of utilitarianism is best developed by listing the forms of ethical doctrine which it excludes. Consequentialism rejects all forms of morality and practical philosophy which do not base judgements solely on effects, including any claims that actions should be performed or rules obeyed because of duties arising out of God's will, the human condition or the nature of reason. This condition alone excludes the overwhelming majority of ethical thinking over the course of history. The aggregative quality excludes all utimately distributive moralities. Thus it rejects egalitarian public philosophies which argue that either treating people equally or making people more equal are legitimate ends. It is also opposed to most theories of justice, including that of John Rawls, which judges social arrangements according to the position of the worst-off individual within them rather than according to the aggregate.[5] Sensualism rejects the inclusion of entities in the aggregate which do not translate into feelings. Of the question of whether fox-hunting should be allowed by law, it allows evidence to be considered only about whether sentient beings are better off if hunting takes place than if it does not. Sentient beings may be co-extensive with human beings, or it may be taken to include foxes and other creatures affected (such as the wood pigeons which the foxes themselves might hurt). This remains an important ambiguity.

Broad Utilitarianism as I have defined it rejects also certain other forms of utilitarianism. Firstly, it rejects what may well be still the most common use of 'utility' and 'utilitarian', the demand that things should be useful or efficient. At its most foolish, this is a kind of mindless instrumentalism which insists that everything be assessed on the basis of its capacity to produce something else. If we say that something is 'purely utilitarian' what we normally mean is that it does its very limited job without offering any kind of bonus by way of being charming, interesting or aesthetically satisfying. It was this kind of utility which Wordsworth had in mind when he wrote his sonnet opposing the proposed railway to Windermere. He wrote of the lover of the land:

> Who scorns a false utilitarian lure
> 'Mid his paternal fields at random thrown . . . .[6]

Paradoxically, this reference remains meaningful, and becomes much more complex, if 'utilitarian' is taken in the broad philosophical sense which I have outlined, but it is fairly clear that Wordsworth only meant it in the ordinary sense. The 'purely utilitarian' is virtually the opposite of philosophical utilitarianism. One virtue of the latter is described by Samuel Brittan as an insistent reductionism which asks of the 'useful' as well as the 'shibboleth' what is its ultimate collection of effects on human feelings?[7] It is the kind of sceptical interrogation to which Falstaff submits the concept of 'honour'.

> Can honour set – to a leg? No: or an arm?
> No: or take away the grief of a wound? No,
> Honour hath no skill in surgery, then? No,
> What is honour? a word. What is in that word,
> honour? What is that honour? air. A trim

reckoning! – Who hath it? he that died o'
Wednesday. Doth he feel it? – no.[8]

It must be stressed that any doctrine of mere usefulness is strictly opposed to the sensualism of Broad Utilitarianism. But it must be realised that fallacies of usefulness are common and persistent. The true utilitarian must demand of 'economic growth', the 'balance of payments' *and* 'the environment' what their relation is to human well-being, as Falstaff did for 'honour'.

The Broad Utilitarianism which I intend to apply in this book must be distinguished from several narrow utilitarianisms which have it in common that they aspire to the precise calculation of right answers. The first of these was the 'felicific calculus' which Jeremy Bentham developed: this required calculations of the balance between pain and pleasure according to their 'fecundity', 'intensity', 'duration' and so on. It is uncontroversial, even among utilitarians, to state that this scheme is a complete failure as applicable theory: the concept of utility simply does not work. Those of use who respect Bentham nowadays do so for his astringent scepticism toward such deontological concepts as 'natural law' and 'natural rights' and for his determination to establish an ethical system which would be consequentialist and aggregative rather than for the precise stipulations of his version of utilitarianism. It is, I suppose, something like the relationship between Marx and some contemporary Marxists.

Subsequent narrow forms of utilitarianism have included 'classical' economics and, as a reaction to that, 'welfare' economics and especially those forms of applied economics, like cost-benefit analysis, which aspire to calculate all the advantages and disadvantages of alternative courses of action. Economics has based its calculations on preference, not utility: the simple difference is between a method which tries to make people as happy as possible and one which tries to give them as much as possible of what they want, taking their own choices on the basic data of assessment and including choices about money, which allow cardinal numerical assessments to be made.

From the point of view of Broad Utilitarianism, such narrow utilitarianisms are *dangerously* narrow. They purport to include all relevant factors, but the bogus precision of their methods means that some are badly under-valued compared with others. They find it much easier to assess the benefits of increases in the measurables which compound into 'Gross National Product' than they do to evaluate tradition or good communal relations or the special sense of belonging to a landscape. Broad Utilitarianism replaces precise calculation by a necessarily murky mixture of intuition, judgement and guesswork, implemented through a variety of institutions including voting and administration. It acknowledges the necessity of using what John Rawls calls 'summary rules' in making decisions: these are practices and procedures which are generally followed because they are useful guides to action, but which may be over-ridden by more precise calculations on occasions.[9] The justification of summary rules acknowledges that rational calculation is often irrational; neither individually nor collectively can we go through life calculating all the advantages and disadvantages of our alternatives. The cost of decision-making is often too high. 'Cost-benefit analysis' suggests that 'cost-benefit analysis' should not be undertaken. The use of 'summary rules' does not mean, though, that it is 'rule utilitarianism' which I will be applying in the arguments which follow. At least in its strongest sense, 'rule utilitarianism' says we should pick the best rules (on utilitarian grounds) and then *always* obey them. This does not qualify as utilitarianism at all under my stipulation: it is the spirit of utilitarianism that all rules should be broken if there is a good enough reason.

It may be objected that Broad Utilitarianism is a ramshackle construction made of such ill-fitting parts as one broad principle, several rules which can be broken, a number of alternative practices and the right sort of attitude. Does this hotch-potch really constitute a distinct ethical philosophy? Yes, it does: honest application of genuinely consequentialist and aggregative criteria is sufficent to distinguish the tiny handful of modern governments which have used these criteria, at least for most of the time, from the rest of human history.

There are forms of neo-utilitarianism which allow the consequentialist-aggregative-sensualist whole to be over-ridden by a rival or higher principle. Arguably, John Stuart Mill was a doubly compromised utilitarian. His belief in the higher culture was such that he was prepared to overrule the Aggregate to further the interests of the more sophisticated intellectual and artistic practices. He also seems, in writing about liberty, to put a clear principle firmly above the Aggregate. Samuel Brittan is a contemporary inheritor of this tradition in that he wants all interpretations of the Aggregate to err on the side of maximising individual choice. Some commentators would infer that Mill and Brittan are both 'moral pluralists', holding to conflicting values without a method of adjudication. A true utilitarian position (such as the one I want to apply here) cannot be morally pluralist: it seeks ways of amalgamating conflicting values into the Aggregate of benefit.[10]

Some remarks on the utilitarian tradition

I have attempted to restate a form of utilitarianism briefly and as a personal commitment which I intend to apply to the issues which will be discussed later in this book. I will now add a number of observations on the context of utilitarian ideas and the problems and ambiguities which they face before proceeding to a preliminary description of 'green' or 'ecological' philosophies.

The historical context of utilitarianism

Utilitarianism was a product of eighteenth century Britain. One crucial feature of that society was that it was a secular or a religious society in that it was no longer a general expectation that people should believe a shared, established religious truth. Another was that it was steadily evolving towards the model of society which Adam Smith typified as 'commercial': a society which conceived itself as consisting of individuals, equal in many respects before the law, who pursued their interests and formed contracts freely within the limits set by the state. Though Jeremy Bentham was the definitive utilitarian, the philosophical positions of Hutcheson and Smith, as well as David Hume and Edmund Burke also contained central utilitarian elements.

As an ethical philosophy, utilitarianism has been most at home in the English-speaking countries, but it has also had considerable appeal, as a radical alternative, elsewhere, especially in societies where Spanish is the principal language. As commercial values and the English language have spread, so has the natural territory of utilitarian philosophy.

Who counts?

I have so far referred to the Aggregate without specifying who is to count. Bentham, of course, said that 'each is to count for one and nobody is to count for more than one' and utilitarians have normally taken this to mean *people* and within the state or society in which one happened to be operating. But both of these underlying assumptions are difficult, if not impossible, to justify. It is a good summary rule, perhaps, that states consider only their own populations and leave other states to govern theirs. But there must be occasions on which state policies effect foreign citizens more than domestic ones, especially where the state is rich and powerful and the society it affects is poor and impotent. To what extent should states take the population of the planet into account in their decisions? There is no definitive answer. Indeed one of the most difficult and depressing problems to be discussed in this book concerns the existence of international and global environmental problems without adequate international and global institutions.

The assumption that utilitarian calculations should include only members of the species *homo sapiens* is even more difficult to justify. For Bentham, *sentience*, not intelligence, was the criterion of consideration and in several passages he suggests the extension of consideration to creatures other than humans, but he did not apply the principle consistently.[11] The debate about what kind of feelings other creatures have is complex and irresoluble, but there can be no doubt that those which possess a central nervous system do have feelings. Indeed, this seems a far better basis for establishing principles friendly to other creatures than for claiming that they have 'rights'. There are several *prima facie* absurdities about claiming that rabbits (say) have rights. Rights are essentially just claims and creatures which cannot speak cannot claim. The core, established, context of rights is within legal systems, none of which have ever proceeded beyond small gestures towards the rights of animals. (It is only in a very weak sense that having an offence of 'cruelty to animals' constitutes a set of rights for the designated animals.) Argument about human or natural rights have often stressed either God's favours to man or the obligations which arise simply from recognition of a fellow-human. None of these established arguments about rights helps the rabbit. But it is undeniable that rabbits have feelings and it may well have been exaggerated that their fears, pains and pleasures are *of a different kind* from those of people. The most impressive arguments for 'animal liberation', like those of Peter Singer, have been based on utility rather than on rights.[12]

At the risk of losing potential allies, let me express a preliminary attitude to the question of animals, which will bear on a number of issues to be discussed later. I accept entirely that animal sensations should be taken into account and animal well-being should not be hurt by policy without a compensating gain. But human feelings of satisfaction and dissatisfaction are to be accounted on a different scale from those of other creatures; the possibilities for a sense of satisfaction (or, inversely, of frustration) which arise in a being which uses propositional language and which is, thus, self-conscious, intellectual and reflective, are much larger than those of other creatures. Rabbits are to be accounted, but as considerably lesser subjects of feeling than human beings.

Time

It would seem obvious that sentient beings include some not yet born, though Bentham specifically discounted the unborn on occasions on the grounds that we could not know how to account them (for instance, we cannot know their tastes). Subsequent developments of utilitarianism have been less stringently short-term in application, but the whole question of time remains an insoluble ambiguity.

We formulate policies which may affect people's options and well-being in fifty, or even five hundred, years time. But our instututions and assumptions (the profit margin, the electoral system) bind us to short-term considerations. Of course, the long-term should count, but as time-horizons extend probabilities become mere possibilities, chains of forseeable causation peter out, our knowledge of tastes and conditions becomes entirely inadequate. I have no resolution of this fundamental ambiguity, except to say that policy calculations should consider the maximum reasonably foreseeable future.

The politics of utilitarianism

To utilitarians, democracy and authoritarianism, socialism and capitalism do not embody attractive values in themselves. They are to be judged on performance, as a means to securing human well-being. Thus, just as Bentham shifted his support from enlightened despotism to democracy, utilitarianism as a whole has shifted its ground between capitalism and socialism. In mid-century, utilitarians were drawn to state socialism because of the miseries and failures of inter-war capitalism: experience and evidence have cast doubt on the capacity of socialist solutions to perform.

Generally, Broad Utilitarianism is conservative and reformist. It is conservative because it can acknowledge no imperative (whether the will of Allah, human equality or the forces of history) which could justify the costs of social upheaval. It is reformist because it is wildly improbable that any society could not contain major faults and inadequacies in the actual performance of the attempt to maximise the well-being of the Aggregate.

The meaning of 'Green'

During the 1980s the idea of a 'Green' perspective on politics became a popular and journalistic commonplace. After the first Bundestag successes of the German Green Party (*Die Grünen*) in 1983 the British Ecology Party changed its name to Green Party and achieved the impressive total of 14.9 per cent of the vote in the 1989 European elections. The achievement was open to dismissal as a cheap protest vote, but it did establish the idea that there were 'green issues' on the political agenda which could not be ignored and were likely to gain in importance.

However, this popularisation of the idea of a 'green' political perspective also involved a complete distortion. In England 'Green' politics immediately arouses images of protecting the Green Belt, a system of restricting urban growth which (among other things) enhances the amenities and property values of suburban inhabitants. Local politicians and planners warned of the dire economic costs of this 'greening' of policy. Even when green issues were conceived on a much less parochial scale – in the consideration of the ozone layer and global warming, for example – the emphasis was on an avoidance of ecological catastrophes so well worth avoiding that they raised no real questions of ethical principle. The popular meaning of 'Green' thus extended from mere environmentalism to specific forms of self-interest, with only the occasional hint that there were broader questions of world-view involved. The distinct impression was formed that millions of people had voted 'Green' on the grounds that such a vote would help mend the ozone layer and prevent the building of further houses in Surrey.

There is, of course, much more to Green thought than that, but the increment is extremely difficult to define. At its broadest, green sentiment starts with the perception that in modern times human beings have ceased to have harmonious relations with nature. From this loss arise both the possibility of ecological catastrophe and the present reality of a sense of spiritual frustration. This kind of sense of loss has been greatest, for slightly different reasons, in Germany and the British Isles. It accelerated in intensity during the first half of the nineteenth century: in 1800 it was a minority interest, but by 1850 it was commonplace.

Broad Green sentiment has constantly returned to several general criticisms of modern life. Life has become restless; it lacks the stability of previous societies and the tranquility; there is constant movement, but without a destination. It is highly destructive: the terrifying economic and technological forces can, overnight, with a mere twitch, destroy things which have existed and developed for millenia or centuries – groves of oak trees, village communities, ancient skills, trout streams. Modern life lacks some of the meaning and satisfaction that was inherent in previous societies. It organises ambition and incentive almost entirely around material wealth, making people slaves to increasing levels of consumption in which they find decreasing satisfaction. The general thesis is of human alienation, not in the relatively technical sense which Marx refined, but in the looser sense which has developed in ordinary usage. Porritt says of 'alienation' that, 'its current familiarity accurately reflects the extent to which alienation has become a part of our lives. I shall be using the word to indicate that sense of estrangement people experience between themselves and their work, their own health, their environment, and the workings of their democracy.' [13]

The range of methods by which 'alienated' modern man has sought to recover his harmony with nature and with himself forms an astonishingly rich menu. There have been 'back to the land' movements ranging from the radical Land Restoration League to the more moderate allotment movement, whose main aims were achieved by the Small Holdings and Allotments Act of 1907, or from the conventional Council for the Protection of Rural England to the Woodcraft Folk and Kinship in Husbandry. Vegetarianism, animal rights and naturism or nudism are all movements seeking greater harmony with nature through individual choice. In religion, there have been a wide variety of developments of Pantheism, significant modifications of Christianity, a revival of paganism and the development of several neo-religions such as theosophy and Rudolf Steiner's Anthroposophism with its eurhythmic method. There has also been increased interest in Eastern religions, particularly Buddhism and Hinduism, which are not tainted by Western industrialism and anthropocentrism. The medical wing of Green thought is generally delineated by 'holistic' medicure: more particularly, it includes homeopathy, herbalism and bio-rhythmics.

As a social movement, Green thinking has overlapped considerably with a long and varied tradition of communalism, including, of course, the *kibbutz* movement. It has played an important part in what Barrington Moore calls 'Catonism',[14] the belief in the moral superiority of a peasant way of life. When combined with a search for national and ethnic roots, it has created movements concentrating on folk music, 'morris' dancing, traditional story-telling and the revival of dead or moribund languages. It is related to a particular strain of feminist thought which looks back to a matriarchal society and sees industrialism and militarism as consequences of masculine domination, a wing of feminism which has had recent expression in the 'peace' movement and, more particularly, in the Greenham Common camp.

The political spirit of all these sentiments and searches is necessarily both radical and reactionary. They are radical in the strict sense in that they adjudge modern arrangements to be *deeply* wrong and not remediable by the normal methods of legislation and institutional reform, but only by fundamental changes of attitude to life. I intend no disapproval by the use of the word 'reactionary' but only to point to the important common factor that all these accounts suggest that modern people have *lost* something important as compared with earlier societies, irrespective of what the loss is or whether it is a net loss. There is always something which our ancestors had which we lack. And we *feel* the lack at some level or other, whether it is faith, community, rootedness to our place or role, self-reliance or whatever. This spirit of reactionary radicalism was well expressed in a lecture by W. B. Yeats given in New York in 1904:

> Whenever men have tried to imagine a perfect life they have imagined a place where men plough and sow and reap, not a place where there are great wheels turning and great chimneys vomiting smoke . . . We wish to preserve an ancient ideal of life. Whenever customs prevail, there you will find the folk song, the folk tale, the proverb, and the charming manners that come from ancient culture . . . We must so live that we will make the old noble kind of life powerful amongst our people.[15]

In this sense most general systems of social criticism are reactionary to some degree and one consequence of this is that they must contain some doctrine of a Fall, a period in which human life declined in respect of important values. The question is: When did man live in ecological grace? The answers are very varied. For the deeply pessimistic group who wrote for *The Ecologist* in the aftermath of the energy crisis of the 1970s, all of history was to be rejected in an attempt to recover the virtues of a tribal, hunter-gatherer society. Edward Goldsmith wrote:

> . . . the human experience during the historical experience in which institutionalised government and objective knowledge were first made use of for the purposes of social control has been one of wars, massacres, intrigues, famines; in other words, of precisely those discontinuities in terms of which one can measure social and ecological instability and which it is the function of social and ecological control to eliminate.[16]

For Goldsmith and others such as Nicholas Hildyard and Henryk Skolimovski only tribal, hunter-gatherer societies can provide people with the regime of 'religio-culture' which suits our spiritual needs and provides for indefinite biological survival. If the degree to which one is 'reactionary' is measured by how far back in history you aspire to travel in search of virtue, then this is the most reactionary doctrine possible.

A later period of disgrace, for many writers, including the theologian Martin Heidegger, was the coming of the Roman empire with its full 'modern' system of ownership, its emphasis on rapid mobility and long-distance trade and its 'exploitative' system of large-scale, *latifundia*, farming. There were strong premonitions of Green objections to modernisation in the writing of Marcus Porcius 'Censorius' Cato (The Cato of Catonism) who died in 149 BC. Cato protested at what he saw as the decline of the rural-republican way of life, the growth of luxury and idleness and the rise of Greek influence in Rome.[17] For some, like the English rustic Marxists (including Blatchford and Morris) and the bucolic anti-capitalist catholics (like Chesterton and Belloc) the medieval period had attractions, and it was the classical revival and the rise of protestantism which constituted the greatest Fall. A large English group focuses naturally on the 'industrial revolution' and the enclosures; Porritt, turning a vulgar criticism on its head, portrays the Luddites as the last great popular protest against the Fall.[18]

Many periods of history have produced writers whose comments are laced with a sharp sense of decline from the simple, natural, honest life. In Thomas More's *Utopia*, the natives 'define virtue to be a life ordered according to nature' and Utopia stands in almost inverse contrast to the England of Henry VIII with its enclosures, its dissolution of the monasteries, its rapidly increasing commerce and naked political opportunism.[19] William Cobbett's *Rural Rides* is a similar tale of broken tradition, destroyed community and the unjust seizure of land by greedy interests.[20] Sometimes we are left asking the familiar and ironic question: Why is it that *every* period in history seems to be the age when the middle-classes rose, commercial values predominated and self-interest succeeded altruism as the chief motive of persons?

One rather complex theory of history, though very much in the spirit of More and Cobbett, is to be found in the writings of John Massingham, often known as 'H.J.' and not to be confused with his father ('H.W.', the editor of *The Nation*) or his brother Hugh, a distinguished political journalist. Massingham was born in 1888 and died in 1952. He was part of a circle of friends and allies which included Lord Lymington, Sir Arthur Bryant, Rolf Gardiner and Henry Williamson, who extolled the virtues of rural English life and deplored the degeneracy of contemporary English life as a whole, and the decay of rural society in particular. He wrote a large number of books and essays, many of them repetitive, on the themes of the English countryside and English history; his particular loves were birds and traditional wood crafts.

For Massingham there have been at least three great Falls, if not four or even five. The Roman Empire was the first, the Norman conquest the second, the Tudor state the third, the acceleration of industrialisation and enclosure at the end of the eighteenth century the fourth, and his own age threatens to be a fifth. Is man's spirit, then, in free-fall, like Alice? By no means: it has had great revivals. In an essay called, 'Rome is Fallen', he sees the Romans as the prototypes of modern, alienated man; 'The Machine Age is seem in embryo in the engineering genius which the Romans devoted to metalled highways . . . In a smaller area the Roman Empire corresponds with Mr. H. G Wells's dream of a world state.'[21]

But the Saxons saved the human spirit in England: 'It was the Saxon invasion which prevented England from going modern for another thousand years'.[22] It is almost impossible to exaggerate the extent to

which Massingham, or his friend, Sir Arthur Bryant, believed that the
Saxon village represented the epitome of social virtue: 'The constitution
of the village community effected an extraordinarily stable balance
between socialism and ownership'.[23] It was essentially democratic; men
had considerable freedom within it; it was stable because its practices
were ecologically sound and based on the objectives of subsistence and
continuity rather than profit and acquisition. It was peaceful. It revived
and improved the virtues of those neolithic villages which had 'continued
singularly unchanged for some four thousand years'. It was eroded,
though in no way completely destroyed, by Norman feudalism. The next
great wave of destruction was the Tudor Age, which 'unveiled the
morning of modernism'.[24]

It seems to me that, insofar as the claims of Massingham and Bryant
about Saxon society and ecology are factual, they have some support
among the relevant historians, but plenty of opposition. As an appraisal
of the quality of Saxon rural life, they proceed more in hope than in
argument since we are faced with a classic example of Herbert
Butterfield's 'impossibility of history': we can never know what it *felt* like
to be a Saxon 'yeoman'.[25] Were they really bored, excited, exhilarated,
frightened, moved by beauty, spurned by would-be friends or lovers to a
greater or lesser extent than us? If they had something we do not have – a
complete and unquestioning sense of belonging to the land, for example
– would they not take it for granted and get no real pleasure out of it?

But at least the likes of Massingham and Bryant gave a precision and a
scholarship, even if both were ultimately rather spurious, to their
nostalgia. In many modern reactions and much social criticism there is
an equal amount of spurious disaffection with the present, but with
much less thought about which past might be superior and why. In late
twentieth-century thought the past has won a kind of triumph over the
future; modernism and futurism have been vanquished by the heritage
industry and the historical novel. For a utilitarian, nostalgia can be as
futile and debilitating as millenarianism. A limited amount of self-
awareness and practical value can be derived from the study of the past,
but the present is the only time we have to enjoy.

A crucial distinction between those societies which John Massingham
admired and those he feared concerns money. Roman and 'modern'
society are essentially monetary; neolithic, pre-Roman Celtic and Saxon
societies were equally essentially non-monetary. There may have been
something which was a means of exchange and a store of value but it was
little developed. It was not an obsession, nor an end in itself. It did not
allow the development of geographically vast interests, of long-distance
trade or a continental or even national division of labour. There is an
instinctive suspicion of trade and of finance: they necessarily imply
power and alienation. There is nothing unusual about Massingham in
this respect; such suspicion has been a common theme in the Broad
Green tradition. Paradoxically, the greatest prophet of commercial
society and the progress which results from an increasing division of
labour, Adam Smith, is treated by Robert Nisbet as an 'ecological'

thinker.[26] But this is an almost wilfully perverse piece of classification, justified by reference to Smith's account of the natural equilibria created by the pursuit of human self-interest. It is common to all ecological thinkers, even in the broadest political sense, that the equilibria produced by the pursuit of self-interest in a commercial society are not equivalent to the kind of harmony which both the planet and its human inhabitants need.

A Green tradition?

The range of sentiments I have described here contains a strong sense of fragmentation. Man has parted from Nature and also from something in his own spirit. There is a yearning for restoration, for a 'wholeness' or 'oneness' which is no longer possible. Industrialism has taken mankind down the wrong road, an accelerating journey towards the deeply unsatisfying destinations of urbanisation, materialism and specialisation. The only hope is to halt this 'progress' and turn back, in some way, to nature and the land. The Broad Green tradition defined like this is anything but a political movement or sect. Its sentiments have appeared throughout the political spectrum of 'left' and 'right'. Only the most dismal economists, the most stringent utilitarians, have set their faces squarely against them. The interesting aspect of Broad Green thought is precisely *not* that it forms a distinguishable social movement or form of belief; on the contrary, it permeates and transcends all modern thought. It defines the modern 'intellectual'.

Who would confess to having no worries about the direction of 'progress' or about what Man is doing to Nature? Who has never felt a tug of rural nostalgia, which can be rationalised into the theory that a simpler, harder life lived closer to the rhythms of nature, might be more satisfying? For most people, it is a question of 'heart' and 'head', Green sentiment against the immediate perceptions of self-interest and the working of the systems with which we are familiar. Green sentiment may dominate the outlook of the artist or the teacher, but it may also play a part in the thinking of the executive who appears at public inquiries to justify the construction of a new motorway or power station, but who reads Wordsworth and worries about the planet. The distinction between 'heart' and 'head' is often reinforced by that between public role and private self.

Even if Green sentiment were not so widely shared, there would be an insuperable obstacle to regarding it as any kind of intellectual or political tradition. At its core is a philosophical indeterminacy, a problem which must be resolved before practical substance can be derived. What is Man's role in Nature? How is it that human beings are both part of nature, but also separate from, even opposed to, nature? To what extent can we go about our business like other species and like them be a harmonious part of an ecological system? If not a very great extent, why not? Which self-denying ordinances should Man take to assure his peace with nature?

Green sentiment – the love of Nature, concern about the human role in nature, suspicion of 'progress', the yearning for a simple life – is everywhere. Green politics can only be generated by answering some extremely difficult theoretical questions and answering in a particular way. The same problem emerges whether we talk about nature or ecology or a pantheistic God.

Narrow Green politics is a much smaller and more peripheral tradition than Broad Green thought. In the period of modern politics, of 'left' and 'right', there have been relatively few people who have taken the view that the issues arising out of Man's relationship with Nature are more urgent and important than those concerning the distribution of material wealth and the organisation of power. There has, though, been an unbroken, varied and interesting lineage of such people, particularly in England and Germany. Their political allegiances have varied greatly and some of their prescriptions have changed considerably, but there remains a clear case of policy which constitutes a Narrow Green agenda.

On this view industry, other than small-scale, devolved manufacture, is bad in itself and must be eradicated. Utilitarian philosophies should be replaced by those which are 'holistic' and ecological. People should live in small communities which produce most of their own goods. The potential to destroy these communities through the development of trade, industry and centralised financial control, must be vigilantly limited. Farming must be 'organic' (which raises the same problems as nature and ecology); more specifically, it must be small-scale, mixed farming not dependant on trade for inputs (like imported fertiliser). Thus, for Narrow Greens in countries like Germany and England there is a thorny population problem since it is not apparent how these traditional methods could support the existing population. These are the bare bones of a Green political tradition; some more particular flesh can be put on them by considering the writings of two English writers of different generations.

Viscount Lymington and the Hon. J. Porritt

Gerard Vernon Wallop, Viscount Lymington and later ninth Earl of Portsmouth, was born in 1898 and died in 1985. He held a large number of posts during his life, chiefly connected with conservation and rural management. He was Hereditary Bailiff of Burley in the New Forest and Vice-Chairman of the East African Natural Resources Council from 1963 until his death; most of his positions had connections with either Hampshire or East Africa. He was closely associated with a group of intellectuals who sought to revive rural England during the inter-war period when it was suffering from agricultural depression and urban sprawl. This group included Rolf Gardiner and John Massingham and tributes to each other are common in the writings of all of them; these take both an overt form and are also evident in flattery-by-imitation. Lymington (which was the name under which most of his books were published) wrote mostly in the first half of his life; his books included *Ich Dien; the Tory Path* (1931), *Horn, Hoof and Corn* (1932), *Famine in England* (1938) and *Alternative to Death* (1943).

Jonathan Porritt, whose father is Lord Porritt (hereditary baronet and life peer), was born in 1952 and is a leading member of the Green Party as well as being Director of Friends of the Earth. His book, *Seeing Green*, was published in 1984 and has been part of the establishment of the image of a 'Green' alternative in English society generally. He has a considerable 'output' in newspapers, radio and television.

Alternative to Death, subtitled *the relationship between soil, family and community* is a very curious book. Lymington, from different angles, is true green, far right and very shrewd. As a general objective he says that:

> All economy and policies must be unsound which do not attempt to bring wholeness to the individual, to the family, to the village and locality and ultimately, to Empire and international relationship. In general the individual can only be called whole who has physical and spiritual health.[27]

This cannot be achieved by increasing material production and consumption, 'which is the unfelt sting causing the unfelt itch of *ennui*', but only by a close, stable relationship with soil. 'Man', says Lymington 'in so far as he is an animal, is bound to the soil . . . When he enters the city he cuts himself off from one side of his own cosmic nature . . .'[28]

The solution must lie in *ruralisation* which requires getting people back to the land and farming on a self-sufficient, labour-intensive, 'bio-dynamic' basis. ('Bio-dynamic' was a translation from the German phrase used by Rudolf Steiner and, after him, many, including the Nazi Minister of Agriculture, Walther Darré, but it is roughly equivalent to organic.)[29] It is to a traditional England that they will return; there will remain aristocrats and estates and Lymington was vigorously opposed to death duties. However there must be opportunities to acquire land and it will be confiscated from inadequate or ecologically unsound farmers by public committees. The country house will change in its nature, becoming much more the centre of a whole community than the exclusive preserve of a narrow elite.

Lymington does offer solutions to some of the most obvious problems about such a scheme. Why will it not degenerate back into commercialism? Because of limitations on imports and on 'usury' and because limited liability will be abolished, to restrict the growth of businesses. Will we not all be poorer? Only in 'paper money', not in any real sense. Can we feed ourselves? Certainly, with sound management and hard work. (He assumes what had become more or less an orthodoxy by the outbreak of war, that emigration and a low birth rate will bring about a substantial reduction in the British population.)

Even in 1943, Lymington was prepared to express admiration for the agricultural and ecological policies of the Third Reich,[30] which held an attraction for many of his circle and generation. There is a certain sense of regret that England finds itself in 'alliance with Russia and the United States, the two greatest machine-driven powers in the world . . .'[31] despite

Lymington being American-born of partly American parentage. But loyalty to the King would be quite sufficient to ensure his opposition to the Third Reich once war had started.

In many respects, Lymington was a shrewd commentator. Writing in 1943 he, nevertheless, had no difficulty in envisaging the future of Eastern Europe as a 'Republic of European Slave States' (RESS). His expectations of the future of intensive agriculture and of the need for European unity are extremely far-sighted. Most people would now accept what he has to say about collective farming (which was partly inspired by Massingham) and about nationalised industries; his comments on both of these subjects were based on a perception that the idea of public ownership was essentially incoherent, a form of ownership without responsible owners. He predicts, too, a continued dissatisfaction in the West with a culture dominated by 'the dole, Hollywood and the headline press'[32] and thinks we will increasingly hark back to a rural 'Golden Age' which is 'a race memory . . . of times when peoples in differing places had achieved a way of living in partnership and harmony with Nature'. Among those developments of his own time, of which Lymington thoroughly approved, were the Home Guard (as a grassroots, low technology, *local* defence force) and the Women's Institutes. One of his more delightfully eccentric proposals is for a jam bank where people would take the jam they did not need (and no fruit would ever be wasted) so that it could be used by those who did need jam.

In *Seeing Green* Jonathan Porritt offers *'the minimum criteria for being green'* (his italics) which consist of thirteen conditions.[33] To demonstrate the change and continuity of Green thought, I shall repeat this list with a kind of attitude-scale response from Lymington:

Porritt	Lymington
a reverence for the Earth and for all its creatures.	agreed, but the emphasis should be on the Earth rather than on all creatures.
a willingness to share the world's wealth among *all* its peoples; prosperity to be achieved through sustainable alternatives to the rat race of economic growth.	full agreement with the second part, but the first raises different questions in the forties when, according to him, the rural inhabitants of India had a much better diet and healthier life than the inhabitants of English cities.
lasting security to be achieved through non-nuclear defence strategies and considerably reduced arms spending.	the nuclear issues are not directly relevant, but general agreement; preference is for a kind of yeoman militia, a bit like the Home Guard.

a rejection of materialism and the destructive values of industrialism.

complete agreement. He, too, sees the USA and USSR as representing 'industrialism', the similarities being more important than the differences.

a recognition of the rights of future generations in our use of all resources.

agrees.

an emphasis on socially useful, personally rewarding work, enhanced by human-scale technology.

agreement, but his emphasis would be much more specifically agriculture.

protection of the environment as a precondition of a healthy society.

agreement, but the quality of *soil* is definitive of the condition of the environment.

an emphasis on personal growth and spiritual development.

complete agreement.

respect for the gentler side of human nature.

not really clear. Doubtful whether he would agree with the feminist interpretation of this, though he does suggest that the causes of violence and conflict are urban.

open, participatory democracy at every level of society.

there should be considerable influence and guidance from experienced, propertied interests.

recognition of the crucial importance of significant reduction in population levels. (Elsewhere he suggests that there is general agreement that the optimum population of the UK is around 30 million.)

not a problem.

harmony between people of every race, colour and creed.[34]

his views on this were complex. See note 34

a non-nuclear, low-energy

the nuclear issue is irrelevant,

strategy, based on conservation, greater efficiency and renewable resources.	of course, but the rest is very much in the same spirit.
an emphasis on self-reliance and decentralised communities.	complete agreement.

The agreement is considerable, despite the two writers being from apparently opposite ends of the orthodox political continuum. Lymington was, after all, a self-styled Tory with a limited admiration for the Third Reich, which he quickly lost in favour of categorisation as a 'slave state' along with the Roman Empire and the Soviet Union. He was a believer in 'aristocracy', albeit one who perceived aristocratic qualities in miners and farm labourers and wanted to open new avenues to social mobility. Porritt, on the other hand, is a supporter of CND and the Greenham Common camp, an opponent of private ownership of land. But even here, the difference may not be as great as it looks. Lymington was in favour of the 'good husbandry' of private ownership and the long-term commitment that comes with the hereditary principle, but good husbandry was to be judged by public committee and failure punished harshly. Porritt is in favour of some kind of 'communal' land holding which is neither private property nor nationalisation. In effect, both might turn out to involve small family farms under close regulatory supervision from a local authority.

Of the two, I must confess to a strong preference for Lymington. There is a quality of oily indecision about Porritt which is ultimately infuriating. He is thoroughly disapproving of the Pope's views on sex and birth control, but pays tribute to the role he plays in the spiritual satisfaction of millions.[35] He doesn't quite agree that the Greenham Common camp should exclude men, but fully understands their point of view.[36] Lymington, on the other hand, is never pusilanimous; he does offer precise solutions to difficult problems. One does not have to believe that his solutions would work in order to respect him for his intellectual honesty. Even where his views would now be considered unacceptable, they are overtaken by a sense of generosity and decency. He doesn't believe that the urban proletariat should exist, but he admires them personally, paying tribute to their strength of character, the 'warmth' of their communities and the 'rich humanity' of their music-hall tradition.[37] He wants the Jews to leave voluntarily for Palestine, eventually, but for the time being, as refugees, they are to be treated as 'honoured guests'.[38]

After the war, Lymington left England to farm in the White Highlands of Kenya. Most of his views remained unchanged, though he moved more towards orthodoxy, both as a farmer and as a conservative. He finally returned to England as a very old man with severe respiratory problems which had their origins in the poison gas of the First World War. He was bitterly disappointed by the consequences of the 'Africanisation' of his Kenyan farm.[39]

Broad and Narrow Green

I have argued that there exist both a Broad Green tradition of thought about Man and Nature and also a Narrow Green tradition. The Broad tradition transcends our culture: it is to be found all around in our arts and thought. The Grey tradition of utilitarianism, which sees society as an economy whose business is the satisfaction of demand and the state's job as the facilitating and improvement of the working of that economy, is a kind of prevailing ideology. But the Broad Green tradition is a prevailing reservation or evaluative doubt about our way of doing things. The Narrow Green tradition, as an unbroken lineage of practical reformers who rate Green issues as the important issues facing society, is small and peripheral and its actors have often, perhaps usually, been dismissed as cranks. (To which they now, quite properly, respond with E. F. Schumacher's observation that cranks are small, useful, inexpensive tools which make revolutions.)

The existence of Green ideas in 'Broad' and 'Narrow' forms accounts for one of the more discerning features of Green thought, which is that campaigns and organisations often juxtapose very orthodox and respectable ideas and personnel with those which are much more eccentric or even deeply unrespectable. The influential collection of essays against urban sprawl, *Britain and the Beast,* which Clough William-Ellis edited, contains pieces by J. M. Keynes (on the cultural role of the state) and by that stalwart of the 'Brains Trust', C. E. M. Joad, as well as statements by politicians of the three major parties. But it also contains a restatement of John Massingham's theory of history and Lord Howard of Penrith writes enthusiastically about the German *Reichsnaturschutzgesetz* Law of 1935.[40] The Soil Association was founded in 1945 with the understanding and preservation of soil quality as its central aim. It has included many respectable scientists from relevant fields and now has an important role in the definition of 'organic' produce. But its journal, *Mother Earth,* has been edited by Jorian Jenks, who was the British Union of Fascists' agricultural spokesman until 1963. The Association's council included Rolf Gardiner, who renounced support for Hitler only in 1943, as well as Lord Lymington. The Kibbo Kift Kin were among a number of organisations devoted to a revival of Anglo-Saxon customs and a return to the land; their uniform involved a Saxon cowl and jerkin and a Prussian army cloak. The membership not only included such predictable figures as Rolf Gardiner and D. H. Lawrence, but also Sir Patrick Geddes, Julian Huxley and H. G. Wells.[41]

Naturally, there is no clear line between 'Broad' and 'Narrow'. Many ideas about planning are offshoots of a Narrow Green political perspective which has entered the arena of respectable adminstration. A prime example is the ideas of the Garden City Movement, which have influenced not only the building of New Towns, but also the entire operation of development control. Any study of the origins and development of Letchworth would be bound to conclude that the actors were motivated by intense versions of Green ideas: they believed in vegetaria-

nism, theosophy, bio-dynamics, back-to-the-land, Anglo-Saxon nationalism and so on. Yet they were brought together, and the project made
to work, by the simple, practical mind of Ebenezer Howard. He believed
in an environmental determinism whose conclusion was that there
should be careful zoning and more parks and gardens. He argued,
correctly as it turned out, that planning in the style and on the scale of a
Garden City was financially shrewd. Howard's views have proved easily
assimilable into utilitarian decision-making, but they were inspired by
something quite different.[42]

There is another influence on planning which also has fairly intense
Green origins, but which has come to be treated as important by
orthodox planners. This is the complex, ecological perspective on urban
development which has been developed in the writings of Sir Patrick
Geddes and Lewis Mumford and which is sometimes called 'synergism'.[43]
It is a vague and complex theory, the substantive implications of which
are elusive. No respectable planner would confess to ignorance of it, yet
its real influence is, perhaps, negative, as a constant reminder that all
values and reality cannot be contained within the perspectives of
environmental determinism and numerical utilitarianism.

The antithesis between Grey and Green

From a Green perspective, utilitarianism, as it is generally interpreted in
policy, must, in the long run, operate to the detriment of the planet and
thus of human beings. It is a blinkered and short-sighted approach which
is incapable of taking into account future generations. It generates a
collective version of the familiar paradox that to pursue happiness can
only result in becoming unhappy. It lacks a sense of 'magic' or
'enchantment'. One of the implications of Robert Pois' account of the
role of Nature in Nazi thought is that, contrary to any loose inference that
getting dewy-eyed about the natural world leads to movements like
Hitler's, it is precisely the *lack* of magic and meaning in people's lives
under bourgeois and bureaucratic politics which drives people into the
fold of messianic figures.[44]

Utilitarians, on the other hand, are bound to regard fundamentalist
Greens as being entirely incoherent, because the concept of Nature is
incapable of being made substantive and there are no logical Green
procedures for resolving policy dilemmas. Green thought is, ultimately,
mystical and dangerously illiberal because it is capable of justifying
deprivations to human beings without corresponding human benefits. Its
incoherence has an irrational quality, consisting of nostalgia for conditions which cannot be recreated and which we have no good reason to
regard as desirable.

Which of these criticisms is valid and which only holds against a 'straw
man' version of the alternative philosophy, is the core subject of this
book. But before I attempt to evaluate the central arguments. I must
examine further some important aspects of Green thought.

Notes

1 Jonathan Porritt, *Seeing Green: The Politics of Ecology Explained*, (Blackwell, 1984). Richard Sylvan, 'A Critique of Deep Ecology II', *Radical Philosophy*, 41, (1985), pp. 10–22.
2 Porritt, *op. cit.*, p. 18.
3 See Lincoln Allison, *Environmental Planning: A Political and Philosophical Analysis*, (George Allen & Unwin, 1975), pp. 124–29.
4 Francis Hutcheson, *Inquiry into the Origin of our Ideas of Beauty and Virtue*, (John Derby (for Williams and John Smith etc.), 1725). Treatise II.
5 John Rawls, *A Theory of Justice*, (Oxford University Press, 1971).
6 William Wordsworth, 'Sonnet on the Projected Kendal and Windermere Railway', dated October 12th, 1844 and appended to *Guide to the Lakes*, (Frowde, 1906), p. 146.
7 See Samuel Brittan, 'Two Cheers for Utilitarianism', in his, *The Role and Limits of Government*, (Wildwood House, 1983).
8 *Henry IV Part I*, Act V, Scene 1.
9 John Rawls, 'Two Concepts of Rules', *Philosophical Review*, LXIV (1955), pp. 3–32.
10 For a fuller expression of my own (and Brittan's) clarification of these positions see Lincoln Allison (ed.), *The Utilitarian Response: Essays on the Contemporary Viability of Utilitarian Political Philosophy*, (Sage, 1990).
11 He asks, 'Under the Gentoo and Mahometan religions, the interests of the rest of the animal creation seem to have met with some attention . . . Why *ought* they not? . . . the question is not, Can they *reason*, nor Can they talk? but Can they suffer?' John Bowring (ed.), *The Works of Jeremy Bentham* (1838–43), (reprinted Russell and Russell 1962), Vol. 1, pp. 142–43n. Also in the *Introduction to the Principles of Morals and Legislation*, Bentham appends another note (to chapter 17 or 19, depending on edition) to the effect that he looks forward to the emancipation of four-legged creatures, as France has emancipated black people.
12 Peter A. Singer, *Animal Liberation: a new ethics for our treatment of animals*. (Cape, 1976).
13 Porritt, *op. cit.*, p. 77.
14 Barrington Moore, Jr., *Social Origins of Dictatorship and Democracy: Lord and Peasant in the Making of the Modern World*, (Penguin, 1974), pp. 491–96.
15 First quoted in R. Ellmann, *Yeats, the Man and the Masks*, (Macmillan, 1949), p. 116.
16 Edward Goldsmith, 'Religion in a Stable Society', *The Ecologist* 4, 9, (1974), p. 321.
17 T. A. Dorey, 'Cato', in D. R. Dudley and D. M. Long (eds) *The Penguin Companion to Literature*, Vol. 4, including 'Classical and Byzantine', (Penguin Books, 1969), p. 48.
18 Porritt, *op. cit.*, p. 129.
19 William Dallam Armes (ed.), *The Utopia of Sir Thomas More*, (Macmillan, 1912), p. 135.
20 William Cobbett, *Rural Rides*, (Dent, 1932).
21 H. J. Massingham, *Genius of England*, (Chapman & Hll 1937), p. 187. See also 'Past and Future' in his *Field Fellowship*, (Chapman and Hall, 1942), pp. 80–84: he compares developments in wartime agriculture to the Roman *latiundia*. I am grateful to Christopher Hall, editor of *The Countryman*, for

lending me the magazine's stock of Massingham's books, none of which are in print at the time of writing.

22 *Genius of England*, p. 186.

23 H. J. Massingham, 'Our Inheritance from the Past', in Clough Williams-Ellis (ed.), *Britain and the Beast*, (Dent, 1938), p. 18. See also Arthur Bryant, *English Saga*, (Collins, 1936).

24 *Genius of England*, p. 185.

25 Herbert Butterfield, *The Historical Novel: An Essay*, (Cambridge University Press, 1924).

26 Robert Nisbet, *The Social Philosophers*, (Paladin, 1976), pp. 355–58.

27 The Earl of Portsmouth, *Alternative to Death: The Relationship Between Soil, Family and Community*, (Faber and Faber, 1943), p. 161.

28 *Ibid.*, p. 12.

29 See Anna Bramwell, *Ecology in the Twentieth Century, A History*, (Yale, 1989), pp. 201–95 and *Blood and Soil. R. Walther Darré and Hitler's 'Green Party'*, (Bourne End, Bucks, 1985).

30 *Alternative to Death*, p. 125.

31 *Ibid.*, p. 5.

32 *Ibid.*, p. 14.

33 Porritt, *op. cit.*, pp. 10–11.

34 Who would disagree with this, depending on the definition and perceived causal conditions of harmony? Lymington's views on these questions were complex. He disavows the concept of race, dismisses petty nationalism and declares the English inferior in most respects to other Europeans (their culture degraded by enclosure and urbanisation). On the other hand, he believes in 'sound breeding' and 'types' of people remaining with the terrain to which they are adapted. Dutch Fen-drainers, Flemish weavers and Hugue-nots are assimilable, but most British immigrants have consisted of 'the marketeer, the unscrupulous trader, the slick higgler, the seditious natural under-dog and agitator . . .' Portsmouth, *op. cit.*, p. 21. These should go somewhere else. This is all rather sinister. The spirit of Lymington's comments is in many respects completely removed from that of Porritt's, but both can be said to be extreme versions of the fashions of their respective generations.

35 Porritt, *op. cit.*, p. 28.

36 *Ibid.*, p. 203.

37 Portsmouth, *op. cit.*, p. 22.

38 *Ibid.*, p. 20.

39 I am grateful to Lady Rupert Neville for information about the latter years of her father's life.

40 Clough Williams-Ellis (ed.), *op. cit.*, pp. 283–91.

41 See Anna Bramwell, *Ecology in the Twentieth Century*, pp. 104–32.

42 See Ebenezer Howard, *Garden Cities of Tomorrow*, (MIT Press, 1965). Since the 1970s I have been taking student field trips to Letchworth. I am grateful to a number of people for additional insights into the period of the town's foundation, but especially to Bob Lancaster of the Letchworth Heritage Museum.

43 Patrick Geddes, *Cities in Evolution: An Introduction to the Town Planning Movement and to the Study of Civics*, (Benn, 1968, First published, 1915). Lewis Mumford, *The City in History: Its Origins, its Transformations and its Prospects*, (Secker and Warburg, 1961).

44 Robert A. Pois, *National Socialism and the Religion of Nature*, (Croom Helm, 1986), pp. 149–160.

2 Aspects of Green thought

The concept of ecology

The concepts of ecology and environment are both products of the third quarter of the nineteenth century. The precise stimulus of their creation was Darwinian biology. The underlying condition which made them of interest was man's changing and accelerating interaction with other things: the astonishingly rapid urbanisation and industrialisation of Britain, setting a paradigm for other nations to follow, and the rapid colonisation of the non-European world, especially the United States.

'Environment', in a loose and rare way, already existed in English; it is an application of the French *environner*, to surround. It acquired a more precise meaning as 'The conditions under which any person or thing lives or is developed; the sum-total of influences which modify and determine the development of life or character'. Herbert Spencer was using the term in this way in 1855, before the publication of *The Origin of Species*. By the 1880s scientists were giving it the more pithy definition: 'the sum total of the external conditions of life'. As German geography became influential in British universities it acquired a meaning with a geographical or economic slant, specifically concerned with human activity, as a translation of the German *umwelt*.

The origin of ecology is more specific. The word was first coined as *Oekologie* in German by Ernst Haeckel in his *Generelle Morphologie* published in 1866. The Greek roots mean 'house-study' and Haeckel defined it as 'the science of relations between organisms and their environment' and this has remained the gist of the academic definition.[1] But the word has developed a systematic ambiguity. It means:

1. The science or study of the system of interactions involving living things
2. The interactions in themselves
3. A belief in the transcendent practical, ethical and intellectual importance of those relations, considered as a whole or system.

The word may have a relatively precise origin, but the ideas associated with it are much older and vaguer in origin. As Robert Nisbet suggests, the predecessors of 'ecology' are the ideas of a 'web of life' and 'great chain of being' which suggest that all creatures have 'purposes' in respect of life as a whole (or of ourselves, which is rather different). His account of a continuous ecological tradition of thought includes Saints Benedict and Francis, Sir Thomas More, Adam Smith and the Physiocrats and many anarchist thinkers, including Proudhon and Kropotkin.[2]

The systematic ambiguity of 'ecology' accounts for the odd status of ecologists. In one sense, the ecologist is an entirely respectable and orthodox creature. The idea of an ecological system, of an immensely complex and potentially fragile set of relations, is universally accepted. So is the fact of ecological change. They are part of scientific orthodoxy and also of popular culture, taught in schools and universities and widely illustrated on television. But 'ecologists' are also strange, peripheral figures, pursuing odd lifestyles and voting for a tiny political party. The difference lies in whether you assume that the concept of ecology has ethical and political substance or not; whether, to put it simply, understanding ecology tells you what to do.

Of course, in some sense ecologists can tell you what to do. When they discover a 'hole' in the ozone concentration of the stratosphere or when they suggest the possible effects of an increase in the carbon dioxide content of the troposphere, we react. The question is not, 'What is the right thing to do?', but 'Do we have the technology and the political institutions to do the right thing? It is not ecologism to react in this way if human life is threatened with extinction or a massive shortfall of expectations; it is not even environmentalism; it is merely prudence to be exercised irrespective of values or theories.

But most observations about man's ecological effects are not about eco-catastrophe and do not threaten extinction or nightmare. They are merely changes, with some advantages and some disadvantages, depending on who you are and over what time period you extend your judgement. It is not just man who changes the ecological system; the weather and the emergence and spread of species have always changed it. Nor is contemporary man and modern technology essentially different from previous periods. It is generally agreed that human beings arrived in America across the Behring Strait and instituted a method of fire-drive hunting which destroyed millions of acres of forest and extinguished most of the large mammals on the continent, including the mammoth. Arguably, one of man's first distinctive bits of technology, deliberate fire, is also his most drastic, ecologically speaking. Yet this change created the grasslands, the prairies and the Native American ways which have often been quoted as epitomes of ecological soundness. Even the rate of change in North America in the nineteenth century – the coming of the railway, the extinction of the commonest bird (the passenger pigeon), the near-extinction of the bison, the use of the plough on unsuitably thin soils – seems far more worrying seen from 1890 than from 1990. Why can't we play our part in the ecological system simply by pursuing our own interests as we have before and as other creatures do? This is, loosely, the Adam Smith view of man's ecological role. I don't want to prejudge the question; it is one of the central questions of this book. But it is clearly a very complex question and, with occasional exceptions, it is not answered by the study of ecology. All that it tells us is that complete ecological stability is impossible and might not be desirable even if it were possible. Other values and arguments have to be imported if we are to make substantive ethical and political judgements.

Ecology as religion: Haeckel and Lovelock

Ernst Haeckel was a scientist; more successfully, he was a populariser of science. He was also a cult figure, the head of the 'Monist League', one of those gurus of the popular magazine and the evening meeting, who thrived in urban society before the advent of radio. Part of this cult was religious: Haeckel developed his own form of Pantheism.

The science which Haeckel popularised was overtly Darwinian in doctrine and content. In *The Evolution of Man* he spends over seven hundred pages explaining the details of evolution and the evidence of man's Ascent. There are special twists, however. In several respects he is more Lamarckian than Darwinian, and allows for the possibility of acquired characteristics being passed on, without apparently realising the extent of the incompatibility between that and Darwin's account of evolution. He also insists that there is a functionally necessary parallel between *ontogeny*, the development of the individual, and *anthropogeny*, the development of the species. In some sense we all go through phases of merely chemical, sentient, intelligent, hunter-gatherer and so on in order to become civilized. (This is sometimes stated as 'ontogeny recapitulates phylogeny', the latter referring to the tree-like shape of our patterns of derivation.)

The essence of *monism* is that the universe is one: mind and body are the same, man and animal are the same. To our minds, Haeckel wages two intellectual campaigns simultaneously: he is for monism against dualism and he is for a mechanistic account of the universe rather than one which is teleological. That is, the basic workings of the universe are not to be understood in terms of any will, intention or purpose. In some respects, it is ironic that Haeckel commits himself so enthusiastically to a *mechanical* view of the universe, since many 'Green' writers have declared that it is the image of a mechanical universe, the whole thing as a machine made up of component parts, the 'God's computer' image of Newtonian physics, which they oppose most fundamentally.

For Haeckel, 'the whole knowable universe is a harmonious unity, a *monon*'.[3] Spirit and nature are the same. Thus the soul or spirit must mean the *psyche* and psychic life is 'a development of the medullary tube', the primitive form of spinal marrow. 'The human soul has been gradually developed in the course of millions of years from a long series of Craniote souls.'[4] Haeckel treats us to heavy little monist jokes about bits of soul being stuck onto the side of sperms. More seriously, 'Every science, as such, is both natural and mental. That is a firm principle of Monism which, as its religious side, we may also denominate Pantheism. Man is not above, but in, nature.'[5] Pantheism is the doctrine that God is everything and everything God. Haeckel's revival of Pantheism is a neat and attractive trick which portrays man as ascending from the swamp, rather than descending from the heavens. But God was already in the swamp, as he is in us. Sometimes, one is tempted to think that Haeckel's Pantheism is more of a satire on religion than a religious doctrine, but over his long life (1834-1919), he was mainly serious.

Taken seriously, it has faults. The idea that the workings of the mind are only the mechanical interactions of forces like any other events, leads him to the view that, 'The magnet that attracts iron filings, the powder that explodes, the steam that drives the locomotive, are living inorganics'.[6] To which I respond, simply, that his semantic trick has led him into semantic absurdity. The distinction between 'life' and 'non-life' no longer exists. What he calls 'life' isn't what we mean by 'life' or what we want to mean, nor does it generate any interesting consequences. Nor does he have a mind/non-mind distinction which is worth anything, but to establish that I have to construct a defence of a form of dualism, which I will in due course. His one-dimensional obsession with the similarities between human beings and other creatures led him into biological errors, like placing the intelligence of ants above that of all mammals except ourselves.

Haeckel's monism-Pantheism is really scientific materialism with a sort of joke or semantic twist added on. In essence, it is perfectly orthodox: modern science *is* monist; it does assume that the universe is made of the same stuff and that no teleological categories can be invoked as explanations. Ethically, it has no substance. The Pantheistic God does not tell us what to do. Monism does not tell us how properly to conduct our role in the ecological system. That is not to say that Haeckel did not have an important effect on political action. The Monist League were largely radicals, opposed to monarchy and orthodox religion, and heralding a new age of scientific rationality.[7] Haeckel's biology reinforced their views. In another direction, his work has been valuable in undermining the narrow interpretation of dualism which sees man and 'animal' as offering no insight into one another. Thus Haeckel's thought has played a part in the development of *ethology*, which seeks to merge the understanding of human and animal behaviour. He has encouraged the insights of Konrad Lorenz, Jane Goodall and Desmond Morris at the expense of the mechanistic behaviourism of Ivan Pavlov. He has also had some influence on the development of holistic ideas about medicine, which see people as a whole in the context of their environment, as opposed to the orthodox tradition of analytic, chemical medicine.

A more contemporary exercise on the frontier of ecology and religion is James Lovelock's 'Gaia' hypothesis. The formal statement of the hypothesis is:

> . . . the physical and chemical condition of the surface of the earth, of the atmosphere, and of the oceans has been and is actively made fit and comfortable by the presence of life itself. This is in contrast to the conventional wisdom which held that life adapted to the planetary conditions as it and they evolved their separate ways.[8]

The name comes from the Gaia (or Ge as in Geography, etc.), the Greek Earth Mother, a rather pithier title than Biocybernetic Universal System Tendency/Homeostasis which might have been the name had not the novelist William Golding, a Wiltshire neighbour of Lovelock's, suggested the classical allusion.[9]

There is no real mystery for Lovelock about the origin of life. It was 'an almost utterly improbable event with almost infinite opportunities of happening'.[10] The mystery is about its persistence, about how the extraordinarily improbable temperatures, range of atmospheric constituents and non-toxicity has persisted despite rapidly changing conditions created by the development of the planet itself and by the energy coming into it from the sun. The only explanation is a systematic self-maintenance on the part of Life itself. It is really not such a surprising conclusion. Folk wisdom tells us that houses and gardens provide for better living conditions if they are lived in than if they are not. It is normal for living entities of every kind to do 'jobs' for the eco-system as a whole which do not benefit themselves. Some plants have long roots which bring minerals to the surface, others compost well, others mulch, others provide food for birds which then excrete richly on the soil. Why should the planet not be a similar system, a system of systems? Organisms certainly do 'adapt' to environments; that is, they survive differentially depending on conditions. But that does not preclude the sum total of organisms from acting as a kind of life-preserver or life-enhancer in respect of the whole planetary environment.

Can we call the Systematic Tendency 'Mother' ? She (for the moment) has inter-connected parts like a living thing. Many of these parts have surprising functions in respect of the whole; many more may turn out to have important functions 'The alga *Polysiphonia fastigiata* extracts sulphur from the sea and converts it to dimethyl sulphide, which subsequently reaches the atmosphere and is probably the normal natural carrier of sulphur in the air'.[11] She is *cybernetic*, possessing self-correcting mechanisms which exercise control as if 'to steer an optimum course through changing conditions towards a pre-determined goal'.[12] To this degree, She can even be said to be intelligent.

Thus we have the prospect – exciting, bewildering, disturbing or whatever – of a religious hypothesis beating science on its own terms. There really are more things, on Earth at least, than we are allowed in the philosophies of Charles Darwin and Albert Einstein. Science admits gaps which only Gaia can fill. Certainly, this has been the reaction of many Greens. Porritt enthuses, 'Were such a hypothesis to be "proved", it would certainly put the kibosh on any lingering anthropocentric fantasies!'[13] Gaia was clearly an inspiration for the award-winning BBC melodrama about nuclear power, *Edge of Darkness*.

But this is a very crude version of the thesis, quite detached from the elegant and subtle argument put by Lovelock himself. In terms of the religious dimension of Gaia the trick (as with so many books of grand theory) is to read carefully the assumptions on the first few pages. Lovelock makes it clear that he is deliberately writing for a general audience and in ordinary language: 'In consequence there are passages and sentences which may read as if infected with the twin blights of anthropomorphism and teleology'.[14] She is absolutely non-sentient. To talk of Her:

> is meant no more seriously than is the appellation 'she' when given to a ship by those who sail in her, as a recognition that even pieces of wood and metal when specifically designed and assembled may achieve a composite identity with its own characteristic signature, as distinct from being the mere sum of its parts.[15]

Gaia, in other words, is analogy – good, profound, detailed, thought-provoking analogy, but never homology. It is, however, a rather more substantial attempt at a scientific Pantheism than is Haeckel's.

When it comes to policy. Lovelock is very far from being a conventional Green. He insists that nuclear power is natural and even nuclear weapons could prove useful in a number of circumstances, such as averting a collision with a rogue piece of cosmic debris.[16] He believes that true global disaster is as likely to stem from attempts at organic farming as from anything else.[17] He sees the best hope for the planet as improving technology based on increased scientific research. He surmises that 'twice the present human population of the world could be supported without uprooting other species, our partners in Gaia, from their natural habitats. It would be a grave mistake, however, to think that this could be achieved without a high degree of technology, intelligently organised and applied.'[18]

Thus it may well be that a clear-thinking utilitarianism can function as a part of Gaia. Certainly She provides no clear imperatives: She is beyond caring about a species here or there and likely to be beyond the kind of harm that foolish action might cause:

> It may be that the white-hot rash of our technology will in the end prove destructive and painful for our own species, but the evidence for accepting that industrial activities either at their present level or in the immediate future may endanger the life of Gaia as a whole, is very weak indeed.[19]

Thus:

> There can be no prescription, no set of rules, for living within Gaia. For each of our different actions there are only consequences.[20]

Although Lovelock deliberately eschews deontological prescription and counsels us to rely on our scientific reason and sense of beauty, his argument is far from irrelevant to practical policy. Gaia issues no absolute edicts against extinguishing species; the smallpox bacillus has been lost with impunity, perhaps locusts could be. But it does suggest extreme caution and research; the algae might be a vital part of the system, and they might be destroyed by kelp farming. It is also suggestive of a certain cautious awe, of a mechanism which created us and which we need, the complexity of which defies comprehension.

The religion of nature and the religion of God

It is often remarked that Pantheism is the oldest and most widespread of religions, the belief that God is all of nature predating and extending beyond the animism which sees God in certain objects and the polytheism which posits several Gods as moving in nature. But even the name suggests an overlap, the Greek *Panthea* being statues which carried symbols of several deities, the Roman *Pantheon*, a building which held statues of many Gods.

But the formal statement that all is God and God is all is no more useful as a substantive concept than the theist's formula that God is the omniscient, omnipresent, omnipotent creator of the universe. The two definitions overlap: according to these definitions, theism is also pantheistic because God is everywhere and in all things. Theologians have distinguished between *acosmism* which starts with faith in God and *pancosmism* which starts with the unity of the world and extrapolates God. Acosmism is much closer to orthodox religious belief. There is no doubt that, according to this distinction. Haeckel was an apostle of pancosmism. One contemporary theological critic wrote, comparing him unfavourably to Spinoza, 'Haeckel . . . uses the word "God" only as a fig-leaf to hide the nakedness of his materialistic monism'.[21] According to that critic, Haeckel's pantheism was mere naturalism. In summary, we can say that pantheism is a concept with fraying elastic boundaries, spilling over into theism, animism, polytheism, perhaps deism and certainly into some kind of vague reverential mysticism which says that 'This thing is bigger than all of us'.

Western theology and the 'Judaeo-Christian tradition' are notoriously unsympathetic to pantheism compared with Eastern religions like Buddhism and Hinduism. It has often been treated as a Paganism, a worship of false Gods more reprehensible than atheism, perhaps because it is closer to Satanism. Despite this, much pantheistic thought and sentiment have survived in the West, principally in two forms. The first can be called Folk Pantheism, common to people who work with land. Intimacy tends to anthropomorphise a sense of the land having a will of its own, which makes rules, which punishes and avenges, which can be appeased. I confess that it is not only superstitious peasants who develop such relationships with land. On lone, long-distance walks I have often had Pantheistic sensations – of Nature dancing threateningly around me in the forest on a winter night or giving me a hard and fair contest in the Highlands on a spring day. Who hasn't, who has been close to the land?[22]

The second Western form is in the high culture of the Romantic Movement. One does not have to attempt the formidable task of defining Romanticism in order to state that the movement was largely a reaction to rationalism and utilitarianism. It was deeply attracted to the dark and the primitive; its chosen goddesses were Mother Nature and Rosy Nostalgia. These attractions were a relatively small part of the intellectual life of 1780; they had become extremely important by 1840.

The most familiar forms are to be found in the mysticism of William Blake's 'Tiger, Tiger' or in the 'Auguries of Innocence':

> To see a World in a Grain of Sand
> And a Heaven in a Wild Flower,
> Hold Infinity in the palm of your hand,
> And Eternity in an hour.

Or Elizabeth Barrett Browning's,

> Earth's crammed with heaven,
> And every common bush afire with God.

Romantic Pantheism often expressed approval of Folk Pantheism. Wordsworth quotes the story of a 'yeoman' neighbour who was advised to cut down a 'magnificent tree' for profit. ' "Fell it" exclaimed the yeoman, "I had rather fall on my knees and worship it" ' [23] Wordsworth's position was complex; if not contradictory. In 1837, in 'Steamboats and Railways', he said:

> In your harsh features, nature doth embrace
> Her lawful offspring in man's Art.

But seven years later he was protesting against the arrival of the railway by the banks of Windermere and demanding:

> Is there no nook of English ground secure
> From rash assault? [24]

The idea of human technology being nature's lawful offspring is a neat statement of the central problem, but it offers no solution. In Hindu thought the problem is expressed by an argument between the guru, Shankara, and the guru, Ramanuja. Shankara taught that Brahman is everything and everything Brahman. To which Ramanuja responded, 'How can one worship oneself? '[25] In vulgar terms, the inference is that, if God is everything and in everything, human and non-human, 'good' and bad, why would his existence matter a ha'porth? It explains nothing that does not demand further explanation; it offers no moral prescription.

The sentiments of Romantic or neo-religious Pantheism may lack substance, but this is not to say that they lack influence. That the Lake District is a National Park a quarter of which is owned and managed by the National Trust is due, in no small measure, to Wordsworth's influence. To some degree, we revere or worship the Lake District. That we do so is anathema to the mainstream of the Judaeo-Christian tradition. At least one important element in this tradition emphasises that God, the Creator of Nature, but distinctly outside it, has given the world to man. He has 'dominion' over it, it exists for his *use*. Thus, in Genesis, one of the most frequently quoted verses in the bible:

And God said, let us make man in our image, after our likeness: and let them have dominion over the fish of the sea, and over the fowl of the air, and over the cattle, and over all the earth, and over every creeping thing that creepeth upon the earth.[26]

For a long series of commentators, principally German, this is an unacceptable statement of Nature's status. Ludwig Feuerbach wrote:

> The doctrine of the Creation sprang out of Judaism; indeed, it is the characteristic, the fundamental doctrine of the Jewish religion. The principle which lies at its foundation is, however, not so much the principle of subjectivity as of egoism. The doctrine of the Creation in its characteristic significance arises only on that stand-point where man in practice makes Nature merely the servant of his will and needs, and hence in thought also degrades it to a mere machine, a product of the will.[27]

Thus, 'Utilism is the essential theory of Judaism'[28] and the central symbolic act of Jewry is eating.[29]

This is no isolated criticism, but part of a consistent theme in German thought which sees the German tradition of harmony with Nature as in direct opposition to a Jewish tradition of the use of nature. According to some commentators, 'The Religion of Nature' is a consistent strain of modern German thought, manifesting itself not only in such phenomena as naturist and nudist social movements, but also in the Nazi party and *Die Grünen*.[30] Certainly, the naturist element in Nazism was an important attraction for its intellectual supporters, not only in Germany, but also in England. Some of these took to referring to 'Indo-German' ideas. In doing so they utilised a linguistic contingency because 'Indo-German' is the German way of referring to what is elsewhere called the Indo-European family of languages. It is the supreme irony of Indo-Germany that the swastika is the emblem of the Jain cult, an adjunct of Hinduism, whose adherents pray when they rise every morning that they will not harm any living thing.[31]

Of course, this theological opposition to Judaism is only a small part of the whole phenomenon of anti-semitism. An important related factor in the traditional European image of Jewry was what I would call 'Merchant of Venice syndrome'. Gentile restrictions, and the will to preserve their own identity, led the European Jews to lead a double life. Within their own community, their relations were of a *gemainschaft* form: they supported each other in difficulty, accepted communal rules and punishments and lent money without interest. But in the wider community they were forced into a *gesellschaft* mode, living by the stern letter of enforceable contracts. They had to be (as Antonio put it) creatures of 'gold and silver' and not of 'ewes and lambs'.[32] Thus the image of the Jew always wanting his 'pound of flesh', his claims to contractual rights unconstrained by any broader sense of decency. It was a composite image of finance, greed, individual ambition and removal from things 'natural', a sociological reality which confirmed Genesis. On alien territory the Jew was the symbol of hard-hearted commerce. On his own, in the *kibbutzim* by the Sea of Galileee, tending his soil without individual financial reward, he is a potential Green hero. The theology may be the same, but the image is very different.

The relationship between this aspect of Judaism and Christian theology is complex. It has always been acknowledged that there are two other major influences on Christianity; besides the Judaic, there were important Greek and Eastern influences. The latter, certainly, and the former, more dubiously, modify the biblical notion of 'dominion' over nature. In any case, much Christian practice has simply absorbed Pagan practice and Pagan assumptions about nature have never been eradicated by Christian churches. Consider Christmas: mistletoe, Christmas trees, Santa Claus, feasting, Yule logs and presents all have pre-Christian origins in forms of celebration of the relationship between Man and Nature in Winter. Most of them are Nordic or Germanic in origin and have been revived in the past two centuries. Harvest Festival is another example. Until the late nineteenth-century there was no celebration of the harvest in most Christian churches. Harvest suppers were a purely secular affair, barely tolerated, often opposed, by the churches. In the 1890s, starting in Cornwall, the Harvest Festival was introduced as a distinct service in the Anglican church, becoming universally celebrated in the twentieth century. In the 1980s the Roman Catholic church in England bowed to popular pressure and began to celebrate the harvest as well.

It could be argued that Christian attitudes to nature have effectively been dominion-oriented and Judaic in origin. In influential essays published in the 1960s, 'On Christian Arrogance Toward Nature' and 'The Historical Roots of our Ecological Crisis', Lynn White Jr revived the argument that Christianity has been the historical enemy of nature.[33] White's thesis has met with considerable agreement and enthusiasm, though there is no acknowledgement in it of the long German lineage of such analyses. For half a millenium now 'Christians' have destroyed stable 'native' economies and cultures, burned forests and short-sightedly ripped up the earth's surface in search of profit from minerals and large-scale crops. As I write, this process is continuing at a greater pace than ever in Brazil. Absurd extremes of Christian disapproval of nature can be quoted: Pius IX refused to allow the formation of a Society for the Prevention of Cruelty to Animals in Rome because this would imply that human beings had duties towards animals. The *New Catholic Encyclopaedia* states boldly that 'experimentation on living animals is "lawful and good", even though animals may suffer severe pain in the process'.[34] Lynn White writes that, 'Especially in its Western form, Christianity is the most anthropocentric religion the world has seen'.[35]

But this would be a very partial picture of Christian ethics and theology: Christianity has remained a broad church, an area of philosophical pluralism. It may be the 'most anthropocentric' of religions in that it rejects a reverence for Nature *per se*. But it does contain an alternative tradition to that of 'dominion', that of 'stewardship'. In *Man's Responsibility for Nature*, John Passmore suggests that the tradition of Man as the gentle, far-sighted, gardener of Nature is an alternative meaning of 'dominion'; this image has a long lineage from the early church through the Franciscans to the 'creation theologians' and 'New Age Christians' of today.[36] As 'stewardship' moves towards 'partnership', Christian moves towards Green. James Lovelock also quotes the 'stewardship' tradition with approval and suggests that reverence, if that means letting Nature be, will no longer serve Her well. What is now required is man-as-gardener, far-sighted management using the highest level of technology.[37]

As the 1980s came to a close, on December 5th 1989, Pope John Paul II issued a statement called *Peace with God the Creator, Peace with all of Creation*. It was the first papal document ever to address the concept of ecology and the problem of man's ecological role. It attacked the 'selfishness, greed and disregard for nature in industrialised countries' and said 'The increasing devastation of the world of nature is apparent to all. It is the result of a callous disregard for the hidden and perceivable requirements of the harmony which governs nature itself.'[38] It would be excessively cynical to dismiss this Papal move as 'jumping on a Green bandwagon' as an inconsistency and an over-reaction. But it does draw not only on an ancient idea of Christian stewardship of nature, but also on John Paul's consistent opposition to 'materialism' and 'instant gratification'.

The spectrum of Green politics

The magic number in Green philosophy and theology is one: oneness, wholeness, monism are ever-present themes. In politics, the magic number becomes three: the programme and philosophy are a 'third way' (not, of course, the only third way in twentieth century politics) which cannot be identified with left or right, with capitalism or socialism. Porritt says:

> The claim made by green politics that it's 'neither right, nor left, nor in the centre' has understandably caused a lot of confusion! . . . But it's really not that difficult. We profoundly disagree with the politics of the right and its underlying ideology of capitalism; we profoundly disagree with the politics of the left and its adherence in varying degrees, to the ideology of socialism. . . . The politics of the Industrial Age, left, right and centre, is like a three-lane motorway, with different vehicles in different lanes, but *all* leading in the same direction.[39]

The main thrust of this claim can be fully substantiated. Green thought does not belong in any particular part of the left/right continuum; it has a legitimate place in *almost* all established political positions. There are two main reasons for this. The first is that the spectrum is concerned primarily with issues of property and distribution, which are largely irrelevant to Green thought *per se*, though they may be important to individual interpreters of the Green tradition. But a more profound reason is that the idea of a 'continuum' or 'spectrum' of politics is really nonsense and the net value of it has been to obfuscate matters of theory and policy.

Take the notion of being 'conservative' or 'right wing'. What is the relationship between them? What is the most 'right-wing', a divine right monarchist in the style of Louis XIV, a libertarian believer in natural rights and the legitimate acquisition of property like John Locke or Robert Nozick or a 'Fascist' ? Which is the most 'conservative' ? The latter question would surely depend on the *status quo ante*: currently Eastern European and Soviet believers in the restoration or maintenance of central planning, monolithic ideology and the leading role of the Communist Party, are described as 'conservatives'. I have argued that, in one sense, 'conservatism' does not exist; there is nothing of philosophical importance which all conservatives believe.[40] What they do have in common is opposition to the humanist progressivism which has been so influential in the world's affairs in the last two centuries, but they can come to that opposition from nationalist or internationalist, materialist or spiritualist, sceptical or faithful, positions.

In England some of the most passionately and bitterly Green thinkers (including Lymington and Massingham) have considered themselves Tories. But it is also certain strains of Conservative which are most likely to be overtly opposed to Green thinking and to dismiss it as Communism in disguise. Robert Whelan, author of *Mounting Greenery*, a pamphlet published by the Institute of Economic Affairs in 1989, dismisses Green thought as irrational, religiose and reactionary. He says:

> The best way to provide for future generations is to exploit resources, not conserve them. Market forces and human ingenuity will take care of shortages by providing solutions which leave us better off than we were before.

At the time of writing, many ordinary Tories remain deeply Green and conservative in their views on the individual and the community, the relationships between people and land, the benefits of economic growth and several other broad issues. But many of the Party's most articulate ideologists have exactly the opposite opinions.

National Socialism and Fascism

A number of recent works of scholarship have stressed the importance of the 'religion of nature' in the ideas and appeal of Nazism. The *Reichsnaturschutzgesetz* Law of 1935 set up the most ambitious system of nature conservation the world had seen. Translated into post-war English terms, it included a system of protected species and the designation of Nature Reserves, National Parks and Areas of Outstanding Natural Beauty. The prolegomenon of the law owes much to the concept of ecology and the religion of nature. It suggests that previous attempts to preserve nature could not succeed because their object was at odds with the essential forces in society: 'It was only the transformation of the German man which created the preliminary conditions necessary for an effective system of protection of Natural Beauty'.[41] The protection and expansion of forests was a consistent part of the Third Reich's policy: Hitler quarrelled with Mussolini over the destruction of 'German' forests in the Alto Adige and German troops entering Poland were told that part of the reason for their mission was to save the forests of East Prussia from the ravages of the Polish peasantry.

Walther Darré, Minister of Agriculture from 1933–42 was in many ways the most 'Green' of Nazi ministers and pursued a policy of encouragement of small holding and organic farming (*lebensgesetzliche Wirtschaftsweise*). The Fuhrer himself was a vegetarian and nature-lover. His deputy, Hess, was a follower of Rudolf Steiner, a naturist and believer in 'bio-dynamic' agriculture (a slightly stronger concept of the 'organic' than the officially accepted version). Even Fritz Todt, who designed most of the *autobahn* programme was a fervent believer in *oekologie* who wanted his motorways to be part of the landscape.[42]

The 'Green' content of Nazism is interesting and, until recently, had been underplayed by writers about the Third Reich. But its significance should not be exaggerated. It is highly irrational to play the 'Hitler card' and rely, in argument, on the assumption that if Hitler believed it, it must be wrong. It is equally irrational to equate political philosophies with political movements and read into the latter a conspiratorial coherence which is not there. The Party contained multitudes: Hess and Darré were eventually disgraced; Nazis like Reinhard Heydrich always thought that ecologism and rural nostalgia were degenerate. The 1935 Law contained a codicil stating that all of its provisions could be overridden for military or transport purposes. Anybody who has read *Mein Kampf* knows that the Fuhrer's individual mind contained almost as many multitudes as the aggregate in the Party.

In other words, the Nazi party, like most political organisations was contained and embraced a contradictory jungle of political ideas, many of them crudely absorbed and poorly digested. It was not Ernst Haeckel with a silly moutsache and a goosestep; nor was it G. W. F. Hegel or J. G. Fichte or F. W. Nietzsche, nor even Richard Wagner, in disguise. The 'religion of nature' was part of its outlook and was connected with its anti-semitism. But one could also portray the British Labour Party as 'naturist'. It has strong links with many organisations enthusiastic about nature, ranging from the Woodcraft Folk to the Fabian Society. Most of its major historic figures can be pictured in shorts and with rucksacks at some stage of their lives. Between 1945 and 1950 it enacted the whole of *Reichsnaturshutzgesetz*, though without the prolegomenon. Even so, to portray the Labour Party as essentially a naturist organisation would be a ridiculously one-dimensional picture which would have to ignore, *inter alia*, the role of Trade Unions in its history and outlook.

For those who want to argue that there is (or was) a general category of 'Fascism' which can be taken to include National Socialism, attitudes to nature and ecology provide a serious obstacle. Italian Fascism was in many respects quite opposite to National Socialism. Gentile and Mussolini were influenced by Futurism and by similar strains in Italian thought which sought to reject the dead hand of the past and create a powerful, respected Italy of clean lines and gleaming machinery. Fascism added to that the over-whelming force of the 'will' of the people under its almost supernatural leader. 'Nature' existed to be tamed: marshes were drained, forests chopped down and superb *autostrade* cut straight lines through the mountains.

It is true that Mussolini's regime did a great deal to revive Italian farming, but that was largely a question of power, of securing a power-base for the regime and maximising Italy's economic autonomy. For all the Futurist influences, there was also an element of nostalgia. But this was nostalgia for ancient Rome, not for the simple life of Cato's honest republican ploughmen, but for expanding, trading, urban, technological, domineering Imperial Rome.

Other 'fascisms' add even more confusion. In Spain, José Antonio Primo De Rivera, the founder of the Falange party, spoke a rhetoric of 'third way' which portrayed capitalism and communism as (almost) equally satisfactory. His thought was more influenced by Mussolini than by Hitler and he published an account of meeting Mussolini, as an introduction to the Spanish edition of *La Dottrina del Fascismo*, which would be nauseatingly sycophantic written by any interviewer about any subject.[43] José Antonio's thought was also mixed up with specifically Spanish themes, notably the nature of relationships between the state and the Roman Catholic church and the perennial problem of those Latin countries without successful industrial 'take-off', land reform. He was in favour of rural revival and the redistribution of land, but these beliefs hardly mark him out as a greatly original thinker. Much of it was expressed in mystical rhetoric about 'Spain's indivisible destiny'. It is as well to remember that José Antonio only lived to be thirty three and was a young man passionately upset about the condition of his country. Of his theoretical and prescriptive response to the problems Spain faced, Hugh Thomas comments, 'This accumulation of discordant ideas scarcely amounted to a political philosophy'.[44] It was to become yet more discordant when the Franco *coup* absorbed the Falange party.

In Eastern Europe there were a variety of 'Catonist' movement parties which opposed, with varying emphasis, foreign influence and invest-ment, the decline of agriculture and cities. As *glasnost* spread through Eastern Europe in the 1980s many of these themes began to re-emerge. They had, to differing degrees, been absorbed by local Communist Parties. The picture provides a salutory lesson for those who still believe that anything substantial can be said about politics in terms of a continuum between 'left' and 'right'.

Green Marxism?

It is not impossible to trace a lineage of Green Marxist thought from the young Marx to the present day. The starting point must be with selected passages of *The German Ideology*, those which discuss alienation and the freedom of future communism. Engels was influenced by Haeckel: in his essay, 'The Part played by Labour in the Transition from Ape to Man' he said that, 'we by no means rule over nature like a conqueror over a foreign people, like someone standing outside nature – but that we, with flesh, blood and brain, belong to nature, and exist in its midst, and that all our mastery of it consists in the fact that we have the advantage over all other creatures of being able to know and correctly apply its laws'.[45] Communism would save man and nature from the 'senseless and unnatural' contrast been them which is implicit in capitalism and Christianity.

At a time when Engels' essay was finally published, in the 1890s, England contained varieties of rustic Marxist – prophets of a future, rural English communism – in Robert Blatchford, who edited *Merrie England* and William Morris. The dream-future portrayed in Morris's *News From Nowhere* is a society without money, where work is associated with skill and considered a privilege.[46] Almost all motive for crime has disappeared; people freely join and leave communes which seem to owe something in their spirit to both the medieval monastery and the Victorian weekend party. Women remain beautiful and sexually attractive at sixty years of age because they have lived free and fulfilling lives. This tradition is very much alive in continental Europe today: Marxists like Rudolf Bahro and André Gorz, disillusioned with 'orthodox' communism, have become self-consciously 'Green' in outlook.

But this description of Green Marxism describes at most a minority sect within the 'ism'; much of it may amount only to an ambiguity. For Marx, one of the progressive aspects of capitalism was its rejection of the 'deification of nature'. It was a good thing that 'nature becomes for the first time simply an object for mankind, purely a matter of utility'.[47] This is the mainstream of Marx's legacy, a humanist inversion of capitalism and Christianity which finally releases man, in Trotsky's vision, for a complete, managerial domination over the earth.[48] It is this mainstream which has made Communist governments as much enemies for Green critics as are capitalist companies for their disastrous, anthropocentric, arrogance. Tourists to the Soviet Himalayas are sold a pretty picture of far-sighted public management of the wilderness. But *glasnost* has allowed us to evidence fully the death of the Siberian Forests and the Sea of Azov, the disappearance of the Aral Sea and the catastrophe of Chernobyl. Soviet Communism in practice has been anthropocentric industrialism at its most extreme.

Mao Tse Tung looks, at first sight, rather different. He was radically anti-urban, seeing cities as 'beggars with golden bowls' and successfully pursuing policies which kept peasants on the land and gave urban labour 'brigades' experience of agricultural work. But his form of 'Catonism' turned out to represent a peculiar, nature-hating, aspect of peasant life which included attacks on the Confucian tradition of reverence for nature and deliberate attempts to wipe out all the wild birds from Chinese agricultural areas.

Green Marxism is not a logical impossibility, but it is a historical eccentricity.

Anarchism

For the mainstream of the anarchist tradition, nearly all that is wrong and discordant in human society can be attributed to the consequences of re-inforcing institutions. Money creates property, which requires law for its definition and the state for its protection. The state requires power, authority and repressive punishment to function. The institutions of repression and exclusive ownership create human beings who can only be regulated by repressive means if they are to be restrained from destruction. In the typical anarchist vision of future society, people are able to live and associate freely without destructive impulses or desires for acquisition which exceed need. *News from Nowhere* could be considered an anarchist vision just as much as a picture of future communism: it is not the working of society which differs, but the means of getting to that condition of society (and the absence of a 'dictatorship of the proletariat' in Morris's historical account of Nowhere, is closer to an anarchist than a Marxist history in important respects).

The defining core of anarchism consists of an institutional analysis of human behaviour and a prescription for a form of society in which human relations are radically different. Anarchism is not essentially concerned with nature. But anarchism seeks to create a society of powerless relations and to abolish the motivation for most acquisition. Large-scale industry and an insistence on economic growth are its natural targets just as much as they are targets for ecological critics. As Yeats suggested, all utopias or ideals are naturally pure, pre-industrial, clean and green. Anarchy and eco-Utopia must overlap massively. Prince Kropotkin's *Mutual Aid* is a text for Greens as much as for Anarchists.[49] In the American tradition of anarchism, which stretches from H. D. Thoreau in the mid-nineteenth century to such contemporary writers as Murray Bookchin and Theodore Roszak, the fit between anarchist and ecological critiques of contemporary society is almost complete.[50] This is a consistent tradition of individual retreat from the urban mainstream of society, of the simple life and of communalism; it is a tradition best summed up by Roszak's rather Gramscian phrase, *'counter-culture '*.

As a literary *genre*, anarchy and eco-utopia are vast and diverse. But what are they as politics? They must always be confronted with the obstacle of the utopian paradox, which suggests that their kind of arrangements could only exist if people were very different and people could only change sufficiently if the arrangements they recommend were in place for generations. The criticism is not merely that they do not have a programme, it is that they never could have a programme.

An important implication is that utopians can have no practical approach to power. Porritt chides Michael Allaby for saying, 'Ecology activists are not concerned with power: they have no wish to take political or economic power from one section of society and give it to another'. Of course, he replies, they want to take power away from certain people. Then Porritt affirms, 'the belief that *everyone* should be empowered to determine the course of his or her own life within the constraints of a finite planet'. [51] To which the world-weary political theorist is bound by professional duty to point out that whoever gets the job of defining 'the constraints of a finite planet' will have enormous and unprecedented power, greater, even, than that of his predecessors who allowed people freedom within God's laws or within the historical needs of the state. Ecology cannot be improved without stopping a lot of people from doing things they would otherwise choose to do; the Porritt formula is either a recipe for ineffectiveness or a license for authoritarianism. It may, indeed, be both: the 'worst case scenario' is massive authority based on a badly-constructed theory of 'the needs of a finite planet'. The question of the relationship between ecological improvement and programmes for the diminution or devolution of political power is a mighty obstacle for Green thought and must be carefully examined.

Nationalisms

Nationalist movements are inevitably broad churches: many interests and principles are co-opted into the project for greater independence and what defines a 'nation' can vary greatly from one to another. But a common core of nationalist programmes is the rejection of alien influences prescribing a retreat to 'natural' values and the re-establishment of a pure form of the national way of life. For M. K. Gandhi, Indian nationalism was about the re-assertion of a rural, quietist, spiritual India, a simple and contemplative way of life threatened by Western materialism. Eamonn De Valera sought to re-create a 'frugal and ascetic' Ireland, isolated from outside influences by the Gaelic language and the maintenance of a peasant economy. Language is the principal issue of Welsh nationalism, but many Welsh nationalist writers insist that the language question is inextricably linked with a totemistic response to features of the landscape and to the rural way of life. To be a full participant in Welsh culture, according to these accounts, is to read not only the language, but the landscape; it requires an understanding of the history and legends of Wales, which must be put into the context of language and geography. Even Scottish nationalism has an element of this kind. Most commentators agree that the Scots, unlike many other small nations, do not perceive a threat to their identity *per se*. The boom in Nationalist support in the 1970s had every appearance of being, for the most part, an assertion of Scottish economic interests rather than a protection of Scotland's identity. But there has always been a pure, 'Sinn Fein', element in Scottish nationalism. Malcolm Slesser's book, *The Politics of Environment*, seeks to protect a spacious, healthy, mountain-climbing Scotland from the sicknesses of a materialist world. [52]

It would seem natural that 'Green' nationalisms should arise where industry and modernisation come from outside. It is more surprising to find such a movement in England (though the parallels with Germany are important). But the cult of the 'Anglo-Saxon' in England was, to some extent, such a nationalism. It had a number of elements. Perhaps the prime use of 'Anglo-Saxon' was as a theory of racial supremacy which arose out of Victorian racial biology and functioned to justify empire. Being 'Anglo-Saxon' was a parallel identity to being 'Teuton' and the racial characteristics of Anglo-Saxons were contrasted with those of 'Celts' and more distant natives as well as those of European rivals. There were numerous different accounts of the virtues of the 'Anglo-Saxon', but the most common themes were sturdiness, honesty and a capacity for action rather than speculation. Such accounts of race were either explicit or implicit in the majority of 'Imperial Yarns' published between 1870 and 1930. Mercifully, no 'Anglo-Saxon' racial programme ever had a noticeable direct impact on English politics: the idea was abandoned by many in favour of the self-image of a 'mongrel race'. Paradoxically, the 'Celticism' which was a reaction to it has been enormously important in Ireland and Wales.[53]

But not all accounts of 'Anglo-Saxons' were necessarily racial. Literary Anglo-Saxons like C. S. Lewis took the theories of Hegel and Fichte and made *language* the key to identity: it was linguistic roots which made us different. Knowing who we are must start with a grasp of the Anglo-Saxon language.[54] For Bryant and Massingham, it was the nature of Anglo-Saxon society – stable, egalitarian, ecologically sound – which made the identity important. Their account of history paralleled the popular legend of the 'Norman Yoke' descending on 'Merry' England. An extension of this argument portrays Anglo-Saxon virtues and institutions surviving in rural England until industrialisation when the English way of life came under renewed attack from alien values. This gives rise to some interesting scholarly nostalgia such as Peter Laslett's *The World We Have Lost*.[55]

A changing shade of Green

Earlier I poured some reasonably determined scorn on the idea of a 'spectrum' of political thought or (the ideas tend to be confused) a continuum stretching from 'left' to 'right'. But, insofar as those images of spectrum and continuum are established in people's minds, they are important; they create identities and self-fulfilling prophecies.

In terms of these identities and prophecies, the main focus of Green politics has shifted along the political spectrum. In the late nineteenth-century it was largely revolutionary and Marxist, as Blatchford, Morris (and Engels) looked to the workers to overthrow industrialism. The leading Green group in inter-war England saw themselves as Tories, but they had little in common with what has now become the dominant wing of the Conservative Party. They were bitterly resentful of the enclosure movement and wrote disparagingly of 'capitalism' and trade. To widely differing degrees, they admired aspects of the Third Reich. The 'ecologists' who were cast into the limelight in the crisis of Western capitalism following the energy difficulties of 1973 were so reactionary and radical that both 'left' and 'right' would, for the most part, wish to disclaim them.

Throughout the 1980s the perception of the Green movement, from within and without, has moved leftwards. One reason is that the decline of faith in socialism has released personnel of a critical spirit for a different kind of attack on contemporary Western societies. The success of *Die Grünen* (in terms of elections and publicity, if not of policies) has made Germany the influential paradigm, in this respect as in others. On the other side, the rise of the 'New Right' as the most self-conscious opponents of Green thought has helped polarise issues. The low-brow, Tory individualist, response is that Greens are wolves in sheep's clothing, commies in disguise. Finally, the issues of nuclear power and weapons have helped concentrate Green attacks on recognisably 'right wing' targets. For a utilitarian, debates about nuclear issues ought to be precise considerations of cost-effectiveness and risk-assessment. But for the Green outlook nuclear issues are fundamental: both forms of nuclear technology exemplify man's ill-considered and dangerous Promethean arrogance and the threats to life and liberty from existing structures of power.

Green and Grey metaphysics

The constant theme of Green thought is *holism* (or *monism* as Spinoza and Haeckel have it); it seeks to portray reality as *essentially* a wholeness, a unity or a 'oneness'. In opposition to holism is either (or both) dualism, the belief or assumption that reality consists of two separate kinds of stuff, usually mind and body, or some form of atomism, which insists that reality consists of individual particulars, of essentially separate things.

Much Green writing on philosophical subjects suggests an ancient and vitally important clash between two opposed *weltanschauungen*. One side of the chasm is holism; reality is essentially a unity; persons are animals; all are part of Nature: ethically, all entities must be respected. This generates holistic medicine, ethological understandings of both persons and other creatures and a spiritual outlook which has at least something in common with pantheism. In the other corner is the orthodox, Grey, world view: an analytic physics which assumes reality is a set of separable mechanisms; a fundamental distinction between people and other animals, in that only people have 'souls'; man and nature in opposition: a mechanistic medicine and behavioural biology. The religious choice is between reverence for a God who is like man (or, at least, far more like man than He is like any other known entity) and a bleak materialistic atheism in which man is a fairly incompetent driver of a spaceship on an endless Circle Line.

As drama, this dichotomy is superb. The idea of two world schemes fighting it out to the philosophical death, each logically complete, with a co-ordinate set of approaches to every branch of theory and knowledge, the opposite and inverse of the approaches of the other, is extremely attractive. Unfortunately, the history of this drama is that it has never quite been staged. It is rather like one of those pub fights in which a small, aggressive drunk shouts abuse and swings punches at a group of well-heeled citizens by the bar and they respond by ignoring him. It is a one-sided fight because it has been considered important by only one of its participants. The well-heeled men at the bar are preoccupied with their own habitual quarrels between theists and atheists and between 'left' and 'right'.

Naturally, descriptions of what is at stake come only from one side and tend to be rather biased. It is the Judaeo-Christian and scientific Western world-view, ultimately sterile, destructive and alienating, against pantheism and holism, harmony and nature. It is very rare to find proponents of maximum economic growth attacking Haeckel or the Eastern influences on Christianity. But it is fairly common to find Green writers attacking the luminaries of Western science and philosophy. Porritt turns his attentions on Isaac Newton for assuming the world to be a sort of machine-puzzle set by God. Several writers tell the story of Rene Descartes' wife's dog: because the creature had no soul, he cut open its leg and examined it while it was fully sentient. The wife later left him.[56] John Massingham equated Thomas Hobbes with Satan as an epitome of evil.

Descartes, Newton and Hobbes have a great deal in common. All of them lived most of their lives in the seventeenth century and they all feature prominently in books and chapters on 'the scientific revolution'. All of them contributed to the intellectual background in which technology and industry were to make geometric progress. This intellectual background encouraged a rigorous contempt for animist superstition about nature and for anthropomorphic sentimentality about animals. Recent historians have documented the growing 'de-humanisation' of animals since the seventeenth century.[57] To this extent, Hobbes, Descartes and Newton are proper villians for the Green movement.

But sadly, for lovers of drama, the dichotomy between Green and Grey does not really work. Orthodox science *is* holistic or monistic. It does insist that the universe is made of the same stuff. Indeed, it is important to note that this is *all* that defines the project of science as such. Science seeks a coherent account of the universe. The criterion of coherence is *only* that all phenomena should fit the same model, that we should aspire to a description of the universe which is uniform, in which all phenomena obey the same 'laws'. It is not an assumption of science that we should know these laws at any particular time, nor that we should be guaranteed of ever finding them, but only that we must look in order to be scientific.

Criticisms of scientists or of particular scientific practices are not criticisms of the idea of science. It may well be that much existing 'science' is wrong. It may also be the case that 'departmentalised' science, in which Professors of physics, chemistry and biology blinker their researchers and defend their empires, is institutionally crippled and disadvantaged from making radical progress, as James Lovelock suggests. Scientists may operate narrow and repressive views of dissent, and be able to implement those views far more effectively than priests or politicians, as Paul Feyerabend has consistently argued.[58] But these are criticisms of the practice rather than of its underlying philosophy which is holist and maximally open. That many of the mediaeval popes were not 'good Christians' is suggestive, but it is not firm proof that Christianity is steeped in philosophical error.

What, then, of 'dualism', the doctrine which made Descartes such a cad? One form of dualism has been stigmatised by so orthodox a philosopher as Sir Gilbert Ryle as 'the doctrine of the ghost in the machine'.[59] Ontological dualism, the belief that mind and body have entirely separate existences, that human beings and natures are distinct substances, has few philosophical friends in the modern world and they are to be found in orthodox religion rather than in science. But a more serious consideration must be given to logical or semantic dualism. By this, I mean a view of humanity and the universe which acknowledges a single causal reality, but maintains the propriety and necessity of two independent ways of talking about it. In this view, human beings are animals and part of nature, but they have another dimension. Because we have language – symbolic, representative, systems of communication – we have minds: we have beliefs and intentions; we decide and act, we debate and form obligations. To be human is to acknowledge that there are other humans, quite different in kind from non-humans because we understand them in a different way (by appreciating what they believe and want) and we are capable of being ethically bound to them in a different way (by forming obligations, making promises and signing contracts).

I confess, then, in the important dimensions of logic and ethics, to being that metaphysical enemy of all things Green, a dualist. The argument for this kind of dualism is that it is a pre-condition of any rational, human discourse that we divide the world into two categories, entities with minds and entities without minds. Without the distinction we can neither understand ourselves nor formulate an ethics and a politics.

Some charges of dualism must be acknowledged. If it is true that only one species on this planet can be said to have minds, it is only contingently true: it might have been different, it might change, perhaps we have got it wrong. If chimpanzees can enter discussions and make promises, we should treat them as essentially 'human' even though they are not *homo sapiens*. Since chimpanzees, according to accounts of the 'Nevada experiment', have made some progress along these lines, that is worth thinking about. The form of dualism to which I confessed does imply a form of 'anthropocentrism', but it does not imply the anthropo-chauvinism which says that my species must be the only one worthy of consideration because it is my species. Nor does it suggest that the dualist distinction is the only distinction worth making. The distinction between sentient and non-sentient beings is also important. If the allegation against Descartes is true, he wilfully inflicted pain on a sentient being for a very bad philosophical reason: he said the creature was incapable of feeling pain. This is not the position of Benthamite utilitarianism; many commentators have suggested that the primacy of *sentience* in Bentham's philosophy offers the best available philosophical basis for the benign treatment of sentient beings other than man.

Since the early 1970s a number of philosophers have attempted to offer a fully-formed philosophical basis for the outlook of the Green tradition. One starting point was an essay, in manifesto form, by the Norwegian philosopher Arne Naess called, 'The Shallow and the Deep, Long-Range Ecology Movement. A Summary'.[60] Naess summarises the 'Shallow Ecology' movement very briefly: 'Fight against pollution and resource depletion. Central objective: the health and affluence of people in the developed countries'. Deep Ecology has a more complex definition. Its ethical implications include:

- *Biospherical egalitarianism* – the 'equal right to live and blossom' of all creatures.
- *Principles of diversity and symbiosis* – 'Diversity . . . the richness of forms' as ends in themselves both within human cultures and the natural world.
- *Local autonomy and decentralisation* – this conceived entirely in human terms, the principal arguments drawing on man's potential for ecological destruction in large organisations.

But the statement starts with metaphysics:

> Rejection of the man-in-environment image in favour of *the relational, total-field image*. Organisms as knots in the biospherical net or field of intrinsic relations. An intrinsic relation between two things A and B is such that the relation belongs to the definitions or basic constitutions of A and B, so that without the relation, A and B are no longer the same things. The total-field model dissolves not only the man-in-environment concept, but every compact thing-in-milieu concept – except when talking at a superficial or preliminary level of communication.

One must admire the attempt to put the distinction between holism and dualism on a clear metaphysical basis. But the consequences are bizarre: the ontological priorities defy all logic. It is like saying that energy and economic systems exist, but particular motor cars or factory chimneys do not. In some senses, of course, both do. But in a very important logical sense, motor cars and chimneys exist and energy and economic systems do not: we can construct a coherent and useful, if limited, discourse without the relational categories. We cannot do so without individual particulars.

The image of 'Deep Ecology' is part of a fashionable trade in 'deep' versions of things, but the analogy in this case is fundamentally misleading. It is *not* that 'Deep Ecology' is what you get to if you dig deeper, if you follow the implications of Shallow Ecology down to a satisfactory level. On the contrary, 'Shallow' and 'Deep' are fundamentally opposed ethical systems which, Naess himself insists, are based on radically different metaphysics. Shallow is not the superficial version of deep, it is the opponent. It would be foolish to dwell too long on Naess's particular formulations. He suggests that they are 'rather vague generalisations' and that they are *suggested, inspired, and fortified* ' (his italics) by the nature of ecology, rather than implied. He has, apparently, changed his formulation several times. What is interesting is not one or another precise version of Naess's manifesto, but its effects. A brief, modest, cryptically expressed collection of thoughts has, nevertheless, received enormous attention. It has been attacked, developed and re-formulated, albeit by a limited group of ecologically-oriented philosophers. 'Deep Ecology' has most aspects of a cult, including the footnoting and discussion of remarks and unpublished papers. It is difficult to think of an analogy, unless it is Filippo Marinetti's *Futurist Manifesto* of 1909.

Some critics have attached Naess's moderation, suggesting that he is 'bio-centrist' and insisting on the rights of inanimate entities. Others, like Richard Sylvan, though fundamentally sympathetic to the project, consider it a failure.[61] What is certain is that Naess's manifesto raises philosophical issues which are now troubling many people. There are few answers, though. The general (if familiar) problem is that, whatever you think of the metaphysics, no substantive ethics can be inferred from it. What are the limits of man's legitimate 'interference' with nature? Do our ethical duties to the planet also bind our attitudes to the colder, infinitely bigger, conception of the universe? Does not all this talk of non-human rights and intrinsic values necessarily reduce to a particular kind of talk about human satisfaction? Deep Ecologists have made little progress in satisfying themselves on these questions and are far from coming to meet those of us of more orthodox Western persuasions who might have the odd doubt in rejecting the possibility of sentient non-human creatures having 'rights', but who cannot see what it could reasonably mean for a tree, which can be owed no contractual dues, which can articulate no claims and which has no feelings, to have rights. There is a Green ethics, there are some interesting Green metaphysical questions, but there is, as yet, no metaphysical basis for Green ethics.

A note on Green art

The project to establish metaphysical coherence may be in some difficulties, but there can be no doubting the enormous influence of Green art, nor its (artistic) success. Unlike philosophy or politics, art does not have to clarify concepts nor make difficult decisions. Its protests can echo unanswered, its 'statements' be judged on their style rather than their content. The vast empires of the romantic and the pastoral have been enormously important in music, in poetry, in painting and in fiction. They fill us with the worship of Mother Nature and Rosy Nostalgia; they reinforce the Green heart that often lies below even the Greyest of heads.

In art, the Green dominates and vanquishes its enemies. In a number of countries, including England, the Green perspective has been far more important than its enemies (rationalism, futurism, modernism) in the arts and more important, also, than alternative perspectives of social criticism such as Christianity and socialism. Many of our most prestigious writers offer a critique of existing society which is at least aesthetic if not ecological (in its emphasis on future instability, alienation from nature and spiritual *malaise*). Many of the most popular offer reactionary nostalgia, pictures of previous conditions of society which were hard and unfair, but closer to nature and, ultimately, more satisfactory. The subject is so vast it can be summarised quite quickly. But I would like to emphasise two related points, one about English writers of the inter-war period and the other about children's literature.

'Cultural despair' typified English inter-war intellectuals. Britain's Empire was at its greatest extent, but the *cognoscenti* knew that it was an untenable sham, that real world power lay with the USA and that Britain's capacity to resist Germany or Japan was limited. At home, they perceived, in differing proportions, social injustice and vulgarity. It was the peak period of urban sprawl and mass production. Cheap semi-detached houses spread quickly over an economically depressed countryside. Cheap motor cars began to penetrate the land: 'The motorist from Birmingham' was everywhere. An ancient culture was engulfed, as many saw it, in a tide of '78' records, Hollywood films and canned food. At no other period have so many intellectuals been attracted to a radical condemnation of English society and led to seek hope in foreign powers like the Third Reich and the Soviet Union. Many were also drawn to images of a rural past and projects for rural revival, the most prominent being in the loose circle which included Lord Lymington and John Massingham.

Henry Williamson, author of *Tarka the Otter* and *Salar the Salmon*, was an extreme case, attracted to traditional farming and to support for Hitler. He was very briefly interned during the war, but continued to write, broadcast and run his Norfolk farm. His views did not change much. This is clear from *The Gale of the World*, the last of his fifteen-novel sequence called 'A Chronicle of Ancient Sunlight'.[62] It was published in 1969 and is dedicated to Kenneth Allsop, the television presenter, who had made some efforts to rehabilitate Williamson. It is set in Britain in the immediate post-war months and its opening chapters are among the bleakest prose I have read. The characters ramble round a half-starved, half-destroyed London. The news from the Nuremberg trials is treated with ironical comparison to contemporary Soviet activities; the view is defensible, but the style is heavily didactic. One of Williamson's few attractive characters is a virtually undisguised Sir Oswald Mosley, called Sir Hereward Birkin. The country as a whole is described as a 'redundant airstrip'. The mood (to borrow a contemporary phrase from H. G. Wells, who was having a similar experience from a very different perspective), is of 'mind at the end of its tether', on a vision having met its Nemesis, the visionary living through his darkest possible nightmare. For Williamson, Hitler had been the man who would bring into being an Anglo-German peasant paradise, a glorious Northland which would leave the sordid problems of industrialism behind.

Williamson was probably not a very nice man. One of his former workers refers to him as an 'irritated, frustrated man blowing his top over something that had gone wrong on the farm'. But he was highly intelligent and the same former worker, who later became Obituary Editor of *The Times*, comments 'He could not perceive wrong and evil even when both were plain . . . As a Labour voter, I still find it unlikely that he would have been a traitor'.[63] The extremities of Williamson's cultural despair are only marginally less forgivable that those of his many contemporaries attracted to Stalin.

There is a direct Norwegian parallel to Williamson in Knut Hamsun, the novelist who extolled the virtues of simple and peasant lives and derided the world of the 'Protestant Jews' of urban Britain and America.[64] He was awarded the Nobel Prize in 1921, but supported Hitler and the German invasion of Norway. After the war, he was conveniently declared insane, but embarrassed his captors by writing a long and coherent account of his views. It is said that many of those condemned to death at Nuremberg read Hamsun in their last hours. Post-war Norwegian intellectuals often have extremely ambivalent views on him: they admire and are attracted, but are fascinated and repelled by his politics.

J. R. R. Tolkien, author of *The Hobbit* and *Lord of the Rings*, shared some of this outlook, but not the politics of Williamson and Hamsun. He was what Anna Bramwell describes as a 'Northlander', but wrote in 1941 that Hitler had permeated and destroyed 'that noble northern spirit, a supreme contribution to Europe, which I have ever loved, and tried to present in its true light'.[65] His presentation has been extremely successful, inspiring such diverse movements as the Californian students and hippies of the 1960s and the *Nuova Destra* Italian youth of the 1980s.

It is difficult to think of English writers of this period who were not Green, in the sense both of being bleakly critical of contemporary society and of harking back to ancient, rural ideas. Even H. G. Wells could not warm to the realities of progress and wrote admiringly of Hamsun. Of writers of any great prominence, only J. B. Priestley seems to have had any real affection for the time he was living in and for its popular culture. In his writing alone do you get the idea that football stadia, popular theatre and dance halls might have something to offer which was lacking in fields, farms and forests.

An astonishing proportion of what is regarded as 'good' children's literature is the product of a green and nostalgic mentality. Much of it is English and from the first forty years of this century: A. A. Milne, Kenneth Grahame, C. S. Lewis, Arthur Ransome and the later Kipling as well as Tolkien and Williamson. Moving on to the school study of English literature, we find that D. H. Lawrence is the most studied twentieth century writer. What strange stuff it all is, compared with the utilitarian ideology of a supposedly capitalist society.

We have the habit of bringing up the children in what Tolkien called *Faërie*:

Faërie is a perilous land and in it are pitfalls for the unwary and dungeons for the overbold . . . The realm of fairy-story is wide and deep and high and filled with many things: all manner of beasts and birds are found there; shoreless seas and stars uncounted; beauty that is an enchantment, and an ever-present peril: both joy and sorrow as sharp as swords.[66]

I confess to some doubts about the utilitarian value of Faërie. Certainly, it is good to stretch children's imagination and they 'need a world of fantasy'. But it is not good to encourage the view that the real life of the higher self is lived among deserts and forests and mountains and not down here among the motorways and supermarkets. An exclusive diet of Faërie can encourage the development of W. S. Gilbert's 'idiots', who cannot see the benefits of their own time and place. And Faërie takes many forms: in the 1980s it has reinvaded in disguise, as films about a future which look remarkably like the Victorian version of the Middle Ages, complete with swords, princesses, wizards and magic spells.

For my generation, there *was* an alternative. You could save your own money (parents wouldn't encourage it) and buy one of the D. C. Thomson comics like *Rover, Hotspur* or *Wizard*. There you would find sturdy, populist urban characters and values. There was Alf Tupper, the welder who ate nothing but fish and chips and thrashed 'toffs' at running and Matt Braddock who thumped officers to get at his plane to shoot Germans out of the sky. But even Thomsonland has borders with Faërie: one of its best-loved heroes, Wilson, lived on the moors on a diet of herbs and, as a consequence, was still able to beat the world's best runners at the age of 195.

The milieu of Green thought

A glance at the EC elections of 1989 might suggest to the casual political scientist that support for Green parties was fairly widely distributed throughout Europe. Where a clear 'Green' party stood they achieved well over 5 per cent of the vote. Only in Ireland (3.7 per cent) and Spain (2 per cent) was this not true: no 'Green' party stood in Greece or Portugal. Britain had the highest Green vote (14.9 per cent) followed by Belgium (13.9 per cent), France (10.6 per cent) and West Germany (8.4 per cent). The political scientist might then begin to look at rates of economic growth, the extent to which existing parties had responded to environmental demands and the other sorts of contemporary, measurable phenomena which political scientists like to examine.

He would only find half the truth by doing so. Green parties may get all kinds of voters, for protest and 'environmental' reasons, but Green thought and sentiment is much more deeply rooted in some countries than it is in others. Its natural home is in Northern Europe, in England, Germany and Scandinavia and the smaller countries bordering them. It is in those cultures that scepticism about the benefits of economic growth is most advanced, perhaps because of, rather than despite, the fact that at different periods they have all led the standard of living league. They have the most profound and favourable responses to nature in their spiritual and intellectual traditions.

Until 1989 the equation of Britain and Germany might have been considered rather odd. West Germany had the most established of Green Parties which had had elected respresentatives at federal level since 1983 and also had elected members at state and European levels. The British party had been established in 1972 as the 'People's Party' and had subsequently changed its name to 'Ecology' and then 'Green', but its vote had only ever been derisory. Even before any political successes *Die Grünen* were recognised as an important social and ideological movement, with communes and 'alternative' businesses and newspapers. But the classic comparative questions, 'Why has Britain not had a Green movement/party like that in West Germany? ' could not be answered by reference to any relative lack of response to nature in Britain. The British are notorious lovers of nature and animals: surveys show an enthusiasm for the subject which goes so far as a majority willingness to pay extra taxes to protect wildlife. There are numerous voluntary organisations concerned with conservation and wildlife, including Europe's largest, the Royal Society for the Protection of Birds and the National Trust.

Part of the reason for the Green failure in Britain was simply attributable to the electoral system, the 'first past the post' requirement making it very difficult for small parties to attract votes. But another was the enormous range of opportunities for the expression of environmental principles through the planning machinery, more than fifteen hundred local 'amenity' groups and through national organisations like the Ramblers, the RSPB, and the Council for the Protection of Rural England. As a result, there were a range of policies in place which seemed to put Britain at the top of a conservationist league table until the 1980s. These included the system of National Parks, Areas of Outstanding Beauty and other designations which 'protected' more than 50 per cent of the land surface and the well-publicised efforts of the local authorities and regional water authorities in reducing air and water pollution respectively. It was only with the widespread realisation of the effects of modern agriculture and the discovery of new problems (lead pollution, radio-active contamination, the inability of current methods to cope with litter) that the image of relative success was undermined. At the same time, Britain was overtaken by several other European countries in fields such as sewage treatment. Even then, by the end of the eighties, Britain had not suffered for a generation the kind of environmental traumas which the Germans had experienced in the form of Rhine pollution and 'forest death'. Such traumas tend to divert minds towards ecological thought or, at the very least, convince the consumer-voter that a price has to be paid to restore the 'quality of life'.

In the post-war period the English emphasis in describing German culture has been on the differences between us and them. According to this account, they are preoccupied with systematic thinking, with building *weltanschaungen*. They gravitate towards forms of idealism and suffer from *angst*. We are pragmatic and empirical; scepticism and utilitarianism are our philosophical responses. Our typical spokesman is perhaps Bertrand Russell who, when challenged that he didn't believe in anything (that is, he didn't have a *weltanschaungen*) replied, 'I believe today is Tuesday'.

In the generations before 1914, the image of Germany was quite different. It was, admittedly, possible to draw on images of the alien Hun, but in university and intellectual circles Germany had a Most Important Nation status. German ideas were immensely influential in history, geography, music, philosophy and all the sciences. They were considered assimilable and important precisely because we shared so many underlying cultural values with the Germans. (According to Victorian racial theory, the English, though not the Welsh nor the Scottish Highlanders, *are* a kind of German).

Both perceptions are true. The English and the Germans do have common cultural roots and these show in attitudes to nature, travel and the countryside. But it is the differences in culture which often determine the form of expression of values. John Ardagh, in his *Germany and the Germans* argues that Germans make rigorous choices between systems of thought and values which the English successfully fudge.[67] For a young West German in the 1970s and 1980s there was a choice of lifestyle. You could support established ways of the 'alternative', the *Aussteiger* outlook. It was the Mercedes and conspicious consumption or the Citroën, the beard and the vegetable. In England it has always been possible to be 'a bit' of something: a bit left-wing, a bit of a hippy, a bit Green. Thus Green sentiment in England has not provided a clear alternative, but has permeated many aspects of society and politics. As Martin Wiener argues in *English Culture and the Decline of the Industrial Spirit*, an anti-industrial affection for nature and the countryside has inhibited English economic development in ways ranging from the high proportion of English capitalist families who have deserted industry for the land and the nobler callings (like the church and the army), to the severe restrictions that development control has put on the location of industry.[68] For all the determinedly pro-industrial views of Margaret Thatcher and her closest advisers, elements of Tory support have remained resolutely anti-industrial. The five European constituencies in which the Green Party won more than 20 per cent of the vote in 1989 were Sussex West, Cotswolds, Hereford and Worcester, Somerset and Suffolk. All were overwhelmingly Conservative constituencies and there is no doubt that many previously Conservative voters switched to the Greens. This may seem a massive transition to a party which, apart from anything else, wants to confiscate the Queen's estates. But English culture (and the English electoral system) are such that one can occasionally vote for a party without taking its *weltanschauung* seriously or even at all.

Beyond the Anglo-German-Scandinavia Northland, the roots of Green thought are less deep. That Northland has colonies, however. A Green tradition is extremely important on the West Coast of the USA (though much less in other parts of the country), as well as in Australia and New Zealand. The New Zealand party calls itself, simply, the 'Values Party' suggesting that their values are so basic and important that they need no further description (much like the optimism of the 'People's Party' in England). There are echoes of Germanic Green sentiment in the 'slavic' countries, but very few in Latin and Islamic cultures. The civilisation of the Far East have been traditionally admired by Greens. So have many of the primitive and aboriginal peoples of the world, but that admiration does not, in most cases, extend to the nationalistic, growth-oriented governments who represent them.

Within developed societies it is conventional to assert that Green sentiment is primarily a 'middle-class' phenomenon. Taken literally, the statement manages to be both false and misleading; one suspects that the truth people actually want to assert is that Green sentiment is not, relatively speaking, a working-class phenomenon. The sense in which the statement is meaningless arises because what is described as the 'middle-class' in contemporary Western societies is no longer a class, if it ever was. Consider three of its elements:

- publicly employed professionals with *Beamte, fonctionnaire* of other quasi-tenured status.
- owners of small businesses, which can be taken to include certain kinds of contracted manager and franchise-holder.
- highly salaried staffs (including sales, managerial and technical staffs) of major multi-national corporations.

The interests of these groups are clearly different. What a multi-national sales executive wants most from the planning system is likely to be the preservation of the environment of his dwelling, which would imply the minimisation of traffic, of further development etc. The controllers of small business are likely to want the easiest possible conditions for the expansion of trade, including their own trade and the general volume of local trade. Both kinds of business have a contrary interest to the publicly employed professionals in the general level of tax and public expenditure. The principles generally held among the three groups are bound to differ and not only because of differing interests. Each group has its own mini-ideology, arising out of its occupational norms and experience. Crucially, the time-horizons must differ. People who have to make a quarter- or half-year profit are necessarily different in outlook from those who can make five-year plans based on the assumed resources of enormous organisations, public or private. In French terms, *petite commerce* often looks at life from the opposite end of the telescope to the *fonctionnaires*.

In other words, there is no 'middle-class': the factors which divide this residual group are more important than those which unite it. It is the professional and intellectual groups in society who are most often drawn towards the Green outlook. That is the sense in which statements about the 'middle class' are meaningless. The sense in which they are false is that a very important component of Green thought arises from an aristocratic or *upper*-class outlook.

Edward Banfield, who defines class entirely in terms of time horizons, sees it as the unique, defining condition of upper classes that members have effective time-horizons which extend beyond their own life expectations.[69] I would add that they identify more with larger communities than do most people. They say 'we', meaning the villages, the country, the nation or the entire species. 'We' are being very silly with our planet. That global 'we' is in many respects unrealistic: most people do not think of themselves in planetary terms and there are no effective institutions for making decisions at that level of collectivity.

Both Jonathan Porritt and Lord Lymington are thoroughly aristocratic in outlook, which is why I stressed their titles earlier. They are above the ordinary sense of struggle and self-justification. They think instinctively in terms of the broad 'we' and the long term. They are deeply suspicious of trade and commerce. Both are contemptuous of vulgar pleasures. The aristocracy finds common cause with the 'endowed clerisies' of the church and the universities, who easily become an aristocratised salariat. Conservation organisations in England tend to be dominated by Lords and Dons. *Die Grünen* are dominated by *Beamten* from the teaching profession.

This insistence on the aristocratic quality is not intended as a criticism. On the contrary, I would wish to construct broad utilitarian defenses of both aristocratic economics on the grounds of the aristocratic breadth of vision and length of time-horizon and of an aristocratic politics, because of its aloofness from the narrow egoisms of the career-forming classes. But even aristocracy has its drawbacks and they may include unrealistic assumptions about human behaviour and a failure to appreciate the existence of tastes other than one's own.

The realities of Green politics

I have argued that the broad tradition of Green thought has been an important part of the culture of certain developed countries. Yet narrow Green politicians always talk as if they were complete outsiders, criticising a world in which they have no influence and for which they have no responsibility. How can ideas be so important and yet so powerless?

Part of the answer lies in the dilemma faced when a Green movement comes to power. It is the choice between what have been called, in the German context, *realo* and *fundi* approaches to politics. *Fundis* want to change the whole basis of society and are not prepared to trade the integrity of their principles for influence in the short term. As Petra Kelly has put it,[70] if you believe you are right and will eventually win, tarnishing your principles with compromise, sacrificing the purity and integrity of your beliefs, for a tactic that may only delay real victory, is purposeless. *Realos* want to exercise attributable influence, to get policies on the ground in the short or medium-term. In the case of a Green party holding the balance of power in a *Land* parliament, this may mean accepting a programme of industrial expansion in return for a system of cycleways or investment in recycling waste. But the same dilemma awaits Green groups which are represented at British public inquiries about motorways or nuclear power stations. They can attack the whole principle of new motorways or nuclear power; it is certain that the inspector will take little or not notice of their views if they do, but the seeds of ideas are sown in elite debate and public opinion. Or they can join with other groups in pressing for the motorway to run round, rather than through a moor, or for the nuclear power station to be smaller.

In effect, Green movements have had considerable influence on policy in both Britain and Germany over the last century, but it is in the form of a compromised, publicly argued, environmentalism that they have had such influence rather than in changing the basis of society. It is difficult to attribute much direct policy influence to the German Greens in their period in elected office. True, West Germany is setting standards for the rest of Europe in the regulation of pollution and in some forms of recycling. But this cannot be attributed to *Die Grünen.* Environmentalism (and perhaps a certain cultural obsession with nature, purity and cleanliness) runs throughout German society; the Bavarian CSU are keen to boast of the cleanliness of their state in comparison to the dirty SPD *Länder* to the north. When this kind of conservative environmentalism has run into conflict with *Die Grünen*, as it has in a major way on nuclear power, it has been easily victorious. West Germany has expanded its nuclear capacity up to 40 per cent of its energy needs, one of the biggest nuclear programmes in Europe. This is abhorrent to true Greens, but the CDU and CSU have argued for it on environmental grounds, claiming that in measurable terms the burning of fossil fuels is more damaging to the environment than is fission generation.

What of Green governments? Of all governments, which has been the most sympathetic to a fundamentalist Green outlook? Trying to answer this question raises an unpleasant theory for Greens to consider. There seems to be something inevitable about the state's pursuit of maximum economic growth. All states seem to be pushed by popular demand from below and also pulled by the competition from other states into maximising their growth and power. They frequently talk the rhetoric of extinction if they are outgrown by their traditional enemies and rivals. Even where governments have been initially sympathetic to a Green vision of the future, it has been abandoned at some stage. In India, Ghandi's ascetic rural vision was immediately abandoned by Nehru in favour of a programme of rapid industrial development. In Spain the last vestiges of a distinctively Falangist 'third way' were abandoned by Franco in 1957 in favour of the 'years of development'. The Buddhist-inspired socialist government in Burma would be a candidate, but that regime appears to be slowly collapsing at the time of writing. The series of Irish governments dominated by Eamonn De Valera might have some claim in respect of their consistent avoidance of industrial growth for thirty years after 1927. But the De Valera period in Ireland did achieve the unique distinction that over half the population left the country. And, when he was removed from real power, his successors quickly abandoned the policy. It is, at least, very difficult for a modern government to avoid industrialisation and to refrain from offering its electorate (or potential electorate where there are no competitive elections) the maximum economic growth.

Notes

1. The information on 'environment' is from the last, pre-computer, full edition of the Oxford English Dictionary, published in 1933 except that I have added the additional comment on geography. On 'ecology', Anna Bramwell gives an account of the early use of the world and the rival claimants in her *Ecology in the Twentieth Century, A History*, (Yale, 1989), chapter 3 note 2, pp. 253–54. The consensus appears to be that Haeckel established the continuous use of the term ecology and its present sense, though there were earlier uses, such as the English word 'ecology' appearing in a letter by H. D. Thoreau in 1858. Perhaps, as so often, it is a case of 'great minds think alike'.
2. Robert Nisbet, *The Social Philosophers*, (Paladin, 1976), pp. 323–85.
3. Ernst Haeckel, *The Evolution of Man: A Popular Scientific Study*. Translated from the Fifth (enlarged) Edition by Joseph McCabe, (Watts, 1910). Vol II, p. 748.
4. *Ibid.*, p. 745.
5. *Ibid.*, p. 748.
6. *Ibid.*, p. 749.
7. See Bramwell, *op. cit.*, pp. 52–53.
8. J. E. Lovelock, *GAIA, A New Look at Life on Earth*, (Oxford University Press, 1979), p. 152.
9. *Ibid.*, p. 10.
10. *Ibid.*, p. 14.
11. *Ibid.*, p. 119.
12. *Ibid.*, p. 48.
13. Jonathan Porritt. *Seeing Green. The Politics of Ecology Explained*, (Blackwell, 1984), p. 207.
14. Lovelock, *op. cit.*, p. x.
15. *Ibid.*
16. *Ibid.*, p. 147.
17. *Ibid.*, pp. 42–45.
18. *Ibid.*, p. 121.
19. *Ibid.*, pp. 107–108.
20. *Ibid.*, p. 140.
21. A. E. Garvie, 'Pantheism', in James Hastings (ed.) *Encyclopaedia of Religion and Ethics*, (T. & T. Clark, 1917), Vol. IX, p. 609.
22. I am referring particularly to walks which I have done for the purpose of writing about places. I did a series for *New Society* from 1979 to 1984 and one for *The Countryman* since 1984. See Lincoln Allison, *A Journey Quite Different, Collected Walks*, (Manchester University Press, 1988).
23. William Wordsworth, 'Kendal and Windermere Railway', appended to Fifth Edition of *Guide to the Lakes*, (Frowde, 1906), p. 146.
24. *Ibid.*

25. E. G. Parrinder, *A Book of World Religions*, (Hutton, 1985), p. 154.
26. Genesis I: 26, Authorised Version.
27. Ludwig Feuerbach, *The Essence of Christianity*, translated from the German by George Eliot, (Harper & Row, 1957), p. 112.
28. *Ibid.*, p. 113.
29. *Ibid.*, p. 114.
30. See Robert A. Pois, *National Socialism and the Religion of Nature*, (Croom Helm, 1986) and Bramwell, *op. cit.*
31. See Parrinder, *op. cit.*, pp. 112–13.
32. *The Merchant of Venice*, Act I, Scene 3.
33. Lynn White, Jr, 'On Christian Arrogance Toward Nature', in Robert Detweiler, Jon N. Sutherland and Michael S. Werthmann (eds), *Environmental Decay in its Historical Context*, (Scott, Foresman & Co., 1973), pp. 19–27 and 'The Roots of Our Ecological Crisis', *Science*, 155, 10th March 1967, pp. 1203–1207.
34. Miriam Rothschild, *Animals and Man*, The Romanes Lectures for 1985, (Oxford University Press, 1986), p. 11.
35. White in Detweiler *et al.*, *op. cit.*, p. 24.
36. John Passmore, *Man's Responsibility for Nature*, (Duckworth, 1974), pp. 28–40.
37. Lovelock, *op. cit.*, pp. 141–50.
38. Reported by Leslie Childe in *The Daily Telegraph*, 6th December 1989, p. 11.
39. Porritt, *op. cit.*, p. 43.
40. See Lincoln Allison, *Right Principles, A Conservative Philosophy of Politics*, (Blackwell, 1984) and 'The Nature of Conservative Thought', *History of Political Thought*, Vol. IX, no. 2, (1988), pp. 379–83.
41. Translated and quoted by Lord Howard of Penrith in 'Lessons from Other Countries', in Clough Williams-Ellis (ed), *Britain and the Beast*, (Dent, 1938), p. 284.
42. See Bramwell, *op. cit.*
43. José Antonio Primo De Rivera, 'Man is the System', in Hugh Thomas (ed), *José Antonio Primo De Rivera, Selected Writings*, (Cape, 1972), pp. 70–4.
44. *Ibid.*, p. 33.
45. Karl Marx and Friedrich Engels, *Selected Works*, (Moscow, 1950), Vol. 2, pp. 82–3.
46. William Morris, *News from Nowhere*. (Routledge and Kegan Paul, 1970). Krishnan Kumar in *Utopia and Anti-Utopia in Modern Times*. (Blackwell, 1987) rates Morris with More 'among the best' of Utopias judged from a literary standpoint (p. 25). He also comments, 'So far as I have been able to establish, nothing like the western Utopia and Utopian traditions exist in any non-western or non-Christian culture . . . this . . . must almost certainly have something to do with the nature of Christianity as a religion, and its unique blending of a terrestrial and non-terrestrial, supermundane, paradise, 'a new heaven and a new earth' (p. 425).
47. David McClellan (ed.). *Marx's Grundrisse*, (MacMillan, 1971), p. 94.
48. Leon Trotsky, 'Revolutionary and Socialist Art' in *Literature and Revolution*, (Michigan, 1966).
49. P. A. Kropotkin, *Mutual Aid*, (Penguin, 1939); *The Essential Kropotkin*, edited by Emile Capouya and Keitha Tompkins, (Macmillan, 1976).
50. Murray Bookchin, *Towards an Ecological Society*, (Black Rose Books, 1980). Theodore Roszak, *The Making of a Counter-Culture: Reflections on the Technocratic Society and its Youthful Opposition*. (Faber and Faber, 1970).

51. Porritt, *op. cit.*, p. 8.
52. Malcolm Slesser, *The Politics of Environment, A Guide to Scottish Thought and Action*, (Allen & Unwin, 1972).
53. See L. P. Curtis, *Anglo-Saxons and Celts: a study of anti-Irish prejudice in Victorian England*, (Bridgeport, 1968).
54. See Roger Lancelyn Green and Walter Hooper, *C. S. Lewis, A Biography*, (Collins, 1974).
55. Peter Laslett, *The World We have Lost*, (Methuen, 1965).
56. For instance, it is quoted in Rothschild, *op. cit.*, p. 11. I have not traced the contemporary origin of the story, but readers will appreciate that I am more interested that the story is quoted now than in whether it is true or false.
57. See Keith Thomas, *Man and the Natural World*, (Allen Lane, 1983); Harriet Ritvo, *The Animal Estate: The English and Other Creatures in the Victorian Age*, (Harvard, 1987).
58. For example, 'How to Defend Society Against Science', *Radical Philosophy* 11, (1975), pp. 3–8.
59. Gilbert Ryle, *The Concept of Mind*, (Penguin Books, 1963).
60. Arne Naess, 'The Shallow and the Deep, Long-Range Ecology Movement. A Summary', *Inquiry*, 16, (1973), pp. 95–100.
61. See Richard Sylvan, 'A Critique of Deep Ecology' I & II, *Radical Philosophy*, 40 & 41, (1985).
62. Henry Williamson, *The Gale of the World*, (MacDonald, 1969).
63. Colin Watson, 'Winter with Williamson', *The Countryman*, 94: 4, (1989–90), pp. 132–36.
64. See Bramwell, *op. cit.*, esp. pp. 150–60.
65. Letter to Michael Tolkien, 9th June, 41, quoted by Bramwell, *op. cit.*, pp. 131–32.
66. J. R. R. Tolkien, 'On Fairy-Stories', first given as a lecture in 1938 and published in 1947 in the *Dublin review*; quoted here from *Tree and Leaf*, (Allen & Unwin, 1964), p. 1.
67. John Ardagh, *Germany and the Germans*, (Hamish Hamilton, 1987), esp. pp. 421–47.
68. Martin Wiener, *English Culture and the Decline of the Industrial Spirit, 1850–1950*, (Cambridge University Press, 1981).
69. See Edward Banfield, *The Unheavenly City, the nature and future of our urban crisis*, (Little, Brown, 1970).
70. See Porritt, *op. cit.*, p. 14.

3 Green Utilitarianism

In many respects Green and Utilitarian criticisms of the assumptions and procedures of contemporary society are not opposites; they take aim from different positions but are directed at the same targets. It is my objective in this section to isolate and clarify such criticisms as green and utilitarian thinkers might both wish to make.

Much of our intuitive common sense suggests powerful combined reservations about modern economic achievements. You are sitting on the M25, the London Orbital Motorway, in your car. There are too many vehicles on the road, so progress is frustrating. These vehicles are emitting untold volumes of gases which, if they were not quickly dispersed, would kill you in minutes. The verges of the road are strewn with unsightly litter. You are alone and your only current relationship with fellow human beings is an aggressive rivalry when you try to change lanes. There is a danger that another vehicle will smash into yours from behind, a danger which is increased considerably by any hint of frost, fog or heavy rain. You are suffering with tens of thousands of others, but you have none of the companionship with them which helps alleviate suffering.

Yet the sequestration of useful and attractive land for the route of the M25 and the vast direction of resources for its construction were specifically, in our culture, done to make us better off. It was built not to appease some dark and powerful force which insists that we build such things or be punished, but in order that we, aggregatively, can have more of what we want. Sceptical questions come easily to mind on the M25. What are the benefits which we gain from such a transport system? Are they really worth it? [1]

These questions suggest three kinds of comparison. The immediate and individual comparison for the commuter or commercial traveller is between his present life and livelihood and a much simpler one in which he retired or took a less well-paid job nearer home and spent more time reading, watching video tapes and gardening. Might he not be better off, taking everything as a whole? One aggregate and long-term comparison might be with a peasant agrarian society, in which we tilled our own fields and consumed much of our own produce. Was that not a more peaceful and satisfying system of production and consumption? Finally, there might be a comparison with a world in which everything is the same except that there is no M25. This suggests the same volume of traffic, even slower and polluting more strongly, this time grinding its way past schools and houses.

The last comparison might initially suggest that the decision to build the M25 was a 'good' one. But important doubts have been expressed about the validity of that kind of comparison. Much of what I have said about the M25 might have been said with equal force about California's Bayshore Freeway or (even worse) about the E5, the Bagdad Road through Istanbul, or a thousand other motorways. But an argument has been put with particular force about the M25 which suggests that the reasoning behind its construction was incorrect. It was based on the principle that new roads do not create new journeys, but only those which would occur anyway. A criticism which is now widely accepted is that this is a false assumption: *ceteris paribus*, new roads create new journeys just as certainly as areas of low pressure create winds. Traffic flows on different sections of the M25 when it opened were all greatly in excess of projections; in some cases they were more than double.[2] The real choice was not between congestion and decongestion, but between the same levels of congestion on different scales. The real decision should not have been made on the basis of a narrow comparison of 'costs' and 'benefits' in which almost the entire data used was about traffic flows or land values, but in terms of a much broader consideration of the advantages and disadvantages of alternative levels and means of transport in society in relation to the corresponding alternatives in production.

Our common discourse acknowledges considerable doubts (to put it minimally) about the worth of some of our decisions and policies when they are placed in a broader frame than that used by the decision-makers. We sometimes talk about 'progress' with real satisfaction at the improvement of the collective lot, but more often we use the word cynically to mean something which could not be avoided but which has at least as many disadvantages as advantages. *Fortschritt* in German has the same ambiguity.

The idea that our everyday wants and ambitions represent something narrow and petty, hostile to goals which are more profound is an ancient one and a theme of many religious teachers. In the Bible there are many warnings against being 'greedy of gain' (as *Proverbs* has it), not least St Paul's to Timothy:

> But godliness with contentment is great gain. For we brought nothing into this world, and it is certain that we can carry nothing out. And having food and raiment let us be therewith content. But they that will be rich fall into temptation and a snare, and into many foolish and hurtful lusts, which drown men in destruction and perdition. For the love of money is the root of all evil: which while some coveted after, they have erred from the faith, and pierced themselves through with many sorrows.[3]

Christianity is highly ambiguous in status. Is the warning against 'hurtful lusts' and 'many sorrows' simply a warning against a life which turns out to be foolish because it overestimates the satisfactions and underestimates the costs of certain goods (such as money and sex) in themselves? Or does the calculation only prove negative when we introduce everlasting life and an omnipotent God? There has always been a certain wavering, a hint of having one's cake and eating it, in the way that the religion has couched its appeal.

The sayings of the Buddha, by contrast, are more clear philosophically. In his original form he can be interpreted as an ascetic kind of utilitarian: the problem starts with suffering. Suffering arises from craving. But when particular cravings are satisfied, they are merely replaced by different cravings. So the solution to suffering lies not in the satisfaction, but in the eradication of craving; the complete eradication is Nirvana. But the 'Middle Way', the 'Noble Eightfold Path' which the Buddha recommended is not a method of starvation and self-annihilation; it is more like St Paul's recommendation of being satisfied with the simple basics of life.[4]

K'ung-Fo-tzu (Confucius) also warned that the worldly costs of worldly satisfactions might prove too high: 'Wealth and rank are what every man desires; but if they can only be retained to the detriment of the Way he professes, he must relinquish them'.[5] The Way is profoundly conservative, emphasizing traditional manners and the maintenance of allotted place, deeply suspicious of all kind of ambition.

Thus most religion has cast doubt on the extent and authenticity of the satisfactions to be gained from worldly things. In most of human history religion has been formally acknowledged as the dominant intellectual activity. It is only as societies have become 'modern' and 'western' that scepticism about spiritual 'higher' questions has become dominant and policies and ethics have been justified entirely by 'material' considerations. Even so, there have always been powerful and impressive voices maintaining the tradition of a spiritual critique of utilitarianism. These voices have not only been representatives of 'green' and orthodox religious alternatives, but have also been in the core of the prevailing ideology, so to speak. John Stuart Mill's reservations about and modifications of utilitarianism in favour of 'culture' and the 'higher' pleasures were, in my opinion, the greatest of Victorian contributions to this genre.[6] But there have always been economists, as well as philosophers, who argued that economics had become too narrow and often suggested that it had become the contemporary religion, whose practitioners did not have to question their assumptions at all nor to justify their arguments except to each other.[7]

A particularly rich vein of meta-economic critique was produced in the late 1960s and early 1970s in what one might call the 'affluent society' period. The name fits for two reasons. First, most of the thinking was done in a time of high economic growth, in the expectation of future growth, before the oil crisis and recession and the return of 'old-fashioned' economic problems like unemployment and resource shortages. Secondly, because the writings were influenced to some degree by the problems discussed in J. K. Galbraith's earlier book, *The Affluent Society*. In a classic description of the new American prosperity, Galbraith contrasts private wealth with public squalor:

> The family which takes its mauve and cerise, air-conditioned, power-steered, and power-braked car out for a tour passes through cities that are badly paved, made hideous by litter, blighted buildings, bill-boards, and

posts for wires that should long since have been put underground. They pass on into a countryside that has been rendered largely invisible by commercial art. (The goods which the latter advertise have an absolute priority in our value system. Such aesthetic considerations as a view of the countryside accordingly come second. On such matters we are consistent.) They picnic on exquisitely packaged food from a portable icebox by a polluted stream and go on to spend the night at a park which is a menace to public health and morals. Just before dozing off on an air-mattress, beneath a nylon tent, amid the stench of decaying refuse, they may reflect vaguely on the curious uneveness of their blessings.[8]

The books I have in mind are, principally and in order of publication, E. J. Mishan's *The Costs of Economic Growth*, E. F. Schumacher's *Small is Beautiful*, Tibor Scitovsky's *The Joyless Economy* and Fred Hirsch's *Social Limits to Growth*.[9] All of these works begin with the perception that the economic miracles of the post-war age have not produced the degree of human happiness that would have been assumed *a priori*, that making two ears of wheat grow where one grew before, both literally and by extended metaphor, has not been the all-round problem-solver it was expected to be. They are all by men who have come through and transcended economics and who want to criticise its narrowness. They describe the economic achievements of the post-war age as being excessively narrow: in each case the argument is that the contemporary western political economy has a genius for doing one thing well and then assessing itself as if that one thing were the only thing that mattered. In Scitovsky's case, the American economy has successfully heightened levels of 'comfort', but has proved poor in the provision of culture, stimulus or joy. For Hirsch, growth beyond a certain level is merely a zero-sum game, a keeping-up-with-the-Joneses system in which progressive numbers of people have cars or possess university degrees or own second homes, but are aggregatively no better off because these goods merely become needs for one person in respect of society as a whole. Galbraith distinguished between the efficient provision of marketable and privately consumed goods and those goods which are 'public' either in the economists technical sense (as, in the pure case, goods like clean air or street lighting which can supply infinite demand) or in the more ordinary sense of being provided by 'public' bodies. Mishan's core criticism is that we massively underestimate the costs of producing goods, because we barely account the 'external diseconomies' of production. Schumacher argues more broadly that we are obsessed with the large and the material against what really counts, the spiritiual dimension of human existence: he assumes mantles of both 'Buddhist economics' and Christian quietism. Sadly, it is true of all these writers that, though they achieved both popular success and professional respect, their influence on the study of economics has been minimal. The discipline has continued to develop in directions which are ever more narrowly technical and quantifiable and is less willing than ever to face the philosophical and ethical questions which lie at its core.

Economics has absorbed quite easily the technical criticisms of markets

and of 'capitalism' as methods of production. These have included
theories of market instability (the 'trade cycle'), of monopoly and the
tendency to monopoly and of skewed distributions. These criticisms have
informed public policy in all countries, changing the role of the state in
financial management and the regulation of economic activity. To some
extent, but only some, proponents of the market have regained ground
through 'public choice' theory which suggests that in many areas,
though markets have faults, state bureaucracies are intrinsically even
worse. But economics has proved much less permeable to the more
fundamental criticisms of 'materialism' or 'industrialism' which suggest
that it is our assumptions about the value of production and consumption which are wrong, rather than the particular methods of 'capitalism',
'communism' or 'social democracy'. Academic economists, business-men
and bureaucrats, of all political persuasions, tend systematically towards
simple objectives and precise criteria and away from ethical and philosophical complexity.

   In considering the alliance between green and utilitarian criticisms of
the way the world works, I am faced with a difficult triangular relationship between three shifting points. Utilitarianism is a broad and flexible
doctrine, but at least I am expressing my own (broad and flexible) version
of it and am thus entitled to judge what it will tolerate and what it will
not. The 'Green' perspective is very loosely defined, an equally broad and
shifting set of associated ideas, but defined in this case by no one writer or
organisation and not resting on any particular philosophical foundation.
But at least I have already gone to some lengths to map out those ideas,
distinguishing between a 'broad' green tradition of social criticism and a
relatively 'narrow' Green politics. The ideal of 'the way the world works'
or 'the assumptions and procedures of contemporary society', as I called it
earlier, is even more nebulous. I mean mainly 'western' society, but
communist governments have generally demonstrated the same faults.
Lovelock is most worried about 'third world' societies but, arguably, it is
the influence of western ways upon them which is the problem. The USA
is the paradigm 'western' society, but it does things rather differently in
many respects from most Western European countries which are, in any
case, different from each other. Being English, and most concerned about
England, my passions and upsets are largely focussed here. There is no
simple way of identifying the target, but I would insist that the narrow,
'economic', utilitarianism which I am criticising has come to prevail in
business and policy in much of the world and add that, where a criticism
is particular, I intend to direct it as precisely as possible. It is in the light
of these stipulations that the following applications of broad, and
relatively green, utilitarianism should be interpreted.

Scepticism about growth

Considering how seriously economic growth is regarded as an objective
of policy, it is a relatively new concept. The idea of seeing economic

activity in terms of a national income, and corresponding national product, was developed only in inter-war England by Arthur Bowley at the London School of Economics. As Hirsch puts it, 'The central achievement of modern economic analysis has been to add up: to develop a theoretical basis and an associated accounting frame for the aggregation of economic activity within an integrated system'.[10] Insofar as people still aim to make society more Godly, they are pursuing an objective which has been formulated, in different ways, for thousands of years. But insofar as they attempt to maximise the growth of national income, their objective has only been formulated in the lifetime of existing people.

Of course, as Hirsch hints, it is as well to remember Molière's 'Bourgeois Gentilhomme' who said, '. . . il y a plus de quarante ans que je dis de la prose sans que j'en susse rien'. ('I have been talking in prose for more than forty years without knowing it.') The essential ideas of national prosperity and the 'standard of living' are much older than the precise concepts and they have a hundred names. Even so, observations of the standard of living always generated puzzlement and paradox. By the Great Exhibition of 1851, Britain had more than half of Europe's industrial production and its economic expansion was the wonder of the world. But the legions of writers who chronicled the realities of the time observed how unhealthy many people seemed, how their leisure time had declined, how crowded their dwellings were and how the number of people who could not afford shoes appeared to have gone up rather than down. Their reflections suggested several possible conclusions: the prosperity was unreal; it was not to be equated with happiness; it was badly distributed.

Thus the very nature and history of 'growth' and related concepts suggest scepticism. But scepticism is quite different from hostility: sceptical arguments about a concept may generate opposition to positions which take that concept seriously; they cannot imply hostility to the whole complex of phenomena supposedly denoted by the concept. Both Mishan and Schumacher, for instance, are actually opposed to economic growth. Schumacher argues that, beyond a certain level, growth is necessarily a bad thing:

> . . . that economic growth, which viewed from the point of view of economics, physics, chemistry and technology, has no discernible limit, must necessarily run into decisive bottlenecks when viewed from the point of view of the environmental sciences. An attitude to life which seeks fulfilment in the single-minded pursuit of wealth – in short, materialism – does not fit into this world, because it contains within itself no limiting principle, while the environment in which it is placed is strictly limited.[11]

This is a development of the Malthusian view, that the earth is a 'fixed factor', a strictly limited piece of capital which must, at some point, limit the growth of incomes. The fallacy of Schumacher's position (analogous to that in Malthus's) is that it treats growth as if it were concerned with 'matter', with physical 'reality'. It is not so concerned: concepts of national income, and therefore of growth, are measurements of transactions in terms of money. Provided people are prepared to transact and the transaction is recorded, it counts towards growth. Thus growth, as it is normally accounted and discussed, is not related to the supply or availability of any particular commodities. Take, for example, that forgotten element of economic life, Soviet economic success. In 1985 Soviet production of what had been in 1960, the six most important products in the American economy, exceeded U.S. production by the following percentages.[12]

Steel	+80%
Cement	+78%
Oil	+42%
Fertiliser	+55%
Iron ore	+500%

Truly, the Soviet Union had fulfilled Nikita Khruschev's promise of overtaking the United States. To use a Leninist phrase, once a favourite of British trades unionists, the economic 'high ground' of the Soviet Union had become higher than that of the USA. But economies are more like seas than land masses and levels of production are more like waves than hills. Growth statistics are not essentially concerned with particular goods. The massive expansion in western prosperity in the period 1960–85 was about electronics, restaurants, foreign holidays and financial services rather than about coal and steel. It is less obviously true of any of these that they face 'environmental' constraints, though the happiness generated from them may be subject to Hirsch's 'positional' constraint, that their meaning decreases as their distribution spreads.

The economy of William Morris's 'Nowhere' provides an interesting companion to the Soviet Union.[13] Production is concentrated on goods which are produced 'labour-intensively', though the labour is mainly of a kind which is both highly skilled and creatively satisfying. Hand-woven silks, organic vegetables, jewelry, carved furniture and ornamental leather are among its best-known products. (The relative value of all of these products tends to go up in highly developed societies, as a matter of fact.) Clearly we can imagine a situation in which the national income of Nowhere grows, even *per capita* : there would be more and better ornamental leather and organic vegetables for gift and exchange. One obvious source of such growth would be an increase in skills. There would, of course, be a problem of measuring such growth because the Nowherians have no money and regard the whole business as a bit silly. But that would be a very small obstacle to the ingenious economists in measuring their growth. He would happily introduce a hypothetical pricing system based on the bartering rates of goods and services. He might go a step further and compare Nowhere with (say) the USA. Perhaps it would be the case that we might value their arts and crafts very highly and they value our television sets and motor cars very lowly, that they would turn out, in some demonstrable way, to have a higher standard of living than us. In other words, their growth might be 'real' economic growth, but it would not be constrained by Schumacher's assumption of limits.

Being sceptical about growth implies that either nothing very interesting or coherent is expressed by the aggregate figures of national income or that what is contained there is no guide to human well-being (and, therefore, ought to be no guide to policy). Of course, both may be true. The following examples may serve to reinforce one of the branches of a sceptical argument:

ANOTHER GAMBLER'S FALLACY

Viscount Omnium, Julian Smith-Jones-Dalglish and myself are Oxford undergraduates. Our favourite activity is a game of cards, preferably brag. Being young men of dash and panache, we risk large sums on the table. But because we are of an even standard, and play ten hours a week, we end up pretty well even over time. What has happened to the economy during our games?

Nothing, officially. National income accounting requires properly formed transactions. Simple activities in which we produce and consume for ourselves or as part of an economically informal relationship do not count. These include gardening and enjoying the products of the garden, cooking and housekeeping for each other and playing cards. But if I were able to convince the national income accountant that my game of cards and the money it turned over were a service I offered my friends, the income from which I spent on reciprocal services, then we might be said to be increasing national income substantially. Certainly, if I spend five of my ten hours working as a barman and the other five spending the money earned in the cinema and a pub, my activities would count, though not, of course, in anything like the sheer quantity of income and expenditure which the gambling would have to count if it counted at all.

This example reinforces scepticism in both senses. It reveals the arbitrariness with which things count or do not count and thus the lack of relation between national income and the general well-being. And there is a suggestion that some of the services, especially the financial services, which *do* count might be no more and no less significant than our three-person gambling school.

ON PLEASURE FROM WORK

Let us adopt one of those two-product models of which Marx and the classical economists were so fond. There exist only food and drink and a food factory and a drink factory which make them. Everybody is involved in producing one and consumes both. Let us also assume, in the traditionally unrealistic way of economists, that production and consumption of both products can be expanded indefinitely, but is subject to labour constraints.

Less conventionally, let us make some assumptions about working conditions. Each individual has a capacity for work. People are happiest, *ceteris paribus*, when working at about 85 per cent capacity; this gives them time for the little rituals of working together, including conversations, jokes, tea breaks, fairly leisurely meals and so on, which allow work to be a communal experience which has a 'lighter side'. Above 90 per cent capacity, people's pleasure from work deteriorates steadily; above 100 per cent it goes into stressful, nightmare, 'free fall'. Going backwards, it deteriorates slowly below 80 per cent as boredom sets in – or, at least, the additional boredom of under-employment.

Now suppose that new managers arrive at both factories. They feel no general responsibility for human happiness, but regard it as their duty to increase production, productivity and profit. By diverse means, they enforce a much more hardworking regime: shorter lunch breaks, no tea breaks, no talking on the job, payment by results. Production and productivity rise in both factories; there are more food and drink in the shops and wages are higher. But the normal workload in relation to capacity pushes up to an average of 97 per cent, 101 per cent for some.

In some respects the population is better off. In other respects, it is worse off. What is certain is that the national income accountant sees only the increase. What is possible is that, in utilitarian terms, the decrease outweighs the increase. Of course, as they say, it is only a model.

THE QUALITY OF SOCIAL LIFE

Much intellectual fun has been had, over the past century, from hypothesising the services of the 'housewife' onto the market. Classical economists, feminists and even civil servants have pursued this line of enquiry. After all, here is an unmeasurable, and unmeasured, component of the service sector of the economy. Wives do the job of escort, cook, prostitute, nanny, housekeeper, etc. (To be fair, husbands usually offer a package of services, too, which may include gardener, carpenter, accountant, lover and bodyguard, but few people would wish to claim that these services, on average, would be as valuable as those offered by wives.)

By some standards, marriage is a fairly inefficient arrangement. It is asking a great deal of anybody that she should be a good cook, prostitute, nanny, etc. There would be greater efficiency from greater specialisation; one could be escorted by an escort, have one's meals provided by an expert cook and made love to with a trained, specialised prostitute. Arguably, the general level of service-provision would rise considerably; certainly economic growth would be high.

Orthodox economics more or less suggests that such steps in the marketisation or commodification of life would be a good thing. Kenneth Boulding's best-selling textbook demonstrates how the world is better off if doctors pay gardeners to do their gardens: the gardeners gain and the doctors are released for more doctoring which not only pays for the gardening to be done, but leaves plenty of money over.[14] (It's only a small step to suggesting that really highly paid executives should hire toy boys to sleep with their wives.)

But less orthodox economists put specific arguments against such tendencies. Hirsch points to the 'commercialisation effect' and argues that, in many cases, making a transaction of something actually reduces its value.[15] The gift, the prize, love freely given, the home-grown vegetable: all of these are worth far more to us because they do not have to be paid for. Processes of commercialisation may, therefore, raise growth (and, in some senses, efficiency) while reducing well-being. To Scitovsky, the crucial problem concerns the disadvantages of specialisation, a process which makes us richer, so far as the national income accountant is concerned, but at the cost of a loss of novelty, stimulus and the individual capacity to lead a full life.[16]

Proverbs has it that the price of a good woman is 'far above rubies'. A good man might be worth a few pearls, for that matter, and a good marriage far above either of them – a good community and a good cricket team have great worth. The quality of such social relations as these is the real stuff of a good life. Yet, purely logically, the concept of economic growth does not merely exclude them, but in certain circumstances – specialisation, commodification and overwork, for example – it stands to them in an inverse relation.

Further arguments which are both utilitarian in assumption and 'green' in direction, will also suggest reservations about economic growth. In these three cases the import has not been to suggest that economic growth is impossible or necessarily a bad thing. Growth, *per se*, is meaningless or trivial. It would be as foolish to be against economic growth in itself as it would be to be for it. Later on, I will construct further defences of economic growth against its outright opponents.

But the trouble with a concept like growth is precisely that people are systematised and institutionalised into being in favour of it *per se*. They commit the sin, for a utilitarian, of mindless instrumentalism, of pursuing an objective which is not reducible to the general well-being and, possibly, is increasingly divergent from it. Of course, a loose equation with well-being is not the only reason for pursuing economic growth; it is also associated with state power and national prestige.

The association between growth and power is an habitual one and has been reinforced by such historians as Martin Wiener and Paul Kennedy writing as if nations rose and declined as such.[17] A more complex model might suggest that political, cultural and economic standings might move independently. Adam Smith, for instance, was concerned that a 'commercial' society would be militarily inferior to pre-commercial societies because its citizens would not have the cast of mind for fighting. His fear was informed by the record of 'soft' societies in classical times, but also by the abilities of the Highlander, as opposed to the Lowlander, in the Scotland of his own time.[18] The Vietnam War would have confirmed Smith's view of the relationship between economic power and the military virtues. It is equally odd to believe that economic 'strength' brings all goods with it in a world in which the world's two most successful economies, Japan and West Germany, have achieved only moderate levels of international power and low levels of cultural penetration.

Nevertheless, economic growth is treated as immensely important not only by governments, but also by individual members of nations. *L'anno dello sorpasso*, 1987, when Italy overtook the United Kingdom and others in *per capita* national income, was celebrated in Italy as the expunging of a national inferiority complex, even though the reality, for much of the country, was congested towns and roads and polluted coast and country. Conversely, the British have taken the frequent predictions that by 2000 we will be the poorest country in the European Community (or above Portugal only) as a definitive statement on national failure, despite its consequences being hard to detect in daily reality and, arguably, being increasingly trivial as 2000 approaches.

Growth competition may have some of the typical benefits of any competition: there is the pressure to improve and the satisfaction of winning. But there is also the possibility of it being a destructive and obsessive game, in which abstract economic status is pursued without regard to actual well-being. Developments in the Soviet Union suggest two quite opposite conclusions. The country has had an impressive rate of growth in comparison with previous historical periods, but it has lost a growth race with Western countries in the view of its citizens and is demoralised as a consequence. Had the 'West' not existed in its present form, the mood might have been complacent or even self-congratulatory. But what do we infer from this? Was it a good thing that the Soviet Union was subject to that kind of competition? Or would it have been better if it had not been gripped by macroscopic envy? The judgement is one of those which are too big for a utilitarian to make unless he has to and it depends, too, on what you think are the virtues and vices of that particular society.

Contemporary Greens often talk about 'sustainable growth', which sounds sensible enough. But sustainability is ambiguous and insubstantive. It could have at least the following meanings:

- *That a particular number, n per cent, is simply too high to be sustained indefinitely.* This is a Malthusian error: there is no reason to suppose that any growth rate cannot be sustained, given a changing 'basket' of goods and services.
- *That the current increase in the current basket of goods and services cannot be maintained.* Of course, it can't and never has been: we are always running out of resources, rendering particular goods 'uneconomic' and substituting others for them.
- *That a given number, n per cent, is ecologically undesirable.* There are two problems here. First, ecology requires the importation of other values in order to generate rules and constraints. Second, whatever form or level of ecological deterioration one declares to be

unacceptable, there is no reason why a number should break the rule.

The planet as a system of external diseconomies

In introducing the subject of diseconomies, Mishan says:

> The operations of firms, or the doings of ordinary people, frequently have significant effects on others of which no account need be taken by the firms, or the individuals, responsible for them. Moreover, inasmuch as the benefits conferred and the damages inflicted – or 'external economies' and 'external diseconomies' respectively – on other members of society in the process of producing or using, certain goods do not enter the calculation of the market price, one can no longer take it for granted that the market price of a good is an index of its marginal value to society.[19]

Thus:

> . . . the *social* value of a good – the value remaining after subtracting from its market price the estimated value of the damage inflicted on others by producing and/or using the good – may not only be well below its market price, it may even be negative.[20]

In less technical terms, Mishan suggests that most economies and diseconomies can be called 'neighbourhood effects'; elsewhere he describes them as 'spillovers'.[21]

A fairly conventional example might be as follows. A man sets up a glue factory: this requires transactions between himself and suppliers of raw materials, a labour force and customers. As a result of these transactions he makes a profit and the other three types of participants all consider themselves better off. These are the only considerations which orthodox economics considers relevant. But there are also neighbourhood residents who have to put up with the nauseous smell of the glue factory. More controversially, one might also mention those affected by traffic generated by the factory, those who dislike the sight of it and the parents of children who might be adversely affected by 'sniffing' the glue produced in it.

This last consideration would be considered inadmissible by virtually all economists, who would argue that glue-sniffing is a voluntary activity which cannot be accounted as an effect of glue production. Certainly, one would concede that there is a large class of voluntary activities which ought not to be counted, including (say) over-eating as a consequence of farming. But there is no simple line to be drawn between the effects of production or consumption and other voluntary activities. The philosophical assumptions of economics are a crude and untenable libertarianism. The contemporary litter problem in the western world (and, perhaps, in Britain in particular) is largely an external diseconomy of modern packaging methods and only very slightly an expression of individual moral weakness, but even single actions contain elements of both.

The history of the concept of externality suggests that economics was late to absorb a wide range of arguments and considerations which a broad utilitarian view would suggest were essential to good decision-making. For economists, the need for a concept arises from loopholes in the theory of marginal-cost pricing. A broader, political theorist's, definition of external economies and diseconomies might be that they consist of those aggregative advantages and disadvantages of human actions of which no account is taken in the criteria adopted by decision-making procedures. 'Decision' here must be interpreted in its broadest sense, to include outcomes in which there is no conscious sensation of deciding and no distinct time and place of the decision. Thus 'decisions' include what political scientists call 'non-decisions'; the term is broad enough to encompass any human outcome in which there was an alternative. Of course, the question of whether there were real alternatives to any particular outcome is partly philosophical and this philosophical element cannot be reduced to semantics or technicalities.

Thus it is not only transactions in well-defined markets or acts of consumption which produce external diseconomies. All human actions which might possibly be called 'economic' produce unconsidered effects, including barter trading, state activity and fully planned economies. At the time of writing, many people's candidate for the status of Europe's most polluted place is Bitterfeld, near Leipzig in the former East Germany. Most of its rivals are in Poland. The decisions which brought about the levels of pollution were pseudo-market decisions, based on an unreflective drive to maximise production, lacking both the refining constraints of the true market and the breadth of judgement of true utilitarianism.

Consequently, in the most interesting and politically important interpretation of the concept, external diseconomics are everywhere. At its worst, the world is a system of external diseconomies. Certainly, they are not only the consequences of markets. 'Free' markets produce many diseconomies; there is every reason to suppose that, however good market systems are as producers, they make poor guides to policy and to support the old saying that markets make good servants but bad masters. But, both careful theorising about the nature of 'public choice' and our knowledge of the real working of planned economies suggest that centralised authoritarian decision-making may be worse either because its productive failures may outweigh its improved breadth of consideration or even because its diseconomies are actually greater. In crowded and weary places like Southern England or the Bay Area of California, people are often pessimistic and assume that all major changes will have disadvantages which outweigh their advantages. Change is a fateful process, a 'progress' which is to be staved off for as long as possible.

What can be done about external diseconomies? The economists' logic suggests that they should be internalised; full real costs should attach to courses of action. Where an indefinite number of people, the 'public', is affected then taxation is the appropriate response: the polluter should pay. Where it is a limited set of people, it is appropriate to re-define the systems of property rights and laws of nuisance which are part of even the most primitive legal system. 'Class' actions, by groups of disadvantaged citizens are the necessary modern development. Mishan, *in extremis*, suggested that the true cost of flying (taking into account the noise and danger of aeroplanes) would be high enough to ground almost all planes. They have, at least, become noticeably quieter since the time that suggestion was made.

But many external diseconomies are either ignored or dealt with by crude political means equivalent to pruning only randomly selected trees and doing the job with an axe (which may, of course, be a lot better than doing no pruning at all). The state's assumption of development rights in Britain in 1947 has, at least, stopped Southern and Central England becoming a megalopolis like some of those in more spacious parts of the English-speaking world. The 'amenity clause' which says that state enterprise should be conducted 'with due regard to the interests of amenity' has had some beneficial effects on public activities in Britain. It was first introduced in the Hydro-Electric Power (Scotland) Act in 1943 and fully generalised by the Countryside Act of 1968. Its effect has diminished with the sale of nationalised corporations; proponents of privatisation have often argued that confrontational regulation – allowing organisations to pursue their own goals, but regulating their activities strictly – will prove more effective than giving them, so to speak, a built-in conscience and a mix of objectives. Public inquiries in Britain essay to subject both private and public developments to the criterion of 'the public interest'. In the USA environmental impact assessments have a slightly different emphasis: they seek to elucidate all effects of development and to clarify how rights will be affected.

American planning has been much influenced by the synergistic ideas developed by Sir Patrick Geddes and Lewis Mumford.[22] Synergism portrays the world as a complex and systematic interaction of a number of factors which is almost inconceivably large. A simplistic 'economic' investigation into the question of whether a motorway should be built may see the decision only in terms of whether an assumed number of possible journeys might be completed more quickly, more efficiently, etc., and assess whether the monetary value of the improvements as a whole (including the relief of pressure on existing roads) outweighs the cost of the project. A more complex model may evaluate external economies and diseconomies and give them values in terms of their effect on property prices and the compensation required to make those who have been dis-benefitted feel that they have not lost. But a synergistic account goes well beyond the realm of such calculations, considering how ecological patterns may change, how 'corridors' of development pressure will be created, how the character of areas and patterns of commuting and the quality of communal life may alter.

The advantage of economic calculation is that it produces answers, even if, to a broad utilitarian, there are reasons to suspect that they might not be very good answers. The advantage of synergism is that it fosters awareness of complexity among decision-makers, though without giving many answers. A narrow and precise treatment of external economies and diseconomies will tend to leave the most important consequences of any decision out of consideration. But a broad definition leaves us with guesswork and philosophical judgement and the knowledge that, if we end life on earth, we could call our mistake a major diseconomy miscalculation.

Things which eventually diminish

In 'classical' economics the Law of Eventually Diminishing Marginal Utility went something like this: If an individual consumes successive units of a good, there must be a unit, number n, which gives less satisfaction than its immediate predecessor, number $(n-1)$. It was famously exemplified by glasses of drinking water, consumed by a man who has just come out of the desert: the fourth may taste even finer than the third, the fifth than the fourth, but there must come a point, eventually, somewhere between initial satiation and a swollen belly, at which a diminution of satisfaction occurs. That this is so is rather more immediately obvious in the case of some acts of consumption (chocolate bars, sexual intercourse) than it is in the case of others (Mozart symphonies, fine views). Nevertheless, the formal truth of the Law must be conceded, even if there are doubts about its practical meaning.

Suppose we define goods very broadly, so that there are only two kinds of goods, material and spiritual. All material goods substitute for each other to some degree, as do all spiritual goods. But spiritual goods cannot substitute for material, nor vice-versa. As a person's prosperity increases, we would see a general satiation with material goods. Assuming that the increase in prosperity did nothing to increase spiritual goods, we would expect an increasing importance of spiritual goods at the margin. Aggregatively, a more prosperous population would be one in which spiritual goods were more important, whether it was more prosperous compared with other societies or with itself at a different period. If, for any reason, there was also a tendency for increases in the supply of material goods to diminish the availability of spiritual goods, beyond a certain point, then the well-being of prosperous societies would need rethinking and replanning. Continuing to assume that increased material prosperity was the highest priority would be a major utilitarian error.

The distinction between 'material' and 'spiritual' is a fatuous one, not intended to be taken seriously. It simply does not work because most things that matter to people are not like either chocolate bars or prayer, they involve both consumption *and* a special meaning unrelated to the price or value of the thing consumed. Family meals, sports events and travel are typical of 'goods' which have both dimensions. But the failure of the distinction does not invalidate the argument that modern economies may be oriented to a class of goods which demonstrates diminishing marginal utility as a class and which also have corrosive effects on other aspects of aggregate well-being. The philosophical economists offer a number of alternative distinctions which could validate the argument.

Fred Hirsch's 'dual economy', partly inspired by Sir Roy Harrod, distinguishes between the 'material' and the 'positional' economy. The definitions are as follows:

> The material economy is defined as output amenable to continued increase in productivity per unit of labour input: it is Harrod's democratic wealth. The material economy embraces production of physical goods as well as such services as are receptive to mechanisation or technological innovation without deterioration in quality as it appears to the consumer.

and:

> The positional economy, which is the basis of Harrod's oligarchic wealth, relates to all aspects of goods, services, work positions and other social relationships that are either (1) scarce in some absolute or socially imposed sense or (2) subject to congestion or crowding through more extensive use.[23]

The focus of Hirsch's argument is on what happens as the material 'pie' gets bigger while the positional 'pie' remains the same size. One consequence is that the price of certain goods whose supply is absolutely limited goes up by hundreds or thousands per cent even in 'real' terms. These include the most prestigious works of art and houses in beautiful and protected areas of countryside.

Hirsch's two economies suggest four ideal types of good:

1. *Pure consumption goods.* As far as the individual is concerned these may be subject to the law of eventually diminishing marginal utility, but even in the most advanced economies there is no forseeable end to the benefits which might accrue from more efficient production and distribution. Good food and drink and medical services are close to this model.

2. *Pure status goods.* These establish rank and order in society and thus (contingently, but inevitably) have important effects on self-esteem. Only one person can be first and, as W. S. Gilbert says it (in *The Gondoliers*),
   > When everybody is somebodee
   > Then no-one's anybody.

   Honours, ranks, titles and championships are of this form.

3. *Changing status goods.* We have been frequently reminded over the past century, by such writers as Thorstein Veblen and Vance Packard, that apparent acts of consumption contain important elements of 'status-seeking'.[24] At different stages the motor car, the foreign holiday, home ownership, the yacht or whatever are badges of having 'made it'. The more widespread they become, the less value they have.

4. *Absolutely scarce goods.* Some things are irreplaceable or all but entirely non-substitutable. This is how Hirsch treats great art and landscape.

This analysis suggests considerable pessimism. We can't expand pure status goods and our expansion of changing status goods has us all striving individually to remain aggregatively in the same place. In the case of absolutely scarce goods we may not only have no way of expansion, we may also be devaluing the experience and destroying the source through pollution and congestion: the cave paintings at Lascaux are deteriorating and closed to the public, Venice is crowded and polluted to the point of having to refuse access to the city on occasion, and the Lake District is suffering from severe 'people-erosion'. Only pure consumption goods seem to offer genuine scope for improvement of the human lot and very little of reality fits that model. This might stimulate nostalgia for the England of the thirties when lobster was affordable, motoring was a joy and you could travel from London to Brighton on a cheap, clean train which served good meals and arrived on time. Or it might tempt us into the apathy suggested by the late Sir Neville Cardus's remark that the sum of human happiness never actually varies from time to time or from place to place.

Education is a curious kind of good which Hirsch discusses in a number of contexts. It is partly a positional good: thus one effect of raising the proportion of people who enter higher education from 2 per cent to 20 per cent (my figures) is simply to raise the entry threshold for a professional career and to exclude almost wholly the remaining 80 per cent of the population. There is an element of pure status good: if you expand the number of first class degrees, then the real *caché* attaches only to 'congratulatory' firsts, or to degrees from those institutions which 'maintain standards'. But those of us who peddle this good cling to the belief that it is partly, if only partly, a pure consumption good which can improve the lot of an indefinite number of people.

The implications of Scitovsky's version of the dual economy are in some respects even more pessimistic about the benefits of prosperity. Scitovsky distinguishes between 'comfort' and a range of alternatives which includes 'stimulus', 'pleasure' and 'culture'. Modern capitalist economies, and most especially the American economy, are very good at providing comfort, but relatively poor at providing anything else. The relevant definitions are: Behaviour to increase comfort consists of;

> . . . relieving or forestalling discomfort. That includes behaviour which satisfies various bodily and mental needs and so lowers arousal that is too high; it also includes behaviour which combats boredom and so raises arousal that is too low. Though somewhat different and of opposite sign, the two kinds of behaviour are alike in that both aim at securing a negative good: freedom from pain, unpleasantness or discomfort. The positive good is pleasure, and it is very different from comfort.[25]

and:

> I shall define culture as knowledge; it is that part of knowledge which provides the redundancy needed to render stimulation enjoyable. Culture is the preliminary information we must have to enjoy the processing of further information. Consumption skills, therefore, are part of culture,

while production skills are not . . . while the enjoyment of comfort requires no skill, only stimulus enjoyment is a cultural activity.[26]

There are two aspects of Scitovsky's argument which he does not particularly need to disentangle, but which need some distinction for the purposes of my argument. He is concerned that advanced market economies are far better at comfort than they are at culture. But he is also particularly concerned that American ideology and tradition create an interpretation of the comfortable life which undervalues culture by a much wider margin than is the case in such countries as England or Italy. There is a 'Puritan Ghost' in the American outlook which militates against doing things with style and as ends-in-themselves. Americans are goal-oriented: they want to 'win', they want 'success', but their response to achieving these things is not relish, but a quest for further goals. Thus Americans work harder, take fewer holidays, spend more time alone and have more clearly defined ambitions than do Europeans; there is considerable statistical evidence for all these differences. The typical achievements of American consumerism are comfort-oriented: they remove or minimise technical difficulty, embarrassment and exposure to climate. They have led the world in automatic cars, fast food, and air-conditioning, but lag behind Europe in the proportion of people involved in the creative arts, community sports or in the maintenance of local tradition. Americans often cannot understand why people in more traditional societies will put up with months of short rations or even bankruptcy, in order to perform their role properly and fully in an important cultural event like a wedding-feast. Conversely, people in traditional societies cannot understand what the purpose of American life is supposed to be.

Only part of this argument is concerned with the special features of the 'American way of life', however. We must always bear in mind the concerned theory that American achievements and problems are simply a developmental stage ahead of those in other societies. Much of the theory concerns the behaviour of *homo sapiens* in the interesting, but unfamiliar, circumstance that he had broken the back of the eradication of discomfort and is moving on to a different set of problems. Philosophically, these new circumstances put us right back to the origins of utilitarianism, to conceptual questons about pain, pleasure and satisfaction. David Hume, roughly speaking a proto-utilitarian, wrote in the eighteenth century that, 'Human happiness, according to the most received notions, seems to consist of three ingredients: action, pleasure and indolence'.[27] Scitovsky comments, 'It is a simple framework, but not simple enough for the modern economist, for he has thrown the insights of his predecessors to the winds and recognises only one motivation of behaviour: desire for satisfaction'.[28] One must add that, in the conceptual move which economics has made from utility to preference theory, the whole logic of 'satisfaction' has altered. It is not longer *people* who are satisfied, in the sense of having a feeling of well-being or achievement. It is *wants* which are satisfied. And the number of possible wants is strictly infinite.

But something of Scitovsky's central distinction can be found merely in returning to Bentham's distinction between pain and pleasure. The relation between pain and pleasure can be portrayed in two quite different ways. The first sees the two as different levels of the same thing, perhaps experienced in different ways, as heat is experienced as ice and water. All life is better than death and the experience of pleasure by movement through a transition stage as things get 'better'. This is the assumption which most utilitarian philosophers have made and to which economics is committed by its replacement of pain and pleasure by the single concept of want-satisfaction. The alternative is to assume that pain and pleasure are different kinds of thing, which can increase together. A certain level of pain-eradication would have to be achieved before pain and pleasure could increase together, but within a margin they could: masochists, explorers, rugby players, *inter alia*, act on this model.

Importantly, what it suggests is that rational people, exploring their own interests, should treat the eradication of pain and the pursuit of pleasure as different kinds of objective. It makes sense to maximise pleasure, but we should only satisfice in the eradication of pain. As I sit here, writing these words, I have a certain amount of pain in my wrist and back and a dog is barking rather irritatingly across the road. But I can 'live with' these things; I do not have to eradicate them in order to seek other satisfactions. It would be oddly boring to spend one's life minimsing pain; nor would the maximisation of longevity, physical fitness or wealth, or the minimisation of risk seem to be possible routes to personal satisfaction: all of these are cases for satisficing, not maximising.

Little thought has been given to the logic of pain and pleasure. The mainstream of most political and artistic traditions and the rhetorics they generate is about pain as the essence of the human condition, and it is considered self-indulgent and irrelevant to the serious issues if one dwells too much on the nature of pleasure. The 'Puritan Ghost' haunts a wider field than the USA. Even an author like George Orwell, given to occasional bouts of great common sense, writes, 'Most people get a fair amount of fun out of their lives, but on balance life is suffering, and only the very young or the very foolish imagine otherwise'.[29] On the whole, our intellectual tradition since the eighteenth century has allowed little room for the discussion of pleasure, because it has regarded the eradication of pain - of poverty, disease, and various kinds of grievance - as being the more urgent task which is far from completed. There may be some good reasons for this assumption, but to some degree it is a failure of clear thinking and a legacy of theological propositions which are no longer generally accepted.

The meaning of life and the pleasure of life

Let me offer a broader definition of culture than that of Scitovsky, which looks at it from a different angle: Culture consists of the institutions and shared values which give meaning to life. The role of culture is to define the identity of people and to set goals which retain significance in the context of an individual's entire lifetime. Thus culture allows people to feel a permanent sense of belonging and a lasting sense of achievement. Because comfort is a different kind of thing from culture, it is possible to live a painful and difficult life, even a tragic one, which is also rich and satisfying.

The old saying that 'the best things in life are free' is not strictly true. Most of the best things in life carry financial costs as a matter of contingency and opportunity costs as a matter of logical necessity. But it remains an important half-truth, more true (in a loose kind of way) than the philosophical assumptions of economists and bureaucrats. Certain activities which locate us in a culture have a value out of all proportion to their cost. Being a part of a local pub or community, playing a useful role in a cricket team or theatrical production, completing a famous and arduous walk as a secular pilgrimmage, belonging to a place, successfully growing and cooking food for family and friends, above all, the cycle of sex, love, parenthood and family life: all of these things have value on a higher scale from rank, wealth and consumption.

Sadly, though, for reasons of theory which I have tried to clarify, our public ways of doing things – markets and bureaucracies – underestimate the significance of cultural goods by subsuming them onto the same scale as comfort-oriented consumption. 'They' turn our local pubs into homogenised bar-restaurants, remove the excitement and communal warmth of the football terraces and allow the motor car to destroy the atmosphere of the countryside.

The American-inspired nightmare

To the defecting Romanian gymnast, America is the ultimate freedom, where you can eat and drink as much as you like of what you like most and make love all day. To the young Pole, interviewed by a BBC reporter, the idea of paradise is simply 'an American supermarket'. But to many West European visitors, and to a section of its own intelligentsia, the USA is 'God's own junkyard', 'The Air-Conditioned Nightmare', the 'Joyless Economy' and a place of permanent 'public squalor'. It has the highest rate of car-ownership in the world, but, with a few small exceptions, it also has the highest rates of violent crime, drug addiction and family breakdown. For all that American political speeches often state that the USA is the most successful nation in the history of the world and that many ordinary Americans believe them in an abstract and ill-informed kind of way, no observer with any comparative perspective could see the USA as a happy society.

The difference between the two perceptions has something to do with all the distinctions which have been discussed in this section: pain and pleasure, material and spiritual, material and positional, comfort and culture. For those below a certain level of development, particularly East Europeans who have been subjected to a grinding sense of backwardness and a crude ideological tyranny, the USA looks like paradise. But to West European and even American intellectuals, brought up in pluralist societies, with relatively high and rising levels of material comfort, it is closer to a nightmare. It has only a kind of mistaken success. The extreme suggestion, though not the reality, of American life is of a world from which all familiar difficulty – unpleasant weather, embarrassing confrontations with strangers, hard physical labour – have been excluded, but so have real pubs, real families, real cricket teams, so that individuals are left playing a kind of success-game, which is ultimately futile.

Alternative versions of the dual economy

Green writers have distinguished between the 'real' and 'paper' economists and between 'sustainable' and 'unsustainable' economic activity. Economists distinguish between the transaction successes of modern economies and the 'external diseconomies' which are never fully considered. Hirsch distinguishes the 'material' from the 'positional' economy; Scitovsky illustrates the difference in the high capacity of the American economy to provide 'comfort' and its failures to provide 'culture'; Galbraith points to the co-existence of a rising tide of *per capita* private wealth with a deteriorating quality of public goods and deteriorating standards of public service.

Let me summarise theories of the dual economy:

1. In considering economic expansion as it affects human well-being, two aspects must be distinguished. In the spirit of such a distinction, rather than in the hope of precision, these can be called the material and non-material dimensions of the economy.
2. In terms of this distinction, economic advance is always disproportionately material.
3. Thus, beyond a certain point, continued economic advance is subject to a grand version of the Law of Eventually Diminishing Marginal Utility.
4. In some cases, at least, the expansion of material production actually diminishes the non-material dimension of well-being.

Taking the stagnation and the dimunition of the non-material aspects of well-being together, there are three types of reasoning behind the suggestion that expansion of material goods is not, proportionately, an expansion of well-being. First, there are analytic arguments which suggest that, by definition, non-material goods cannot be expanded: Hirsch's analysis amounts to saying that much of what we really care about is not logically capable of much aggregate expansion. This may be true, in different ways, of status (and, possibly, consequently, self-esteem) and beauty. Some aspects of Scitovsky's argument also suggest an analytic diminution: it may be precisely because progress removes the need for hard physical labour, for coping with the weather, for dealing with people we have not chosen to deal with, that life means less to us. Secondly, there are causal arguments: arguments about external diseconomies and sustainability generally imply that a material gain often causes a non-material loss. Perhaps the most important example concerns the effect of the increased use of motor cars on security, tranquillity and beauty. But, thirdly, there are some effects, of both stagnation and diminution, which seem purely contingent. This is especially true of Galbraith's consideration of the public and private realms. Why *has* economic growth in many western countries been accompanied by increasing failures to deter crime or to clean up rubbish? There may be a social or psychological link between crime and the acquisitiveness which generates growth in markets. But surely we could afford to pay to clear up the tidal wave of packaging which has accompanied the growth of the retail sector? These consequences are not always or everywhere evident. They seem to rest on a mere marginal technicality, that public expenditure is always believed to be approaching the level at which increased taxation would cause recession or increased borrowing inflation. It is partly a problem of democracy: the provision and protection of public goods by taxation does not seem to pay in votes in proportion to the good it does.

However, all of these arguments and observations, whatever their logical status, have real effects which we experience. They all suggest reasons why a utilitarian should be suspicious of the meaning and consequences of economic 'progress'.

Addiction and poverty

To be addicted to something is to have an acquired need. Individual addiction is such a well-known phenomenon in contemporary society that it can be taken for granted. We distinguish between a strict sense in which the addict suffers from physical dependancy such that he will experience chemical destabilisation and distress if he does not get what he needs and a psychological dependancy in which the addict feels disturbed or insecure if he does not get his bar of chocolate, his twelve hours work or his soap opera.

For utilitarianism the concept of addiction is difficult to incorporate. The economic interpretation assumes that a desire acquired and satisfied makes a person better off; it tends to assume that, *ceteris paribus*, a desire acquired but not satisfied makes a person no worse off. But a broader, more sceptical utilitarian view allows for a much more Buddhist interpretation: the best thing to do with some desires is not to satisfy them, but to eradicate them. They should be eradicated because they cannot be satisfied or, if satisfied, such satisfaction only creates further desires which themsleves cannot be satisfied or the initial or consequent desires can only be satisfied at too high a cost. The cost may be high in terms of money, opportunity, time or the loss of personal autonomy.

This point may be more fully developed and emphasised by Buddhism than by other philosophies, but it is an ancient wisdom common to most systems of thought. Aesop talked about desires being bad masters and Aristotle said, 'I count him braver who overcomes his desires than him who overcomes his enemies'. To St Paul, those who fulfilled 'the desires of the flesh and of the mind . . . were by nature the children of wrath'.[30] A long tradition of Christian morality portrays desire as temptation and as something which 'enslaves'. This cannot, *prima facie*, be subsumed within utilitarianism; much of it is concerned with heaven and hell or with a strict ethical good not reducible to self-interest. But there are hints, even in Christian accounts, that base self-interest is sufficient to prescribe resistance to temptation. It is echoed in common sense by the woman, lighting her cigarette at the bar, who says that, if they'd known what these things were going to do to people, they would have executed Sir Walter Raleigh a lot quicker and banned all importation of tobacco leaves. There is a common and ancient wisdom which counsels that the eradication of potentially addicting wants is better than their satisfaction. It is counsel which utilitarianism can ignore only at the risk of absurdity.

Yet, if the importance of individual addiction is widely understood, the nature of social or collective addiction is not well grasped. By this I mean not merely the aggregate of individual addictions, nor the biological or learned transmission of such addictions in the family, but forms of dependency which are forced on individuals by a pattern of choice outside their control which may pre-date the period in which it exists.

Social dependency can occur because of the working of markets. When motor cars are invented the first purchasers get a good deal: high status and empty roads. But as car ownership spreads the car drives the tram off the roads, makes the train unprofitable, slows down the bus, makes the horse and the bicycle too dangerous, until we all end up in a vast traffic jam travelling slower than ever. For many, maybe most, people there is no option of another form of transport or of living near their work. They are, through no fault of their own, dependant on the motor car. Some dependencies are democratic: government cannot, or dare not, act because of the working of the electoral system. This might be because an intense minority will change votes on the issue (tobacco workers, for instance) or because voters' time-horizons are assumed to be too short. Then there are manipulated dependencies; part of the strategy of any organisation selling in a market must be not only to create dependency, but also to establish norms of consumption. To fall below such norms may be to suffer ostracism of some kind. Junior norms can be particularly powerful: it is difficult to explain the proper Buddhist attitude to consumption to children who feel deprived and despised because they do not have a video-player or are not going on a skiing holiday.

Lewis Mumford regarded addiction as a central fact of modern societies. He said that, 'the unwillingness of cigarette smokers to free themselves from their addiction to cigarettes despite the incontestable evidence of the probable consequences of lung cancer, give a hint of the difficulties we face in redeeming the planet – and ourselves – for life'. His concept of addiction extended to social addiction: 'Our present addiction to private motor transportation alone may prove equally hard to break until every traffic artery is permanently clogged and every city is ruined'.[31]

Mumford's thesis is that we are not sufficiently selective about technological progress; much of what the machine economy does to us is not to make us better off, but to addict us to its products. His historical account of modern society says:

> The expansion of the machine during the past two centuries was accompanied by the dogma of increasing wants. Industry was directed not merely to the multiplication of goods and to an increase in their variety: it was directed toward the multiplication of the desire for goods. . . . Needs became nebulous and indirect: to satisfy them appropriately under the capitalist criterion one must gratify them with profitable indirectness through the channels of sale. The symbol of price made direct seizure and gratification vulgar: so that finally the farmer who produced enough fruit and meat and vegetables to satisfy his hunger felt a little inferior to the man who, producing these goods for a market, could buy back the inferior products of the packing house and the cannery.[32]

The nature of addiction is the core of the explanation of the phenomenon of poverty. The poor are always with us, despite decades of compounded growth. Their existence is a logical necessity, implied by the sociological definition that personal poverty is an inability to afford those goods which are established as minimal norms.[33] Scitovsky quotes figures to show that the single person poverty norm as a percentage of GDP per capita varies little between societies: the Egyptian figure is 21 per cent, the USA figure 25.8 per cent.[34] Thus poverty is virtually ineradicable: if you don't have a car in the USA you *are* poor, not only because you feel poor (in a country in which there are currently about 550 cars per 1000 people), but because there are no remaining safe forms of transport.

Thus, Mumford is able to say that, *'capitalism has not come within miles of satisfying the most modest standard of normalised consumption'* [35] (his italics) because 'the mass of mankind . . . do not have . . . an adequate diet, proper facilities for hygiene, decent dwellings, sufficient means and opportunities for education and recreation'.[36] This is in sharp contrast to the expectations of Adam Smith about industrialism or of John Locke, who claimed that most people in late seventeenth-century England were better off than Norman Kings. The 'standard of living', in any real sense, does not increase on such a scale as paper figures.

One might argue that the alternative systems of economic organisation have done worse; as a modest enthusiast for capitalism, I would so argue. But that does not mean that Mumford's point is not well taken and that the criticism should not be considered seriously.

Time: horizons and slices

Most people recognise intuitively that choosing the wrong period of time
over which to plan one's affairs is a prime example, even a paradigm, of
folly. How much advice from one person to another is counsel against
being 'short-sighted' ? By how much does this proportion go up if only
advice to the young is considered? In the jargon of modern social science,
too many people frame their actions within a time-horizon which is too
short. The old-fashioned scold is often right to warn that, 'You'll regret
this later'. The mistake made by the five foolish virgins in St. Matthew's
gospel is the most familiar of human errors.

A more complex form of error consists of slicing time too thinly and
therefore automatically 'disjointing' the incremental decisions which
make up a strategy or policy. My old car is rusting. Shall I scrap it and
buy another one or spend money on the bodywork? (Most of us probably
know this story.) I choose to spend the money. Then the engine needs a
re-bore and I face another decision; then the clutch, then the gearbox.
Over a two year period I have spent £2,000 and ended up with a car worth
very little. What kind of errors have I made in looking after my own
interests and how could they be avoided?

Of course, there are several. I may make an error which is anthropomorphic and sentimental, believing (in my 'heart of hearts') that the
poor old banger deserves better than the scrap-heap after its years of loyal
service. If my satisfaction at being in the familiar car is sufficiently great,
this will not be an error; on the other hand, if I would have callously
forgotten the old car, then it is. It may be that I simply make one mistake
after another: every time I spend money on the car I am 'throwing good
money after bad'. This could be because I am hopelessly misinformed
about the probabilities of old cars having structural problems or it could
be because I never do a sufficiently clear arithmetical calculation about
the alternative strategies available. Or a more complicated error is
possible in which I make a series of short-term 'emergency' decisions
which are each rational within my horizon at that time, but which add up
to something foolish. The body job makes immediate (three-month)
sense; having spent that money, the re-bore is 'profitable' over six
months. Eventually, the gearbox is justified even over a two-year period,
having already made decisions which turned out to be wrong over a two-
year period.

This is a relatively simple example, involving such trivia as cars and
money. In less arithmetically precise, but more important, ways our lives
go wrong through all these kinds of mistakes. When we move on to the
realm of collective decisions, looking after one's interests becomes even
more difficult, because the structures which build small individual
decisions into collective policies allow no possibility for the individual to
make long-term choices. Thus, what Fred Hirsch calls 'the tyranny of
small decisions' is not so much concerned with individual failure to
'slice' time into big enough pieces, but with institutional failure to allow

people to make the kind of longer-term choices which would provide the kind of arrangements they would prefer.[37]

The 'classic' example is Garrett Hardin's 'tragedy of the commons'.[38] As the common becomes over-grazed, individual commoners might wish that they could achieve a stable and regulated common. A small guaranteed share of that would be preferable to any share of a piece of mud or dust. But there is no mechanism for choosing this option. Each commoner knows that self-limitation is going to do nothing for the common: since it is going to be over-grazed in any case, his only rational policy is to get the most out of it while he can. The sum of such rational decisions can only speed up the destruction of the common. Any preservation of the common is preferable to its destruction of the common. Any preservation of the common is preferable to its destruction, but this can only be changed by a major institutional reform: the common must be enclosed and be the property of one landlord who can 'husband' it or the commoners must forfeit their grazing rights in favour of a collective system of regulation. In practice, it has proved difficult to persuade people to give up their rights and individual enclosure backed by the authority of the state has proved a more frequent solution of ecological problems.

In contemporary circumstances the tragedy of the commons is duplicated by over-fishing and tourism, the tragedies, respectively, of the Peruvian anchovy and the beauty-spot. International waters are a very obvious analogy to common land. But so is tourism: our rush to see it before it is ruined being the spiritual case of which over-grazing is the material paradigm. Mishan has suggested severe restrictions on tourism, to which Wilfred Beckerman, has replied that any restrictions would imply distributive gains for the rich and for certain fastidious, minority tastes.[39] I will make my own recommendations about this problem later on, but part of Beckerman's case – in effect that beauty, solitude, rare habitats, etc., constitute a minority interest – can now be dismissed by the accumulation of evidence since he wrote. They are not minority tastes; there have been geometric increases in the activities which express these tastes. But for a utilitarian the considerations of distribution seem unjustifiable and potentially disastrous; it is better that some should suffer disproportionately in a smaller aggregate loss than that everybody should suffer equally and massively.

Modern planning issues provide many major examples of 'the tyranny of small decisions'. The broad process of suburbanisation, urban 'sprawl', commuting and urban decay is one in which individuals rarely have any rational option except to contribute to major social changes which many of them find repugnant in the long run. In the retail trade there is a move to 'out-of-town' shopping which at its worst leaves us trailing round dreary and soulless hypermarkets which have a monopoly of the local trade while town centres decay and car-less pensioners despair. A similar structure is observable in transport planning: through market mechanisms the car undermines and replaces rival means of conveyance. But this creates a disjointed incrementalism in public decision-making: roads are built to meet 'needs', but these roads create new needs and we end up with roads which (like the cars) we would not have wanted if we had operated with broad strategic alternatives and institutions which allowed us to choose between those alternatives.

Democratic and aristocratic economics

The acknowledged advantages of markets as systems of production and distribution is that they are highly competitive. They constantly force participants to seek increases in productivity and they allow no complacency. The obverse is that market participants can rarely afford to take a long-term view; they must always be looking to the future, but it is usually only to a near horizon. Given the range and plausibility of arguments about market failure – monopolies, oligopolies, external diseconomies and so on – we would have to be sceptical about any possibility of the market acting as an 'invisible hand' to serve broad utilitarian directives unless it was guided by a state whose activities bordered on the level of genius.

But if the regulation comes from a modern democratic state (by which I mean only that politicians are liable to dismissal by an electorate roughly equivalent to the whole adult population) then there are reasons to fear that the regulators will suffer from the same limitations as market participants. Politicians 'have' to win elections, just as businessmen have to make profits. They can only operate within the time-horizons of their electoral system. By election-time they must buy off major interest-groups, re-inflate the economy and put any measures which will put short-term unpopularity well behind them. The electoral system is a very crude market in which electors can choose to 'spend' only one vote; people are likely to use their vote on the issues which most directly affect their interests. The commuter will vote to lower the cost and difficulty of commuting. The worker who is threatened by unemployment will vote to keep his job in being. Neither will take much account of issues like pollution in doing so.

This is the message of modern 'economic' theories of democracy like that of Anthony Downs.[40] Participants in the electoral game, like those in the market game, are rational and self-interested. Voters seek to maximise the extent to which policy furthers their interests; politicians seek to maximise their length of time in office. Typically, politicians build '50% + 1' coalitions in shapes which depend on the rules of the electoral system; they abandon clear principle and parties try to occupy the same ground; the state becomes increasingly involved in protecting and subsidising sectional interests. None of these conclusions suggest a near-maximisation of the long-term interest of the people as a whole, or of the quality of the environment in particular. No wonder Bentham's first inclinations were towards 'enlightened despotism' rather than democracy.

In marking what he called 'the choice of evils' in favour of democracy,

Bentham made the opposite assumption to that of the contemporary models he has inspired: he assumed that people could and should vote altruistically.[41] They are to be altruistic not merely in the limited sense of including the interests of selected others with whom there was an identity of interests or for whom there was affection, but of a generalised benevolence towards the 'public', the aggregate, or an indefinite number of people. Bentham's voter is a public and responsible figure, not a self-seeker, but a benevolent legislator.

The questions of self-interest and altruism and short-term and long-term have an important overlap. 'In the long run we are all dead' as Keynes *bon mot* has it, but there will still be a 'public'; as time-horizons lengthen and as people grow older voting must stretch to an interest in the conditions in which one's children will live and one's grandchildren and thus to a concern for the well-being of society generally. Empirical evidence about voters, as opposed to *a priori* assumption, is thoroughly mixed. Voters are not entirely self-interested any more than they are entirely rational. Principle is not always a good thing, as when electorates put the nationalistic principle which implies guns before the self-interest which implies butter. But there is growing evidence that western electorates are prepared to put trees before butter.

An examination of the structural biases towards time of different institutions suggests a similarly mixed picture. Politicians and entrepreneurs may be confined, for many purposes, to operating within short time-horizons, but civil servants, as part of the quasi-tenured professional classes, have every interest in taking a much longer view. It was 'technocratic' public servants who planned France's modernisation under the Fourth Republic: their power was boosted by the very weakness of politicians in a regime which allowed few governments to last more than a year and which forced politicians into a day-to-day struggle. Planners in Britain and the USA produce plans for periods of twenty years, but their 'best laid schemes' are often nullified by inaccurate projections and the short-term, 'knee jerk', responses of elected governments. Only where power is concentrated and resources guaranteed, in rare conditions like the New Town and the new university, can there be a semblance of over-arching strategies in which a proposal for what will go on at time $T + 5$ years *and* $T + 10$ years *and* $T + 20$ years are all integrated and judged by broad criteria.

In referring to the 'quasi-tenured professional classes' I have already suggested a link between social class and time-horizon. Edward Banfield goes much further than this and defines class by time-horizon. He distinguishes four classes: a lower class with a myopic concern for instant gratification, a working class whose plans and aspirations stretch over about a year, a middle class who have projects for a full career or a lifetime and an upper class whose dynastic aspirations stretch well beyond their expectations of life. Banfield's theory of class says, in effect, that the interesting and important distinctions between people do not concern their present occupation or financial status (the typical sociologists' indicators of class) but the longevity of their vision and projects. It is the time-horizon that defines the man and anybody can break out of a class in the superficial sense. It is easier to have a long time-horizon in certain circumstances than in others, but it is the horizon that ultimately matters, not the circumstances; thus, individual choice and responsibility and the American norm of upward social mobility.

The qualities of an aristocracy include, but go beyond, the characteristics of Banfield's upper class. By aristocracy, I mean a condition of life which is removed from concern about financial security, social status and career success. In this condition there can be no pure self-interest, but a merging of ego with the wider identities of people and land, with the broadening sphere of '. . . the family . . . the village and locality and ultimately, . . . Empire and international relationship' as Lymington put it. The economic motivation of aristocracy is not with the maximisation of profit, but with the long-term maximisation of the capital value of the estate in its broadest possible sense. It is no coincidence, but of immense ideological significance, that aristocrats have been at the forefront of 'green' movements in both theory and practice and that the environment has proved to be the abiding concern of the British royal family.

I should qualify this use of aristocracy. My definition implies only a contingent link (though an important one) with what are generally recognised as aristocracies. Mere possession of a title does not guarantee membership of the aristocratic class as I have defined it, nor does lack of a title exclude. Where formal titles are widespread, as in much of Eastern and Central Europe before 1914, then impoverished so-called aristocrats have to scrimp and worry about status and they sometimes travel by omnibus. The English aristocracy, 'the most democratic' as Lord Macaulay called it, but also the most numerically exclusive, is generally much nearer the model.

The practical recommendations of this defence of the aristocratic outlook are not so much for a government of dukes, as for a Disraelian project to enhance the elements of aristocratic outlook throughout society: security of status, identity with land and community, the long view. This requires noses to be lifted from the grindstones of short-term insecurity. It may sound fanciful, it requires improvements in education and a further professionalisation of work but if it does not happen we are likely to end in different versions, simple and complex, of the plight of the foolish virgins.

General conclusions and their prospects of acceptance

I have argued that, in the content of their social criticism, a broad and sceptical utilitarian philosophy and the 'green' outlook have a great deal in common. Both have good reason to be sceptical about economic growth and to argue that our institutions systematically undervalue certain kinds of benefits and satisfactions and coerce us into excessively short-sighted frameworks of decision-making. The argument can be characterised as a criticism of the narrow, precise utilitarianism which has been evolved by economics and bureaucracy from the point of view of an interpretation of the same philosophy which is unashamedly vaguer and more intuitive.

In many respects the late twentieth century is a ripe time for the expression of this conservative and commonsensical philosophy. With the execution of Nicolai Ceausescu in the very last days of the 1980s the world lost perhaps its last political leader who really believed that he was going to change the nature of society and transcend all familiar problems of the human condition. It was worth razing entire villages and putting a whole people on short rations because society was going through a transcendental change which would make existing problems irrelevant. Since the eighteenth century political philosophy has been dominated by such quasi-millenarians, talking the language of the transformation of man. Marxists, anarchists, fascists, national socialists, have all offered us a revolutionary break with old problems, a spiritual leap to a different level of development. So have some liberal capitalists, most recently represented by Herman Kahn, arguing that the sheer abundance of material goods produced by advanced capitalism would create a different kind of society, essentially without environmental and social problems. There are still many people suffering from mild versions of 'Ceausescu syndrome', powerful and impatient middle-aged men (Vice-Chancellors, managing directors, civil servants, et. al.) who want to push ahead with 'progress' and lay their monuments down without stopping to argue about whether the benefits of what they do will outweigh the dis-benefits, but they are on a relatively small scale. The last great remaining proponent of transformation is the reactionary Utopianism of Islam.

It does help, too, that the world is getting smaller, that air travel, telephones and television coverage are such that there are no longer 'far away places of which we know nothing' but that we realise the inter-connectedness of planetary events and the ways in which a bad harvest or an ecological mistake ten thousand miles away might affect us. One important dimension of the history of environmental planning is a constant movement to greater scale. It started with concern for particular slums, moved on to attempts to control the quality and density of housing in general, then to plans for the distribution of population and industry. Now we instinctively treat whole states as inter-connected 'crossroads' of planning, economic and social issues and are groping towards international institutions for the international dimensions of these issues. Concern for pollution has progressed from worries about the hygenic problems of particular streets and rivers and from particular emissions which landed within a few miles of the place of combustion, to a scale of air and water pollution which nearly always crosses international boundaries and rarely goes unremarked.

One important symptom of these changes is that the burden of proof has shifted. Established ideologies always demanded an absurdly high standard of proof of critical propositions. You had to 'prove' that smoking 'caused' lung cancer or that DDT acted as a cumulative poison or even that large-scale straw-burning did more harm than good. To which the conservative and sceptical utilitarian is entitled to remark, 'What kind of proof must you have! And Why?' and to insist that making rational choice is not like trying criminals: it is perfectly reasonable to act on suspicion, or the balance of probabilities and to prefer the policy with known consequences to the untried.

If I am right that the mood is more auspicious for scepticism of 'growth', 'progress' and of the consequences of much of our productive activity, then my kind of utilitarian and many people of a 'green' outlook can rejoice together. But, despite important common ground, we are not always on the same side and I will now move on to a discussion of utilitarian arguments which, even in my hands, remain opposed to much that defines the green outlook.

Notes

1. See, for instance, Steve Platt, 'Did we really need the M25?', *New Society*, 79: 5, (1986) pp. 20–22.
2. *Ibid.*
3. *Timothy I*, 6, 6–10. Authorised version.
4. English translation in E. G. Parrinder, *A Book of World Religions*, (Hutton, 1982), pp. 120–25. See also Paul Lucardie, 'A State in Moral Development?' in Lincoln Allison (ed.) *The Utilitarian Response, The Contemporary Viability of Utilitarian Political Philosophy*, (Sage 1990), pp. 57–73.
5. Porrinder, *op. cit.*, p. 128.
6. See, *inter alia.*, John Stuart Mill, 'Bentham' and 'Utilitarianism' in Mary Warnock (ed.) *Utilitarianism*, (Fontana, 1962).
7. See, for instance, Barbara Wootton, *Lament for Economics*, (Allen & Unwin, 1938), Joan Robinson, *Economic Philosophy*, (Watts, 1962).
8. J. K. Galbraith, *The Affluent Society*, (Hamish Hamilton, 1958), pp. 186–7.
9. E. J. Mishan, *The Costs of Economic Growth*, (Staples, 1967 & Penguin, 1969). E. F. Schumacher, *Small is Beautiful. A Study of Economics as if People Mattered*, (Blond & Briggs, 1973). Tibor Scitovsky, *The Joyless Economy, An Inquiry into Human Satisfaction and Consumer Dissatisfaction*, (Oxford University Press, 1976). Fred Hirsch, *Social Limits to Growth*, (Harvard, 1976).
10. Hirsch, *op. cit.*, p. 15.
11. Schumacher, *op. cit.*, p. 25.
12. Quoted in Martin Walker, *The Walking Giant, The Soviet Union under Gorbachev*, (Michael Joseph, 1986), p. 53.
13. William Morris, *News from Nowhere*, (Routledge and Kegan Paul, 1970).
14. Kenneth Boulding, *Economic Analysis*, Fourth Edition, (Harper and Row 1955), pp. 93–101. It is slightly unfair to quote Boulding in this context since he was one of the most philosophical economists of his generation. But this is a clear exposition of the argument in a best-selling textbook.
15. Hirsch, *op. cit.*, pp. 84, 89–91 and 95–101.
16. Scitovsky, *op. cit.*, pp. 264–84.
17. Martin Wiener, *English Culture and the Decline of the Industrial Spirit*, (Cambridge University Press), Paul Kennedy, *The Rise and Fall of the Great Powers*, (Unwin Hyman, 1988).
18. Adam Smith, *An Enquiry into the Nature and Causes of the Wealth of*

Nations, Dent edition, ed. by E. R. A. Seligman, 1962, Vol. II, Bk. 5, Part I, pp. 182–98. First published 1776.

19. Misham, *op. cit.*, p. 82.
20. *Ibid.*, p. 83.
21. E. J. Misham, 'The Spillover Enemy', *Encounter*, 33: 6, (1969), pp. 3–13.
22. See Patrick Geddes, *Cities in Evolution: an introduction to the town planning movement and to the study of civics*, with an introduction by Percy Johnson-Marshall, (Benn, 1968). (First published 1915). Lewis Mumford, *The City in History: its origins, its transformations and its prospects*, (Secker and Warburg, 1961).
23. Hirsch, *op. cit.*, p. 27.
24. Thorstein Veblen, *The Theory of the Leisure Class* in *The Writings of Thorstein Veblen*. Vol. 1, (Kelley, 1964 First published 1899). Vance Packard, *The Status Seekers; an exploration of class behaviour in America and the hidden barriers that affect you, your community, your future*, (McKay, 1959).
25. Scitovsky, *op. cit.*, p. 59.
26. *Ibid.*, p. 226.
27. David Hume, 'On refinement in the Arts', *Essays, Moral Political and Literary*, (Liberty Classics, 1985), pp. 269–70.
28. Scitvosky, *op. cit.*, p. 78.
29. George Orwell, 'Lear, Tolstoy and the Fool', *Inside the Whale and Other Essays*, (Penguin, 1962), p. 115.
30. *Ephesians*, 2: 3. Authorised version.
31. Both statements quoted in *The Daily Telegraph* obituary, January 1990, p. 19.
32. Lewis Mumford, *The Future of Technics and Civilisation*, (Freedom Press, 1986), p. 140.
33. See, for example, Peter Townsend, *Poverty in the United Kingdom: a survey of household resources and standards of living*, (Allen Lane, 1979).
34. Scitovsky, *op. cit.*, p. 117.
35. Mumford, *op. cit.*, p. 146.
36. *Ibid.*, p. 147.
37. Hirsch, *op. cit.*, p. 40.
38. Garrett Hardin, 'The Tragedy of the Commons', *Science*, 162: 1243, pp. 1243–48.
39. Wilfred Beckerman, *In Defence of Economic Growth*, (Cape, 1974), pp. 51–52.
40. Anthony Downs, *An Economic Theory of Democracy*, (Harper and Row, 1957).
41. This is a confused and confusing issue. Once he had become a 'radical', in favour of a large suffrage, Bentham risked contradiction with his usual psychological premises if he allowed voters to be altruistic, but demonstrably non-utilitarian policy-making if he insisted on their remaining self-interested. Generally he chose altruism, as John Stuart Mill did consistently. See J. Lively and J. Rees, *Utilitarian Logic and Politics*, (Oxford University Press, 1978), Jonathan Riley, 'Utilitarian Ethics and Democratic Government' and Ian Budge, 'Can Utilitarianism justify Democracy? Benthamism as "Positive Theory" ', both in Lincoln Allison (ed.) *The Utilitarian Response, the Contemporary Viability of Utilitarian Political Philosophy*, (Sage, 1990).
42. Edward Banfield, *The Unheavenly City: The Nature and Future of our Urban Crisis*, (Little, Brown, 1968).

4 Grey Utilitarianism

I am now going to put a series of arguments which will seem, to many minds, more predictable, ideologically, because they direct opposition to Green positions from a broad, sceptical utilitarian base. A common theme will be the opposition between utilitarian calculations of human benefits and dis-benefits and Green concern for harmony with nature or reverence for nature. A caution should be repeated with respect to the content of 'Green' thought: it is not possible to define a coherent web, an essence-with-consequences, of Green thought. I can merely pick out some common and important themes: there may be those who, perfectly properly, consider themselves to be Greens who say, of the propositions I am attacking, 'That is not a part of green thought as I understand it'.

Is there a message or substance to ecology?

In the argument so far I have frequently assumed or asserted a negative proposition: ecology tells us nothing substantive, it cannot cross the logical gap between facts and values. In simple terms ecology does not tell us what to do: there can be no such thing as an 'ecologically correct' choice of policy. Where there appears to be an ecologically correct thing to do that is only because the values we bring to bear on the choice, when combined with our ecological speculations, give a clear indication as to what ought to be done.

This is not a technicality. It is not as if ecologists can claim some 'fundamental value proposition' which lies behind prescriptions, as economists once did. Any recommendation of policy involves contro- versial value-judgements about resources, ethics and aesthetics, which might be capable of synthesis into a utilitarian judgement or might not. Ecological change always happens; there is no option of stability. There are always species which gain and those which decline in population; extinction has been a functional part of evolution; for sentient beings, good times and bad times have always alternated.

In an earlier section, I distinguished three uses of the word 'ecology': it refers to a system of interaction, the scientific study of that system and ethical imperatives arising out of the system. There is no apparent contradiction between the second and third of these, but there is a deep incompatibility between the spirit and purpose of the two kinds of ecologist. Academic ecology has remained, since Haeckel, closely allied to Darwinian theories of evolution. Ecology is about how species change, how creatures evolve; it is concerned with the ebb and flow of populations and the consequences of extinction, all seen in terms of the systematic interaction between species.

Academic ecology remains a study in search of a discipline and a status. Within science it has been considered peripheral and rather woolly. This is because ecologists have not evolved a 'paradigm' or a 'methodology' which would give a hard edge to ecological analysis. By their own account, they have remained rather undeveloped, lumbered with analogies and metaphors which have only progressed to a level at which they are not sure whether they have 'concepts' or 'theories'. Much ecological research looks rather old-fashioned, consisting almost entirely of the collection of data. Such research collects only an infinitessimal fraction of the data that might be collected, the choice constrained by feasability, assumptions about practical importance and the objectives of those who fund research.

In these respects, ecology is a little like politics or psychology and not at all like economics or physics. It is a 'science', but it is logically ill at ease with the other sciences. They are analytic in direction: physics is descended from a long tradition of breaking things down into yet more basic constituents in order to incorporate apparent irregularities. The physics of mass begets the physics of atoms which in turn generates the physics of energy. Ecology is correspondingly rather anti-analytic; its concerns are with systems and connections rather than with constituents. In that sense, rather than the ethical sense, it is an 'alternative' discipline, but it has failed to develop an alternative paradigm. As one current practitioner puts it, 'Economy-of-nature, and balance-of-nature, are excellent catch phrases, and strong on metaphorical content, but have been difficult to transform into theory in ecology'.[1]

This is quite different from substantive 'ecology' in its more popular, green conception. No wonder there are irritations and misunderstandings between the two groups. Martin Spray reports:

> The vogue for 'being ecological' is giving way to the vogue for 'being green', but that ambivalent use of the word 'ecology' does still cause annoyance to many practitioners of the science of ecology; and still these lookers at nature are, somewhat mistakenly, lambasted because they do not automatically associate themselves with conservation.
>
> Gerald Dawe, who runs the Centre for Urban Ecology in Birmingham, reminds me that the British Ecological Society was accorded much scorn during the debates on the Wildlife and Countryside Bill. 'I think the only reference the BES ever made to the Bill was a note under the heading *Miscellanea* in its Bulletin'.[2]

He goes on to say that in the decade since the Bill was debated (in 1981) more professional ecologists have shown a personal commitment to the 'values of ecology'. Even so, the two sides remain opposites in certain respects. Political ecologists are appalled by the 'pollution' of Billingham or Bitterfeld; professional ecologists are fascinated. The one group rushes to its printing presses to condemn, the other gathers around to admire how certain eels and rats and beetles have thrived and searches with excitement for any contemporary equivalent to the 'Peppered Moth'.[3] As a scientific ecologist, Lovelock insists that 'pollution is as natural to Gaia as is breathing to ourselves and most other animals.'[4]

The two ecologies suggest different kinds of religion. Political ecology is paralleled by a substantive pantheism which demands that we observe totems. There are things we must revere, rules we must obey, changes which must not be made. Harmony with nature (like the love of God for certain fundamentalists) must determine our actions, all day, every day. But the scientist's concept of ecology suggests the mystical pantheism of a Haeckel or a Lovelock which says, 'This thing is so big it will roll on with us, despite us, regardless of us . . . we are essentially insignificant . . .'. In theistic terms it is expressed by the third verse of Walter Chalmers Smith's 'Immortal, Invisible' (normally sung to the traditional Welsh melody, St Denio):

> To all life thou givest, to both great and small;
> In all life thou livest, the true life of all;
> We blossom and flourish as leaves on the tree,
> And wither and perish, but nought changeth thee.

Ecological problems

Of ecological systems we can truly evoke Alphonse Karr's insight into change and identity: 'Plus ça change, plus c'est la même chose'. Scientific ecology portrays the 'system' as a vast set of interacting relations, complex beyond full comprehension, always changing. From this perspective the system could only 'break down' when it ceases to exist, an event which could occur as a result of an uncontrollable cosmic event, like a rogue asteroid, or possibly a nuclear war. But, short of breakdown, it is difficult to portray one kind of change as being different in kind from another, except from the point of view of a particular political or ethical theory. Utilitarianism (or egalitarianism, or Hinduism, or Ruritanian nationalism) might be able to distinguish one set of ecological consequences as a 'problem' rather than a change, but ecology cannot.

The relation between the two conceptions of ecology resemble, in important respects, those between Darwinism and Social Darwinism. The essence of Darwinism, as an explanatory theory, is its logical account of adaptivity. Environments change, mutations arise, the most suitable species prosper. 'The survival of the fittest' occurs; it could more accurately be described as 'the survival of the fitted'. How do we know they are fitted? Because they survive, of course. It is an account of the logic of change and adaption which carries no messages about what *ought* to survive. Social Darwinism, by contrast, is entirely concerned with the ought and ought not of survival. The 'race' is weakened, it says, because it is too easy to survive; we have created a society in which 'weaker' elements can successfully breed (at a faster rate, even, than stronger elements) and their offspring survive. The utilitarian, at this point, is bound to question whether we are any worse off for doing this. The strict scientific Darwinist is bound to object that the weak elements are *not* weak if they breed successfully in their given environment.

Darwin was by no means innocent of Social Darwinism, just as Haeckel had tendencies towards political ecology.[5] In both cases there was something illogical about their straying into the prescriptive. In order to do so they have to concede that *homo sapiens* is a partial exception to the otherwise all-embracing explanatory power of 'evolution' and 'ecology'. From the point of view of 'monism' (or the traditional scientific 'uniformity of nature') this is an odd move which restores the messy picture of ape-angel-devil. Man is part of nature, but capable of operating against nature. This conceptual mess raises many paradoxical questions. Why man? We are not unique controllers or changers of the 'environment', only unique intellectually or linguistically. Are we the only species which can operate against nature? What about the over-breeding and destructiveness of the lemming, the deer, the seal and the rabbit, not to mention locusts, aphids, algae and viruses? Indeed, only the behaviour of the great carnivores seems to suggest mechanisms for keeping the ecological system in being *per se*. Man is one of the most successful of species. No other creature of anything like our size is populous on the same scale. From a strictly evolutionary point of view, this would suggest a harmony with nature. If we end up over-populating and therefore starving or self-culling, surely that is nature's way, too?

Man is not the only species to cause drastic environmental change and we are by no means newcomers to the game. The arrival of *homo sapiens* on the North American continent and the use of fire-driving techniques not only transformed the vegetation patterns, but many even have created enough smoke to have climatic effects. Man's use of domestic animals has had, perhaps, the most dramatic effects of all our techniques, an important historical example being the desertification of large parts of North Africa by goats under the Roman Empire. We continue to make deserts and to make them bloom. It is generally agreed by scholars that the ecology and landscape of Greece were transformed by 'civilisation' between the Homeric period (around 1200 BC) and the 'classical' period seven hundred years later. The Greeks 'destroyed' their forests and transformed their ecological system. Attica, according to Plato, became a 'skeleton of a body wasted by a disease . . . The water . . . running off a barren ground to the sea.'[6] But life survived, albeit at a much lower level of protein ingestion, and the life of the mind in Attica is that time is considered one of the high points of human development.

To the question, 'When is ecological change a problem or a decline?' the only available answer is banal (but important): when it is perceived as being a problem or a decline. As conflicts of principle, these perceptions take several different forms.

MAN VERSUS NATURE

At the time of writing there is a new plague of the flying, swarming, migrating grasshoppers known as locusts, throughout the northern half of the African continent. They devour foliage and devastate crops. Locusts may well have revived because of the world ban on DDT and certain other 'persistent' insecticides which did not disperse or decay and which, therefore, increased in concentration as they mounted the food-chain, reaching their greatest concentration in certain hawks and carnivores, to which populations they did great damage. But alternative insecticides have not proved to be sufficiently persistent.

In this, relatively rare, case man and nature seem to be in direct conflict. We might hope for some 'best of everything' solution, like a miraculous system of nets which catches enough locusts to reduce the swarms so much that the food value of the locusts (which are edible and something of a traditional dish in North Africa) is roughly comparable to the crop loss. This would be a 'balance' of sorts and avoid the cumulative effects of DDT. But there is no reason to suppose that such a solution is available; since the existence of such solutions is not a logical necessity, there must be *some* instances in which man is in opposition to nature in this way. The immediate issue is people versus locusts; the implied long-term issues include people versus hawks, people versus certain kinds of ecological change and people starving versus people made sick by DDT.

The utilitarian calculation to be made in this sort of instance may vary enormously. A philosophy which regards human feelings as pre-ponderant, if not exclusive, in the calculation of good and bad, is unlikely to find sufficient dis-benefits in the massive use of insecticides to kill locusts to refrain from doing it. Locusts can cause starvation and social and agricultural upheaval. The calculation becomes very different in the case of red spider mites causing a 30 per cent crop loss in Kentish hops because of an insecticide ban. In both cases, though, the human calculation is opposed in principle to any reverential or 'sacred cow' response to nature.

AESTHETICS VERSUS PRODUCTION

As the American wilderness was opened up in the latter part of the nineteenth century, it stimulated a dilemma and debate which contrasted two kinds of conservation. 'Economic' conservationists, led by Gilbert Pinchot of the National Forestry Service, wanted to manage the wilderness according to the criteria of sustainable production. Their argument was in the tradition of 'good husbandry' and it specifically rejected any romanticisation of the landscape or deliberate (and, perhaps, paradoxical) preservation of wilderness *per se*. The 'Aesthetic' conservationists were inspired by the Scots explorer, John Muir; they included Horace Albright and Stephen Mather and became, with the support of President Theodore Roosevelt, the nucleus of the National Parks Service. They believed in a managed wilderness and accepted the paradox; they helped create what Daniel Boorstin has called 'the cathedrals of America'.

To a contemporary utilitarian mind, Pinchot's view over-estimates the importance of wood-production and the benefits of 'sound' management-for-sustainable-production, much as the expression of farmers' views of the countryside in England always over-estimates the value of food produced in relation to recreational use of the country and the aesthetic pleasure it gives. Equally, the concept of a park-wilderness generates a kind of sham best exemplified by the half-tamed brown bear scavengers of Yellowstone. (Yogi Bear and the Ranger are powerful symbols of the irresoluble ambiguities at the heart of 'ecology'). Even so, the park-wilderness may be a satisfying and sustainable sham and the human desire to commune with nature may be as 'natural' a role for *homo sapiens* as the husbandry of our resources. Lovelock may be right to assert, in his more prescriptive chapters, that our sense of beauty may be our best guide in planetary management. Pinchot was unacceptably puritanical and negative in his disapproval of the wilderness as a successful provider of wilderness-fantasy.

SHORT-TERM AND LONG-TERM STABILITY

The concept and working of 'national parks' raises many interesting questions about both ecology and utility. Over a hundred states now use the term, though what is meant varies greatly from the historic monuments of Israel to the managed wilderness-for-consumption which is the American invention and general paradigm. Somewhere in between is the complex compromise of the National Parks of England and Wales which contain the wilder and more beautiful parts of an inhabited and productive countryside.

A complex ecological debate recurred in the late 1980s concerning fire in the American National Parks. There have always been fires, of course: combustion can start with volcanic activity, over-heating compost or refraction of the sun's rays. Man brings to the possibilities of fire not only a multiplicity of new sources, but also a capacity to extinguish. There is evidence that the latter is preponderant: if we compare the post-war period in the developed world with primaeval landscape, there have been more fires, but they have been much smaller. Man is having more effects by putting fires out than he is by lighting them: it is an important and respectable hypothesis about 'forest-death' in Germany that the forests are suffering the long-term consequences of having all their fires put out. In the short-term, fires destroy forests. Over a longer period they fertilise and alkalise soil, kill parasites and clear space for new and more vigorous growth. In the Yellowstone fire of 1988, the authorities controversially allowed the fire to rage, taking the view that fire was natural and of long-term benefit, against short-term aesthetics and the theory that it was man's ecological role to put fires out.

In Southern England, it became clear in the 1980s that, from the perspective adopted by the Yellowstone authorities, we protected our trees excessively and let them grow too old. That is why so many trees – in parks, gardens, hedges, copses and forests – were destroyed by the Force 12 winds of October 1987. But it was fascinating to visit these areas in 1990 when the damage could be compared with the fresh damage from the Force 12 winds of the early months of that year. Many of the areas devastated in 1987 had assumed an ecological character of their own which was both rich in variety of species and quite different from any other places in Southern England. The rotting vegetation of the crashed forest had created a bonanza for fungi, woodlice, insects and climbing plants which in turn stimulated bird and mammal life. Many areas were almost entirely impenetrable to human being, thus offering habitat for the more 'shy' species. Nobody wants to conclude with the ethically neutered Panglossian sentiment that 'all is for the best in the best of all possible worlds'. But it cannot be denied that ecological change suggests different and contradictory assessments depending on which time-horizon you select, which species you favour, which guesses you make and which aesthetic position you adopt. Or, to put it another way, nearly every ecological cloud has a silver lining, even the creation of deserts. Deserts have a special kind of beauty and, for scientific ecologists, a particularly fascinating ecology.

ECOLOGY AS THE BEARER OF VALUES

One introductory lecture on political philosophy used to start with the concept of nature and the natural (as in human nature, natural law and natural rights) and then proceed to distinguish twenty seven meanings of 'natural'. Most of this range of ambiguity extends to nature in the ecological context, including theories of man's place in nature and our duties towards nature. Homosexuality is 'unnatural', but it seems to come naturally to many creatures, including humans. Nature's laws can never be broken, but they often are and much breath is wasted on preaching against breaking them.

'Nature' becomes a surrogate for many things. For nostalgia: we used to live naturally, expressing what came naturally to us and in harmony with nature (in the sense of things other than us). For deontological ethics: it is unnatural to beat a child, shoot a fox, etc. For social institutions: natural life is lived in villages or communes. (But cities and suburbs developed by natural processes, too.) For aesthetics there is natural harmony in an 'unspoiled' landscape: a Palladian house 'fits', but a power station does not. For religion: abortion is unnatural, but it is used by people naturally following their interests and it keeps population down to levels with which we can more naturally cope.

Thus disputes between interpretations of ecology or between what claims to be ecology and alternative objectives are often disputes between pairs taken from a myriad of ethical and aesthetic values incorporated into social and theological theories. One of the most complex forums for the class of these values is the European, and particularly the English, concept of 'country' or 'countryside'.

The countryside

The concept of the countryside is a strange one. Most people would believe themselves capable of recognising countryside, but there is no adequate definition of it. In old-fashioned logical terms, it is a word stuffed with connotations, but with very flimsy and elusive denotations. The origin of the word 'country' is simply from the Latin *contrata*, meaning 'lying opposite'; 'country' has referred to any kind of territory, however defined, (South Tyneside, a predominantly urban area, refers to itself as 'Catherine Cookson Country'), to England outside London, to the land outside towns, to productive agricultural land.

But 'the countryside' is actually a rather complex problem in conceptual and practical ecology. None of this catalogue of historic meanings captures what we *want* to mean by 'country', which (for its evaluative force) is dependent on what country means to us. Wilderness is not country; nor are the featureless agrifactories of Iowa and Cambridgeshire. Sometimes an urban park or university campus, which has kept its hedges, its copses, its ponds, is much more like country than is agricultural land, though counting as 'urban' land according to formal distinctions.

When William Cowper, in the eighteenth century, said 'God made the country, and man made the town', he may have neatly expressed what many people believed, and still do believe, but he could not have been more wrong. Man made the country: peat-digging made the 'Broads'; sheep-farming made the 'Downs'; aristocratic pretension, imitating art, made the parklands. Since Cowper's time, enclosures have added trees and hedgerows; the railway system added those cuttings and embankments which are now some of the richest habitats. It was made by man, not always in love or in harmony with nature or other people, but often pursuing financial interests, crudely and aggressively, with little or no regard for those he dispossessed, caring about nature only insofar as its aesthetics would assist his social status or its creatures provide him with blood-sport. If man was part of Nature, it was that morally neutral nature which Tennyson described as 'red in tooth and claw' and which 'shrieked' against the love of God.

What we see as 'the countryside' is not just space or nature or ecological complexity or food production or any particular combination of those things. There must be additional elements which fit our images. These include the historical complexity, the image of the 'palimpsest', the surface which has been inscribed and partly erased many times, by Roman *latifundia*, Saxon strip, enclosing hedge, Victorian railway, and so on. We seek an indication of our past, of a traditional way of living and doing. Countryside also requires a sense of harmony, of man living in ways that can be permanent, of a rapport between human beings and land. Violent change may have created the countryside, but it cannot *be* the countryside.

The reality often disappoints when compared to the image. That is why the countryside is always dying. Cobbett's *Rural Rides* recorded one

death, the agricultural depression which started in the late 1870s was
another, Massingham and his contemporaries recorded yet another. In
November 1989 the wildlife writer Robin Page published a plugging
article for his latest book which referred to 'the brutal murder of rural
England'. 'Britain', he said, 'is losing its rural heritage and it is not dying
so much as being systematically murdered.'[7] He complains of the
disappearance of hares, holly blue butterflies and partridges. He admits
the revival of kingfishers, collared doves and frogs. He does not mention
the success of hawks, often taken as a guide to the richness of the
ecological system: peregrine falcons, sparrowhawks and kestrels have all
revived markedly since Page was a child in the 1950s. He is (in my
experience) factually incorrect about partridges: I have never seen more
than there are at the present time.

Do the changes which Page bemoans institute a decline, let alone a
death? It is very difficult to say. Of course, he can complain of the effects
of elm disease, the ugliness of the new garage, the suburban newcomers to
the village and the effects of traffic. But these complaints, or equivalent,
would be true in every period for at least two hundred years. He
complains that 'time has not stood still', but it never did. The images
invoked by those who record rural disaster are often of 'rape' and
'murder'; Page talks about 'a skeletal elm . . . a symbol of crucifixion'.
The analogy is of a mother or goddess; her fate is tragic. An alternative
would be to see the countryside as the legendary Arabian phoenix,
regularly arising from the ashes of its own nest-pile. At the time of
writing, the English countryside has its problems, but I doubt whether it
has ever contained so much game or had such well-preserved old
buildings and well-maintained gardens as it does now.

At the core of the concepts necessary to understanding what we mean
by 'the countryside' – harmony, nature, tradition – are paradoxes, lies and
hopeless ambiguities. Thus when it comes to the practicality of 'preserving the countryside' we can never win. If you allow new housing and
industry in a village, you may help local people to remain, but you
change its look, size and 'character'. If you 'protect' it, it may look very
traditional, but will increasingly become an expensive haven for com-
muters, the two-home class and wealthy pensioners. The 'natural'
progression of farming technique is to farm more intensively and
efficiently, which equally naturally tends to make some farmers
redundant. But farmers (like Page) complain that diversification into
recreation or retailing or being paid to 'set aside' land creates a false,
shallow countryside. Even if you were studiously to re-create the countryside of 1890, it would rightly be denigrated as a 'museum-piece', but the
'living' countryside is always going to contradict our images and
childhood memories.

The countryside is a typically complex ecological concept, involving
man as animal, observer and would-be controller. As with other ecological concepts, it is ultimately elusive, being dependant on notions of
'balance' and 'harmony' which do not fit reality. The temptation might
be to say 'Plus ça change . . .' and to accept that the changes might as well

be considered the best available as there is no objective standard by which to denigrate them. On the contrary: this is very far removed from the attitude I wish to support. I am still a conservationist and environmentalist, but these prescriptions are grounded on broadly utilitarian values. It is because species are important to our sense of wonder and to our genetic resources, that it is nearly always worth paying a high cost to keep them in being. It is because landscape has so much meaning for us that we must have 'island' policies to preserve the variety of places and the perceptions of diversity and tradition. Utilitarianism furnishes values and prescriptions for the preservation of the environment; ecology only tells us it never can be preserved, yet always will be.

In defence of economic growth

I was driving across a rather mediocre stretch of Midlands countryside, a few miles north of Birmingham. In the passenger seat was a young man from China. Until a few days before he had never left his native province, which was many hundreds of miles from Beijing. He had been sent to England on an academic exchange scheme at a high point, for the Chinese government, of liberalism and interest in Western ideas. He barely knew how to get into a car and was completely unacquainted with such things as quadrophonic sound and seat belts. Until the last few days, he had never spoken to anyone whose first language was English. But he was highly intelligent and had read assiduously in English.

I asked him about his strongest impression of England. He thought for a moment and replied, 'the wildlife'. I was quite stunned; I suppose I expected something about full shops, fast cars or busy roads. I put it down to the language problem, but he was clear and correct about what he meant. 'Here, everywhere . . . trees and birds. Where I come from, people chop down all the trees and kill all the birds.'

There is a particular background to this statement: during the cultural revolution there was a systematic attempt to eradicate birds from China in the belief (ludicrous, from an ecological perspective) that agriculture would benefit as a consequence. But it is the general argument which is more important. In a backward part of China, struggling economically to get above the level of production required for subsistence, he had witnessed an environmental deterioration of a most unambiguous kind: resources and beauty had both been diminished greatly. During the same period, I had witnessed much more complex changes: the number of interesting old trees had gone down (not least as a consequence of Dutch elm disease), but the amount of forest had gone up by fifty per cent. New roads had sliced through the countryside but hawks and crows (protected from the pesticides which had reduced their populations during my childhood) had thrived around the roads. I doubted whether the English Midlands had ever been so densely populated with game. Magpies were now ubiquitous, once-rare herons and muntjak deer (ironically from my friend's part of China) were now common.

My friend, as he admitted in an amused way, had made a typical communist mistake (he did *not* describe himself as a communist). He had thought of 'developed' and 'undeveloped' in a one-dimensional kind of way, so that he had imagined the highly developed countries he had never seen necessarily had more of their trees chopped down and more of their surface covered with concrete than did less developed countries.

The implication of realising that 'growth' and 'development' are numerical and abstract is the realisation that they do not correspond to any particular phenomena. The implications of growth for environmental quality are entirely ambiguous. Some things which constitute and create growth destroy habitats and beautiful views. But other implications of prosperity and the sense of prosperity work in the opposite direction. They create enough resources to preserve and enjoy one's surroundings and to appreciate their meaning. On the whole, people who are comfortably off have much nicer gardens than those who are poor. The farms on ducal estates have more trees, more game, more landscape features and more varied cultivation than do those of 500-acre cereal farmers who have large debts to the bank. But the same is true at the collective, public level. Societies which generate new wealth not only can afford to devote resources to husbanding land, they also give rise to the political will to do so. The systems of national parks, national monuments and national forests in North America work well in many respects; attempts to imitate them in South America fall foul of the squatter and the drug baron. States have only been effectively financed in conditions of expanding industry. Judith Brown comments that, 'Pre-industrial societies have rarely generated sufficient wealth to produce a surplus which through tax has financed more than a minimal government'.[8] The comment stands in particular reference to the Mogul empire, but it would have more tragic relevance to Africa and South America in the contemporary world. It is growth which finances conservation, by states and individuals; the less important land is as a source of wealth and income, the more likely it is to be treated according to loving, long-term, totemistic criteria.

Otherwise most of the arguments for economic growth are statements of the disastrous implications of stagnation rather than clear benefits arising from more and better production. More comforts and gadgets may improve human life a little, but not a lot: most grandmothers and the more philosophical economists know that production cannot solve the problems of love, self-esteem and the meaning of life. It is these problems which become more significant as prosperity increases. The more fundamental objections to no-growth concern our inability to live with stagnation. How would we live without the pride and purpose which comes from technological progress, without trying to make new things and improve the production of those we already have? How do we get rid of the drive to have at least some things which are better than those in the past and better than those over our borders? It is all very well to talk about 'lowering expectations'; presumably, if we lowered expectations, we could afford to devote more resources to the 'environment' (and other collective projects) without increasing production. But such a thing is much more easily said than done; it requires the irradication of assumptions which have very deep roots in our culture. When I lived in California in the 1970s the governor, Jerry Brown, offered as the sole solution to many problems that we should 'lower expectations'. The idea faced a simple cognitive gap and the more complex gap between individual and collective action. Individual people said 'we should lower our expectations', while their own continued to rise unchecked. Those who did try to check their own expectations (and those of their children) found it very difficult to do so from a minority position.

We have no model of stability or voluntary stagnation. Western history, since the Homeric period, has consisted of technological and economic progress, often slow, being set back by war, famine, plague and the breakdown of civil order. The only model we have of living in stability with the environment is of hunter-gatherer tribes living at a very low density of population. The women of such tribes normally bore six children in their fecund period. The number was restricted by a four-year period of breast-feeding and four of the six children (on average) died in infancy. Truly, life was poor, nasty, brutish and short. In Australia, Brazil and New Guinea, that sort of life, and its harmony with nature, has existed relatively recently; but it inevitably collapses on contact with other modes of social and economic organisation.

There is no convincing case of such stability and harmony in an agricultural society: the typical history of agriculture is of endlessly disputed and changing property rights and of collapsing systems of debt and public order. In any case, even if we could find an attractive model of pre-industrial society, we would face the problem of supporting a population which is already far too big to be supported by pre-industrial means. We have an immutable demographic addiction to the level of production which only drastic measures, imposed by a highly authoritarian government, could begin to change. Speculation about life at different densities of population, like Porritt's 'generally agreed' 30 million for the UK, has no practical force without such drastic measures.

Other defences of economic growth often emphasise the consequences for justice of restricting growth. Economists and politicians have argued that by restricting growth you primarily restrict the numbers of people who can cross any particular threshold of prosperity. In slogan terms, this is the problem of the differential effect of restricting growth on the 'haves' and 'have nots', though 'have not so muches' would be a less misleading description of the poorer group. It is part of Beckerman's argument and Anthony Crosland used the memorable phrase 'pulling up the ladder behind them' of those who wished to restrict aspects of growth once they had realised their own expectations.[9] It is demonstrable that English planning, by restricting the availability of building land, has raised the price of houses and prevented some people from entering the housing market at all and many more from living where they might have chosen to live. Correspondingly, many people's 'environment' has remained more attractive than it might have become. There is also the problem, less often discussed, of the unjust distribution between those who have growth-oriented tastes (cars, technology, ownership of consumer durable goods) and those who have growth-threatened tastes (tranquility, wilderness recreation, observation of nature).

Utilitarianism is not concerned with justice *per se*. There is no objection to five (or even twenty) per cent of the population being deprived of something by a piece of unredressed historical bad luck unless that deprivation can be redressed with benefit to the aggregate. It is no problem to a utilitarian that we cannot all have Rolls Royce cars or the vast estates of the Duke of Northumberland. There is pleasure to be had from seeing a Rolls Royce or walking through an 86,000 acre estate and wisdom and contentment from such a plain demonstration that we can't all have everything. Houses in the Surrey green belt involve more difficult calculations, but any utilitarian position suggests that there must be some sorts of restriction on growth and that these will be to the disadvantage of some people more than others, the state's capacity to redistribute such disadvantage being intrinsically limited.

Any general utilitarian judgement about growth must be made with the reservation that the same abstract description can refer to many different realities and, particularly, will suggest different values depending on the cultural context and the level of development. But it is a logical necessity that the best of all available worlds is well-planned growth, meaning overall growth which restricts diseconomies and diverts resources to the things people really care about. The worst of all worlds is unstable recession in which starving mobs chop down every tree for warmth and kill every animal for food. Even badly planned growth would be better than such a recession, for at least some people could invest in their private environments. From the point of view of the utilitarian environmentalist, who sees a diverse, beautiful, healthy environment as a very important part of human well-being, there can be no general answer to the question of whether a well-planned recession might work, in the sense of being preferable to badly planned growth.

Implications of and for power

A constant theme of the Green package of principles and policies concerns power: existing power structures should be demolished, power should be devolved to smaller territorial units, people should hold power equally and over themselves. It is easy to identify the images of modern society which give these prescriptions force. They are images of the managing director, the merchant banker, the party boss, the property developer, who, by decisions made in the isolated comfort of his office, can affect the lives of thousands of people whom he has never met and who may be hundreds of miles away. The theory which most closely corresponds to these images is the 'power elite' theory which emerged in the 1950s with the continuing urbanisation of American society and its domination by big business. There was a particular account of the contemporary 'military-industrial complex' in the USA, but also a general account of power in modern societies. According to one meta-phorical account, the power structures of 1890 were like a wide landscape of low hills; those of 1960 were like towering Alps dominating a plain.[10]

From the point of view of someone who wants to establish a position which is both liberal and environmentalist, the prescriptive implications of these theories and images seem doubly unsatisfactory. In the first place, most 'environmental' policies require the firm exercise of power and authority in a negative and universal way. People must be prevented from shooting rare birds, building on beautiful land, tipping waste into rivers, emitting toxic smoke etc., not on a local option system, or by assuming power over themselves, but by enforced regulation at the widest possible territorial level. Considerable problems will occur even if adjacent states have different regulations. Within the European Economic Community the principal two types of problem have concerned the 'exporting' of pollution by the high-level emissions of power stations and into shared rivers and seas and the 'unfairness' of competitition which arises from differential environmental regulation. They have led to strong and successful pressures for environmental regulation on a European level. The logic of the situation seems to lead inexorably to regulation at a wider level, rather than to the devolution of power.

The second cause for concern is liberal rather than environmental. If you really devolve power, so that the village, family, tribe, monastery or commune has a genuine autonomy, you raise the possibility of despotism. As the scale gets smaller, the context more private, the relations more personal, the personnel less able, power becomes more frightening. Genghis Khan and Stalin may be prominent in the history of tyranny, but their evil is cumulatively outweighed by the nameless ranks of fathers, headmasters, tribal chiefs and mother superiors who have operated within systems of local autonomy. It would be good to 'have power over oneself', but as we are not Dr Donne's notorious islands but parts of a whole, the nearest we can get to that is to be part of a clearly regulated large society which offers exits from local institutions, where there is social and geographical mobility and a myriad of ways of making a living.

So far I have constructed these arguments as if I believed in power. But the concept of power does not really work. To put it another way, the meanings of the word 'power' are so complex and ambiguous that quantitative comparisons between different contexts are meaningless and misleading. The metaphorical tale of a transition from low hills to soaring Alps is fascinating, but misses the point of reality and its relation to words. The extent of modern power looks great, when measured by the number of people affected and their geographical spread. The managing director might affect a wide range of people from Basingstoke to Botswana, but his capacities are much less clearly described as power: their fit to paradigmatic notions of the nature of power is much less close. The managing director can achieve little unless he secures a sound financial structure, negotiates with local planners and politicians and anticipates the reactions of his board and his shareholder. If his wife wants to divorce him or his personal assistant wants to take another job (taking his secrets with her) because she has taken a dislike to him, he may well come to envy the kind of power which a tribal chief or an *ancien régime* aristocrat of the sword or a Victorian capitalist actually had. We think of all these 'types' as having 'power', but, actually, the nature of the relationships involved are quite different; time and development have increased the complexity of power and freedom. Modern power is not so straightforwardly the inverse and enemy of liberty when compared to earlier forms.[11]

Let me characterise a modern society: a high level of technology, formal-legal relations like contracts dominate business, a high level of geographical mobility, a majority of people who own some kind of wealth. In such a society, the devolution of power may mean the real increase of power. This is partly because the formal relations of the state allow considerable opportunities for redress and accountability which cannot be provided in old-fashioned 'face-to-face' relations. But it is also because the 'enlightened' qualities of the elite are bound to diminish as society becomes smaller, a point which considerably worried John Stuart Mill about the devolution of power despite his enthusiasm for participation.[12] Devolution suggests charming images of Ruritanian or Rutlander self-determination, but it ought also to raise the spectre of the classic western where the population, 'three days from the nearest US marshall', removed from the ordered tedium with which mature states regulate affairs, lives in a world where 'possession is nine points of the law' and the gun is nine points of possession, where heroic warriors are necessary to the prevention of despotism.

An environmental problem about devolution arises from the tendency of organisations to seek aggrandisement and to compete with their neighbours. Create a thousand cantons and they all want industry, a high rate of growth, a strong economic bargaining position. A genuinely independent Ruritania is soon worrying about falling irretrievably behind Urbania in terms of growth and in instituting development plans to catch up. There is, admittedly, a countervailing tendency, which is that central governments tend to foist their 'dirty public goods' (which offer net benefit to the economy, but dis-benefit to the locality on which they leave their 'externality footprint') on outlying and powerless areas.[13] With devolution the NIMBY (not in my back yard) effect takes over and Green writers are surely correct to imagine that devolution would *tend* to militate against a nuclear power station ever being built.

But which of these two counterveiling tendencies has in fact proved superior? NIMBY may predominate in Surrey, England or Marin County, California which, left to themselves, might not allow so much as another hut to be built on their territory and would turn all dirty factories into nature reserves. But most American states, West German *lander* and Swiss cantons have seen the federal political system as primarily a competition to secure development, a reaction which has been even more generally prevalent among new post-colonial states. Perhaps the typical reaction of politicians in office to new technologies and sources of economic power was Ernie Bevin's to the atomic bomb: 'We want one with a Union Jack on it'.

I have suggested that Green accounts of power are highly unsatis-factory, being vague, pusillanimous and implausible. How Greens might organise power in practice is open to wide interpretation. But one legitimate interpretation stirs fears of the language of personal autonomy being used to justify the extremes of tyranny, an ideological phenomenon which is already familiar through the histories of christianity and communism. Being restricted by the 'needs of the planet', if someone were allowed to interpret those needs, might be restriction on a new scale, particularly if that someone thought it was 'generally agreed' that the population ought to be about half its present level.

The limits of human nature

Considerations about human nature form a part of the premises of most arguments for and against social reform. There is a general question about human nature which implies a number of subsidiary questions. This general question (to put it in roughly Aristotelian terms) is, 'What are the essential, as opposed to accidental, characteristics of human beings?' That question carries a formal aspect, about the definition of human-ness: 'What are the necessary and sufficient conditions for counting an entity as human?' This must imply answers to all questions of the attribution of humanity: why isn't a chimpanzee human? or a computer? Is a foetus? How would we know in the case of a being who stepped, rolled, flew or oozed out of a vehicle which had arrived from outer space? But there are also much more interesting questions about the causal properties of such beings as we define as human. It isn't a defining property of apples that they fall to the ground if they are not picked or rot if left uneaten, but it is often more important to know those general facts than to know what makes something an apple rather than a pear. Falling and rotting are the general properties of an apple in its causal environ-ment. What are the equivalent behavioural characteristics of humans?

These two kinds of question are logically distinct, but we are likely and entitled to bear causal observations in mind when organising the criteria of definition. Diogenes was quite right to point out that Plato's defini-tion of man would qualify a plucked, live chicken. Marx was on the brink of including many species when he suggested that man was best understood as a tool-user. 'Human beings' may be causally equivalent to the zoological category *homo sapiens* but many writers, including myself, have argued that this cannot be a logical definition of human beings, since it is easy to conceive of creatures other than *homines* possessing the essential human characteristics, whatever they are (nor-mally some combination of language, rights or a particular kind of sentience).[14] It is not so easy to conceive of a mature *homo sapiens* with the full range of biological characteristics normal to the species *not* qualifying as a human.

The questions about necessary and sufficient conditions and about causal 'essence' are merely unavoidable pedantries. In arguments about social reform, the practical questions about human nature concern its mutability. In which way might human beings, while still being human, exhibit very different characteristics from those with which we are familiar? That is a question with historical, biological and philosophical dimensions. How differently have people lived in the past? Are there any constraints on prescribing human action which follow from our knowledge of the *physical* nature of *homo sapiens* or of living entities in general? How do historic observations and biological analysis relate to ethical argument?

I will deal with the question of mutability under two headings. The first concerns constraints on reform: does observation of 'human nature' condemn any prescriptions which might otherwise be ethically desirable because they are 'unrealistic'? The second concerns taste: what are the essential tastes, wants, drives and needs of human beings as opposed to the particular and accidental? Which things do we want from the very cores of our being rather than because of the contingent characteristics of our social circumstances? Wants can be manipulated or structured by society. By manipulated wants I mean those which are deliberately inculcated by advertising and propaganda whereas by 'structured' wants I am referring to those which are socialised into us because of the particular characteristics of a society, without it being anyone's intention to create such wants. 'Structure' is much more important than manipulation in this context. The distinct 'power' of isolable entities to make people want (and believe) what they intend has been much exaggerated by social scientists until recently. But the unintended effects of status hierarchies, collective addictions (in Mumford's sense) to technologies and of ignorance of alternatives are undeniably important in forming wants. Conversely, it is the 'deep', 'real' tastes and wants which matter to political theory and which constitute 'the good life'.

The importance of these questions to conventional arguments between 'left' and 'right' is widely agreed. It is particularly clear-cut in comparisons between radical anarchist views and those of conservatives. The latter tend to be 'pessimistic' about human nature and can envisage only very slow and slight beneficial changes in established institutions and modes of behaviour and suggest absolute limits to the extent of those changes. Anarchists reverse this argument and portray existing societies with their repressive states and obsession with the private acquisition of wealth as out of sympathy with the deeper and more spiritual drives of mankind, which only need effective release to operate in a stable and beneficial system. Liberal utilitarianism has tended to take a negative and empirical approach to human nature. In practice this is a rather similar approach to that generally typified as conservative, because both accept arguments against radical change to the status quo, but there is an important difference of principle because the liberal utilitarian view typically regards all human wants as mere contingencies and therefore liable to radical change, at least in the long term.

A number of 'Green' challenges to conservative and liberal approaches to human nature put the problem almost as centrally as do the anarchists. Andrew Brennan, for example, says of liberalism:

> . . . the very basis of the liberal approach can be criticised on the grounds that it ignores relevant considerations about what kind of beings we are and what sort of life is appropriate to us.

This is to be contrasted with a number of quite separate trends in the ecological philosophy. There is 'deep ecology', which argues that:

> . . . human flourishing or self-realisation requires a re-evaluation of our relationship with the rest of nature . . . a prevailing theme has been to urge the abandonment of our human-centred modes of thinking and valuing and – more recently – to undertake a real identification with nature.[15]

But there is also the 'eco-humanism' which Brennan himself espouses believing that,

> . . . among the relevant frameworks that political and ethical thinking ought to use is one deriving from scientific ecology . . . What is revealed (by scientific ecology) is not an obscure metaphysics, nor a new way with explanation. Instead, it requires us to take seriously the notion that we are a part of nature, and that . . . what we are and ought to be is partly determined by where we are.[16]

Brennan rejects utilitarianism for reasons which I find unclear. He embraces what he calls 'ethical polymorphism', which might otherwise be called 'moral pluralism'. Reciprocally, it is not possible for any kind of utilitarian to accept this kind of pluralism: it simply fails to resolve dilemmas. Even in principle it offers no means of choosing between options which are supported by independent moral values except some notion of intuitive balance. Of Harry Truman's dilemma about first use of the atomic bomb, it says only 'On the one hand environmental damage on an unprecedented scale, on the other possible shortening of the war, back on the first a record-breaking breach of any principle of the sanctity of life, then collective guilt'. The game of ethical ping-pong is endless. At least utilitarianism suggests procedures for comparison of these principles and for the rejection of some of them. Though utilitarianism and moral pluralism are both sufficiently vague and flexible that they might be interpreted as providing the same solution in practice by two persons on numerous occasions. The objection to eco-humanism, as to all forms of moral pluralism, is not that it is a dangerous ethical doctrine or founded on false premises (the utilitarian's normal two objections to forms of deontology), but that it is not, in crucial respects, an ethical doctrine at all. It abandons the real work of ethics to be left undone or done by the dice.

On Taste

The problem of taste is classically difficult for utilitarians. There is Bentham's definitive saw that 'The quantity of pleasure being equal, pushpin is as good as poetry'. But there is also Mill's stricture that it is better to be Socrates dissatisfied than a pig satisfied, his distinction between 'higher' and 'lower' pleasures and his defence of 'culture'. I do not believe that the incompatibility is as great as it appears to be and have argued that a reasonable rehabilitation of Bentham's 'felicific calculus', with all its possibilities of taking into account the 'duration' and 'fecundity' of pleasure as well as its intensity, allows in effect, for a scale of higher and lower pleasures.

The whole utilitarian project is 'liberal', though, in the sense that it cannot accept any *a priori* account of the human essence. I mean it must reject any theory which insists, without reference to evidence, that there are certain tastes and wants which are the true tastes and wants of people, which are to be distinguished from those which are superficial, or manipulated. Most of the metaphysical and religious systems in which people have believed, taking history as a whole, have implied such essentialist propositions about taste. They have said that human beings can find unique 'flourishing', 'self-realisation' or 'salvation' in religion, art or harmony with nature (to take three of the most prominent examples). It does not matter that most people seem to get more out of sport, beer or making money. Acceptance of essentialism in this sense is a frontier which one cannot cross and still be a utilitarian. It is epistemologically unsound because it detaches the understanding of human well-being from empirical evidence; it is politically unsound because it offers justification for tyranny, for burning people to save their souls, for 'forcing them to be free', for 're-educating' them into ideas which contradict their institutions and identities. My own rejection is fortified because none of the objectives (and 'socialism' or 'communism' should be added to the list) which have formed the content of essentialism are images I even find attractive, as will become clear in a later chapter. Green essentialism (man in need of harmony with nature) may not be so familiar as the religious or the romantic, but it is no more acceptable.

Rejecting essentialism does not, though, commit a utilitarian to the naïve belief that the satisfaction of all preferences, as measured by any particular market structure or bureaucratic computation of public opinion, is equally valuable. We must accept the inequality of significance of apparent tastes: poetry can be defended as more fecund and a more long-lasting pleasure than pushpin (or pinball, an approximate modern equivalent) which may only require more difficult conditions to be met (more education, for example) before it becomes very obviously a greater source of satisfaction. It is important for the utilitarian to fight against narrow and falsely precise accounts of pleasure, like cost-benefit analysis or the acceptance of market contingencies, and to insist on broad, complex judgements like those recommended by Mill and developed by such contemporary writers as Scitovsky. I find it odd to think of Mill, who understood little of sex and almost nothing of sport, as an expert on pleasure, but in his reflections and dilemmas of principle lies the ambiguous and difficult truth about human well-being.

Do people ever change?

An historical generalisation: human behaviour is characterised primarily by lust, acquisitiveness, snobbery and rivalry. If one compares classical writers like Thucydides and Suetonius with the contemporary world of *Dallas* or Jeffrey Archer, the essential game of life is the same; only contingencies like religious beliefs and political institutions change. The inference must be that any kind of spiritual reformism, which attempts to change people (rather than merely to give them more suitable institutions) must be doomed to failure.

The best sustained objections to this line of argument concerns the inference rather than the generalisation. It is after all a generalisation about *history* and, therefore, a partial, minority account of human life. History is about upper classes, urban society, reading and writing. The great mass of human life has been lived outside of history, hunting, gathering and farming, without written record. It has been quite different in texture from 'history': more certain, more stable, more spiritual. Consider the forty thousand years, maybe even more, of aboriginal life on the continent of Australia before the white man arrived. Consider, on a much lower scale of time, the centuries of stability of predominantly Saxon villages in England. Naturally ancient Rome and modern London seem rather similar: they are very similar in type as one, statistically minor, form of the human experience. I should add that the picture of Anglo-Saxon life given by such as John Massingham and Sir Arthur Bryant is open to doubt. There are alternative, even opposite, inter-pretations such as that of Alan McFarlane, who sees in 'Anglo Saxon' ways the origins of individualistic, dynamic, acquisitive assumptions which generated the first truly modern society.[17] But it is not within my expertise to referee such alternative interpretations. I wish only to infer that, on questions of human nature, 'history' tells us everything and nothing.

The suggestions of biology are as pessimistic, but inconclusive, as those of Darwin. Superficially, post-Darwinian scientific biology con-firms Tennyson's effectively pre-Darwinian image of 'Nature, red in tooth and claw' shrieking against the creed of love. Man is part of nature: like other living things his only ultimate drive, according to one contemporary biological scientist, is the mechanism of the 'selfish gene', a kind of programmatic urge to survive and reproduce possessed by the *gene*. But that scientist, Richard Dawkins, is properly sceptical about whether one can properly make inferences from the chemical observation of the 'selfish' gene to constraints on human thought and action: the translation from genes to people raises hoary philosophical questions about free will and the mind-body relation.[18] But the biological evidence is strongly negative. It does say that there is no scientifically observable drive in people for 'the preservation of the species', for the good of humanity or nature. Any feelings of those kinds have to be acquired, like patriotism.

A third kind of argument, overlapping in some respects with biological analysis and generally considered more promising at the time of writing, comes from the theory of games. The object of game theory is to investigate the effects of different strategies in a world which consists of two or more individuals whose actions and interests are causally inter-related. Game theory is the world of 'the co-operator', 'the defector', 'the grudger', 'the sucker' and more sophisticated creatures like the 'remorse-ful prober'. 'Strategies' are patterns of behaviour which can be predicated of computers or computer programmes, animals and even plants as well as people.

The most famous 'game' is the 'Prisoner's Dilemma', a model orig-inally formulated about prisoners being interrogated and choosing whether to 'sing' or remain loyally silent, though its enthusiasts see it as being relevant to a wide variety of circumstances. 'PD' is discussed in a hundred books covering a score of academic disciplines, as well as being the basis for many computer games. So I will not go through the basic features, except to list the hierarchy of values of its four combination outcomes, from the first person point of view:

Very good:	I defect, you co-operate.
Good:	We both co-operate.
Bad:	We both defect.
Very bad:	I co-operate, you defect.

What I am interested in, for this argument, is the strategies which tend to survive and prosper. In single games there are usually double defections, producing a 'second worst' outcome for each participant. 'Iterated' games which continue indefinitely, generate highly discussable results. There is no absolutely decisive tendency, but in the elaborate 'tournaments' devised by Robert Axelrod the most successful strategy is the simple 'tit-for-tat', doing to the other person what he last did to you, though 'tit for double tat', which allows a 'free' defection before withdrawal of co-operation, is also a good strategy.[19] However, this is dependent on competition against a particular selection of strategies (fifteen altogether in the first tournament) and any strategy can only be said to succeed or fail in respect of the strategies with which it interacts. Any selection of strategies must be arbitrary, so there can be no 'best strategy' for the game *per se*. A 'nastier' selection of strategies would generate a nastier best strategy.

Garrett Hardin's general statement that 'Nice guys finish last' is not necessarily true. As Richard Dawkins insists in the most recent edition of *The Selfish Gene*, '. . . even with selfish genes at the helm, nice guys can finish first'.[20] It is true, though that suckers (naive, constant, co-operators) are eliminated and that 'do unto others as they do unto you' (rather than as you would wish them to do) is the successful strategy: in practice this means a mix of co-operation with the real deterrence of defection and punishment. The model and experience both offer us outcomes of unpoliced co-operation. Dawkins is particularly cheered by the vampire bats who regurgitate blood for their unsuccessful neighbours on their good nights in a system of probable reciprocity, which can be partly explained by the different marginal utilities of blood to successful and unsuccessful bats. German and English soldiers in the First World War had to be policed *out* of co-operative patterns and even footballers can co-operate, as Bristol City and Coventry City did on one notorious occasion in 1977 when both teams needed a 'point' to stay in Division One.[21]

But 'PD' offers fairly strong arguments for pessimism about the nature of evolved beings and rather stronger arguments against trying to change patterns of behaviour. And this is a non-zero sum game in which it is perfectly possible for the participants to co-operate regularly and 'laugh all the way to the bank'. Strategies (and players) are only 'nasty' in the sense that they are greedy or untrustworthy; for that matter, they are never truly 'nice' because they never account the gains of another as vicarious gains. There are two further levels of nastiness as yet wholly unplumbed by this kind of game theory. There is *envy*, formally defined as perceiving one's interests as intrinsically involved in the relative positions of oneself and other players. And there is *malice*, by which I mean the identification of one's own interests with the inverse of the interests of one or more others. With envy, we introduce the possibility of power and status as focuses of desire. At this point the true game theoretician tends to lose interest; games which allow envy and malice are rather less neat and formal than those which do not and they lack the exquisite ambiguity between determinacy and indeterminacy.

Insofar as human life, as we know it, is like the games of game theory, it is like a mixture of games, some zero-sum and some non-zero sum, played simultaneously. We can co-operate for mutual benefit in the exploitation of resources or we can fail to co-operate through greed and mistrust. But we are also involved in conflicts about status and power which are real (and inevitable provided at least some players care) from which we cannot all gain.[22]

Animals other than man show some capacity for envy and malice, but human beings show a uniquely high capacity. In large part, as I shall try to demonstrate, this is simply a consequence of the variety of responses of which contemplative, theorising creatures (who are also animals) are capable. Consider the following assumptions about human beings:

1. Human actions are extremely varied. People react quite differently when faced with the same choices. Their reactions can be judged according to (at least) the following scales:

   self-interest/vicariousness
   acquisitiveness/material satisficing

> envy/autonomy
> short/long time horizons
> malice/benevolence
> timidity/aversion to risk
> clarity/confusion.

2. Action is generally responsive. How we act towards other people depends on how they treat us.
3. Certain types of response reduce chances of survival. Those who remain passive in the face of aggression or unacquisitive in response to land-grabbing suffer as a consequence.
4. There is a general tendency to respond in kind: to trade with traders, laugh with laughers, fight with fighters, etc.

These assumptions are 'liberal' rather than 'conservative' according to the usual stereotypes. They are not overtly 'pessimistic' about human nature, but they do generate pessimistic conclusions. All the logic of response of pure game theory, much magnified by the phenomena of envy and malice, suggest a general effect of the corruption of human nature. Apart from the effects of imposed authority, divine or secular, the creatures with the most varied responses end up behaving worst. Gentle, harmonious, satisficing is destroyed by acquisitiveness; peace is undermined by aggression. Rousseau was right to suggest that one man shouting 'mine' as he puts his spade into the earth is enough to corrupt paradise.[23] Greed and aggression have a ratchet effect on human behaviour. It is not that 'better' societies are logically or causally impossible; it is that they are infinitely corruptible. J. R. Ewing, unaided, might destroy Nowhere.

The pessimistic conclusions of this argument have a particular application to the contemporary world. The level of mobility on the planet now and the inter-connectedness of events, combined with the responsiveness effect, suggest the eradication of cultures which are not individualistic and acquisitive by those which are. Yesterday's aboriginals are today's capitalists and drunken criminals. Any proposal, including any Green proposal, which does not recognise these tendencies of human nature, which requires a fundamental shift in opposite directions, especially in the direction of less acquisitive behaviour, must be subject to stringent scepticism on the grounds of feasability. There is a mechanism for achieving change against the direction of the innate tendency, but it consists of the rigorous and authoritative imposition of values; the greater the change of direction, the greater the imposition must be.

Wants and needs

It is typical of Green, as well as socialist, traditions of argument to try to distinguish between human needs and mere wants. The distinction can then be used to give a much higher priority to the meeting of need than to the satisfaction of wants; in arguments about policy they are to be treated (to borrow Ronald Dworkin's analogy of the concept of rights) as trumps.[24] Any need over-rides any want. There is a long tradition of insisting on the primacy of need which usually involves the condemnation of 'luxury' in a world in which needs are not met. It stretches back to Cato and beyond, stimulated David Hume in the eighteenth century, to defend 'luxury' against its critics[25] and is passionately maintained in contemporary western society by those who think that it is 'obscene' that some people can spend £100,000 on a car or £200 on a meal when others cannot afford accommodation or food.

Porritt, for example, says that in a future Green society:

> There will, for example, be far more attention paid to the distinction between *wants* and *needs*, needs being those things that are essential to our survival and to civilised, humane existence, wants being the extras that serve to gratify our desires. We all need good food; some people want to subsist on a diet of extravagant and often harmful luxuries. We all need to get from A to B; some people insist they can manage such a feat only in the back of a Rolls-Royce.[26]

It is equally typical of the liberal tradition, of which utilitarianism is a part, to deny the validity of such a distinction and to insist that human desire is boundless and seamless. Other mammals generally satisfice: they feed, they breed, they lie down. They do occasionally over-eat or kill (foxes) or store (squirrels) much more than they can consume, but this is waste: there is a natural point of satisficing. There is no such point with creatures who can conceive desires intellectually and who can own and transmit wealth. As writers from John Locke to Bentham to Bertrand Russell have argued, there is no limit to the desires that people can formulate. If they satisfy one, they formulate another; it is possible to want power, dominion or ownership in respect of the entire universe. Typically, they then add that, in the vast range of possible human appetites, there are many possible distinctions, but no conceptually necessary distinction into two major types.

At the conceptual level, the liberal rejection of need is unanswerable. Needs have no denotation without an object. If you say '*A* needs *x*' the statement cannot be explained or justified unless you add 'in order to achieve *y*'. This is not just a pedantic, grammatical point. It makes the distinction between wants and needs dependant on there being a '*y*' which is both clearly defined and broadly supported as a value.

The most obvious candidate is survival, one half of Porritt's definition. But this doesn't work at all. Mere survival is a very low standard, but it is also too high a standard. In individual cases, such as cancer patients, the very old and the very depressed, what people may need (in order not to experience the extremes of agony and humiliation) is to die with dignity. At an aggregate level, putting an unimpeachable value on keeping people alive amounts to a principle of the sanctity of life which is diametrically opposed to both utilitarianism and established practice. We run our health services and our road systems by trading off deaths against such goods as the alleviation of physical pain and the rapidity of transit. And so we should; we would live very miserable and frustrating lives if we used all our resources on minimising death.

Any definition of need which allows for the variety of individual psychology is thereby liable to be all-inclusive and potentially dangerous in its implications. If we say, for instance, that '*A* needs *x*' if severe mental distress or instability would result from not achieving *x*, then it really is the case that not only are there many cases in which *A* needs the love of *B*, which cannot be given, but, in a very clear way, rapists need to rape and killers need to kill. Similar problems follow from the kind of sociological definition, based on existing norms and structural addictions, which I quoted earlier from Peter Townsend's analysis of poverty. People really do *need* cars in Los Angeles and Solihull; children in Royal Leamington Spa do *need* to go skiing in Austria. Rich places and rich people need to stay rich.

Accounts of the concept of need can quickly degenerate into *reductiones ad absurdam* of the distinction between wants and needs. One of the best known is the theory of needs outlined by the psychologist, Abraham Maslow. [Although a professional psychologist Maslow increasingly turned to writing what was, in effect, political philosophy. In his essays, 'Questions for the Normative Social Psychologist' and 'The Good Person and the Good Society' he was unashamedly discussing the issues raised by Plato, Aristotle, Hobbes *et al.*[27] It seems to me inevitable and proper that all the more interesting and logical souls in two or three dozen disciplines, from zoology to theology and history, should end up discussing political philosophy, which is the central forum of human curiosity and bewilderment. They bring the advantages of different perspectives, but sometimes have the disadvantage of insufficient familiarity with the moves, logical tricks and semantic pitfalls of the game.]

Maslow portrays needs in a hierarchy of (about) six levels, from basic to higher.[28] When a basic need is satisfied we move onto a higher level. At the bottom of the hierarchy are the needs of survival, above those are emotional needs and, ultimately, there are the needs of 'self-actualisation'. Thus, by Maslow's own account, the satisfaction of needs is very rare. The condition of true health involves 'peak experience'; it is not a necessary condition of the good life, but it *is* the good life.

There are perhaps two contextual points which can throw light on Maslow's concepts of health and need. First, it is very Californian: Maslow worked in California and was a best-seller in the state. Having lived in Lancashire and California, I regard the two cultures as opposites in their attitudes to health. In California you can meet a tall, bronzed creature with straight teeth and a firm midriff and ask them 'How are you?' and they will tell you about their allergies, their analysis and their skin-cancer check. The same question put, in Lancashire, to a wizened, pallid creature with chronic bronchitis and no teeth at all, will elicit the response, 'Grand'. As a psychologist, Maslow is building on a rather technical ideal of 'need' used in some parts of his discipline: the *International Encyclopaedia of the Social Sciences* says under 'Needs': 'see drives, stimulation, stimulation drives'. The *Encyclopaedia of the Social Sciences* defines need as 'whatever is required for the health or well-being of a person'. In these definitions, and in Maslow's theory, there is neither the possibility nor the necessity of the kind of distinction between wants and needs which would have ethical significance, which would make needs a kind of trump. All significant human wants are also psychological needs; the concept of needs is far too broad to allow for a real distinction.

To debunk the distinction between wants and needs is not necessarily to oppose the prescriptions which Porritt (or anybody else) might rest on such a distinction. Of course, it would often be better to make sure the substantial minority who lack basic nutrition or shelter get what they want rather than allow more people to have caviar or Rolls-Royce cars, if that presents a real dilemma. Certainly, markets can supply material goods which are of no great importance while undermining the availability of spiritual goods which are important. But these imbalances can be explained and rectified more clearly if they are put on a sound logical basis. The first requires an understanding of diminishing marginal benefits and the utilitarian account of redistribution and its practical limits. The second is better understood as a relation between comfort and culture.

This is not just a semantic change, a rephrasing. Neither of these accounts of imbalance is the same as the distinction between wants and needs; rather, it is a case of two conceptual frameworks which have overlapping consequences. There are objections to the ways in which the production of goods is apportioned and to their distribution, but these objections require a sophisticated utilitarian analysis. They cannot rest on the woolly and rhetorical distinction between wants and needs, nor should they prescribe a vague utopia in which everybody gets what they need.

Reflections on hunting

Hunting, in its broadest sense, is the killing of wild creatures by human beings. In the contemporary 'developed' world the purpose of hunting is always explained in terms of 'sport' and its primary reference (including *la chasse* in France, *la caccia* in Italy and 'hunting' in North America) is to the 'rough' shooting of birds and mammals. In the British Isles the word is used mainly to refer to fox-hunting, a practice which developed in the eighteenth century because of the insufficiency of stags and which involves the seeking and chasing of foxes by people on horseback and a pack of dogs. It is the dogs which kill the fox. There is no doubt that hunting, especially in this British sense, raises highly 'emotive' issues: its proponents and its opponents are both passionate.

On the face of it, there is no reason why Greens and utilitarians should quarrel about hunting. Jeremy Bentham was clearly opposed to all kinds of hunting for sport:

Cockfights, bull-baiting, hunting hares and foxes, fishing and other amusements of the same kind, necessarily suppose either the absence of reflection or a fund of inhumanity, since they produce more acute sufferings to sensible beings and the most painful and lingering death of which we can form any idea. Why should the law refuse its protection to any sensitive being?[29]

In any case, fox-hunting (unlike the non-British understanding of hunting) is the activity of a tiny minority to which the majority are clearly opposed. The curious historical fact, though, is that the first two activities which Bentham mentions in the passage above were made illegal in 1835, shortly after his death, while the remainder have survived many attempts at legislation.

But, from the broad utilitarian position which I have developed, the issue is by no means so clear as it was for Bentham. There are two well-established arguments for dismissing public opinion *per se*. The first concerns the intensity of preferences: utilitarians are not concerned with the brute facts of 20 per cent believing *P* should happen and 80 per cent not-*P*, but with the best available calculation of the extent to which people are affected. It is often better to give an intense minority what they want against the wishes of a relatively apathetic majority; this is one respect in which utilitarian principles of aggregation and the working of representative electoral procedures often coincide. There is admittedly an intense minority within the majority which is passionately opposed to hunting, but their existence is quite independant of the existence of the majority opinion. To dismiss them from consideration, one has to invoke a second kind of argument, the unacceptability of 'external' preferences in utilitarian calculation.

This argument says that such calculations can only count the preferences people have which refer to themselves, their 'privately-oriented wants' as Brian Barry calls them.[30] It must not count beliefs (like moral principles) about what other people should want or should be allowed to have. The argument is graphically put by Amartya Sen in terms of 'Lewd', who wants to read dirty books and 'Prude' who wants the law to prevent him.[31] Its force is not merely that it is very inefficient to count external preferences in calculations of what ought to be done, but it also makes the calculation impossible. Prude's beliefs about how Lewd should be treated necessarily involve Lewd's preferences about Prude and so on into an infinite regress. Suppose, for example, that all hunters thought homosexuality should be illegal and all anti-hunters were homosexuals. It is the orthodox contemporary utilitarian view, which I believe not only ensures better calculations, but is a necessary axiom of any determinate calculation, that the homosexuals' views on hunting and the hunters' views on homosexuality should be ignored. This piece of liberal logic insists, so to speak, that we are qualified to express our own preferences, but not to have preferences about whether other people get what they prefer. Of course, to the extent that hunting or homosexuality is a genuine public nuisance (we cannot avoid seeing foxes torn to pieces and have to endure attempts at seduction by members of our own sex), then there are relevant 'internal' preferences. The consequence of this liberal interpretation of utilitarianism is that in the model both hunting and homosexuality should be legally permitted activities (as they are in contemporary Britain).

The obvious objection to this formulation of the 'external preference' argument is that the two cases are assymetrical: there is no equivalent of the fox in the case of homosexuality. I am assuming that foxes do not like being hunted, contrary to the views of a correspondent in the *Sheffield Telegraph* on November 4th, 1936, who claimed, with blithe disregard of all epistemological problems, that 'nine out of ten foxes actually enjoy being hunted'.[32] The defence of hunting must rest primarily on the calculation that the human satisfaction involved outweighs the disadvantages to foxes. It is quite easy to establish that hunting is a part of culture (in the sense that I earlier developed Scitovsky's argument about culture). Fox-hunting is certainly not a comfortable activity: it involves galloping and jumping around the countryside in the depths of winter and is both arduous and dangerous. Those who believe in it are people, as Raymond Carr puts it, 'for whom fox-hunting remains a passion, a poetry and a mystique'.[33] The literature of hunting, from Surtees to Sassoon and, in the broader sense, including Hemingway *et al.* suggests that for *afficionados* (a very appropriate term, since borrowed from the analogous minority realm of bull-fighting), hunting is a deeply meaningful activity for which there is no substitute. It cannot be portrayed as a whimsical activity which has no real meaning and which can easily be substituted, as can certain other forms of cruelty to animals, including most experiments involving animals. The hunt is not a trivial or whimsical business: it is an integral part of the structure of many communities; it means much to its participants and it is a thing of great beauty even to many non-participants.

It also has had an important ecological role. Hunting is a relatively inefficient way of killing foxes; it certainly doesn't threaten extinction. The rural norm that foxes are not shot, but only hunted, has had much to do with their survival and prosperity in Great Britain. Without hunting, the fox might have gone the same way as the wolf; the last wild wolf in this island was killed in either 1676 or 1683 or 1691, depending which account you take. Landscape features have been maintained, and other species habitat's have thus survived, in order to maintain the quality of the hunt. (The same is true of the copses and patches of primeval woodland maintained for pheasants, but the two effects are not complementary, as gamekeepers with charge of pheasant coveys regard foxes as appalling vermin and are not bound by any fox-hunting norms.) This remains an historical argument, however. It can be argued fairly convincingly that the fox might well not have survived the nineteenth century without the hunting norm, but prospects for the twenty-first century, with a very different public opinion and relatively safe habitats on a variety of public land, mean that the fox could easily out-live the hunter.

Man the Hunter

There is an academic suggestion that hunting may even have a uniquely deep meaning when compared with other human activities. In a seminal article published in the 1960s, S. L. Washburn and C. S. Lancaster summarised the 'hunting hypothesis', the argument that man is essentially a hunter in that it is hunting that has made *homo sapiens* what we now are:

> Hunting . . . is a way of life, and the success of this adaptation (in its total social, technical and psychological dimensions) has dominated the course of human evolution for hundreds of thousands of years . . . Agricultural ways of life have dominated less than 1 per cent of human history, and there is no evidence of major biological changes during that period of time . . . human hunting is a set of ways of life. It involves divisions of labour between male and female, sharing according to custom, cooperation among males, planning, knowledge of many species and large areas, and technical skill.[34]

The hypothesis is generally taken to imply that if you do not understand the unique patterns of human hunting (quite different from those of other carnivores), then you understand virtually nothing of human development. Our language, our social structure, the genesis of our long road of technical progress, our ideas about prowess and self-esteem, all begin with the hunting era that made us what we are.

It would be fun, but wrong, to draw immediate prescriptive conclusions from the hunting hypothesis. Nigel Calder remarks that, if God had meant us to farm, He would have given us longer arms and proceeds to describe a world in which we cram our habitation and productive functions (including a highly intensive agriculture) into as small an area as possible, leaving the rest of the planet as a well-stocked wilderness in which the male *homo sapiens* can do what comes naturally.[35] But ethics is logically independent of any account of man's origins. However we have developed, whatever powerful vestiges or tendencies we still possess, we are still complex beings with free will who can choose to do our best to put our past behind us and choose rules to live by which we consider to be right. If it turned out that we were all descended from the original *homo sapiens* species, which had spent half-a-million years practising universal cannibalism, we could still, quite properly, insist on the maintenance of our taboo against cannibalism.

But the hunting hypothesis does suggest an important doubt about certain kinds of Green social criticism. If true, and it is, by now, fairly well established, it suggests that there is something fairly odd, not about *prescribing* a gentle, Franciscan 'harmony' as the relation between people and nature, but about assuming that such a relationship could be 'natural', or that we are in some sense alienated or detached from our true selves if we look on the world in opposite ways. The dreaming, visionary, theological side of our natures has always envisaged a Paradise, a pleasure-garden where man lives in gentle stewardship of nature: an animal analogy is often seen with the gently herbiverous gorilla. But our actual development was as a wickedly ingenious hunter.

As a human being, you don't love the earth any the less for wanting to kill and eat the creatures on it. Quite the contrary, the predatory feelings not only make one feel truly human, they also make one feel more part of nature. I confess that, on solitary journeys, when I see a fat wood-pigeon I think of its breast marinated in garlic and elderberry wine and when a hare bolts away, I think of how nice it would be jugged. These carniverous feelings make me subjectively closer to nature than I would otherwise be. I can empathise with the fox and even see how satisfying it might be to kill *all* the chickens in the coop (something which foxes frequently do). In the same way, though I have never hunted nor felt any desire to do so, I can empathise with fellow humans to the extent of understanding how satisfying it might be to be in at the kill. Tennyson's image of 'nature, red in tooth and claw' may be partial, but cruelty and, even more, a callous acceptance of death and continuity, is a necessary dimension of nature. Although I have done a fair amount of bird-watching and have never hunted, I cannot help but feel that if what you want is to be a *part* of nature, then the bluff squire who daubs his daughter with the bloody end of a fox's tail may have made more progress than the watcher in his hide. Harmony is most clearly explained as playing a part in making nature what it is. Washburn and Lancaster argue that without man's sophisticated hunting techniques the larger mammals in Africa would destroy the vegetation and starve. They cite the experience of the Masai Amboseli Reserve in Kenya and the Murchison Falls and Queen Elizabeth parks in Uganda as evidence.[36] There is a strong parallel with the kind of case that is often put for sporting hunting in developed countries. It is difficult to get close to the spirit of nature if you approach it in search of our artistic and theological images of Paradise: it will always disappoint. It is better to start with the robust callousness of the old Yorkshire song, *Ilkley Moor ba't 'at*. When you die, we shall bury you:

> Then, t'worms'll come an' eat up thee,
> Then t'ducks'll come an' eat up worms,
> Then, we shall come an' eat up ducks,
> Then, we shall all 'ave eaten thee.

In many respects the juxtaposition between a Green opposition to hunting and a utilitarian defence of the practice, though a real and important contrast, is highly paradoxical. It was enlightened, 'humane' utilitarians who led the campaigns against cruelty to animals in the nineteenth century. Those who opposed them invoked nature, tradition and rural values and were contemptuous of industry. Many an English backwoodsman who hunts has far more in common with the stated aims of Green thinking than he does with most company directors. The Humanitarian League, which was founded by two Fabians and which lasted from 1891 to 1919, does look like a proto-modern Green movement (pacifist, women's rights, anti-vivisection, against capital punishment) as well as opposing hunting. But Richard Thomas comments that its 'crank' views lost it a lot of the support which its opposition to hunting had gained, particularly after the start of the First World War.[37] It is still the case that utilitarians (like Peter Singer) often put the most coherent case for a better treatment of animals and those who agree with much of Green policy, especially anti-industrialism, have little time for 'humanitarian' arguments.[38]

Nevertheless, from many utilitarian perspectives, including my own, the anti-hunting aspect of Green thought, and also the vegetarian element, are profoundly suspicious. The suspicion is that the true sentiment is a deontological puritanism which says that certain practices are wrong *because* they are enjoyed and does not take serious cognisance of estimating arguments about consequences and compensation. The suspicion is, essentially, that anti-hunters are against hunting not because they love foxes, but because they hate people. It raises the formal fear, for utilitarians, of a killjoy world, the rule of the external preference, an institutional structure in which people are too easily able to stop others from doing what satisfies them. This suggests a larger worry that, on many issues, not just on hunting, the Greens have assumed the mantle of the utilitarian's oldest and wickedest enemy, the puritan. As with feminists and socialists, we are entitled to a critical suspicion that what they suggest is recommended, not because it can be justified in benefits to human beings or to sentient beings, but from a position of arbitrary disapproval of many sources of pleaseure and even of pleasure itself. Thomas comments that the journal *Cruel Sports* 'has a straight-laced sense of morality and frowns at indulgence of all kinds.' It was exceptionally horrified by events at the Tiverton Staghounds Hunt Ball in 1972. It reported that 'when the band played a pop number called "Jump up and down and wave your knickers in the air" a young woman hunt member did just that'.[39]

The 'Puritan Ghost', as Scitovsky calls it, still lurks and threatens and disguises itself in the shrouds of many kinds of argument. Later, I will suggest that we ought to maintain the critical suspicion that Green opposition to hunting is typical of puritan opposition to pleasure; that, disguised behind an apparent concern for the weak or for the future or for the souls of people is a negative and malicious disapproval of the way life is actually lived and enjoyed.

Time and risk

Earlier I suggested that a utilitarian attitude to the planet becomes increasingly similar to reverential attitudes as the utilitarian extends his time horizon. The connection is necessary and intuitively apparent. If we plan for now + 25 years, the planners will, on the whole, envisage themselves as being alive by the end of the period. If we plan for now + 50 years, we still feel a direct sympathetic concern about (say) what kind of housing stock will be available to our children, what kind of national parks they will be able to visit and whether it will be safe to swim in the sea. But when we move to now + 100 years, it is much more difficult to translate what we know of wants and interests into a policy. As the time-horizon extends, the known network of interest fades; the people we are planning for become total strangers. The uncertainties multiply: we don't know what kind of tastes people will have or what kinds of options technology will give them. To take the most obvious example, will nuclear fusion ever become a practical source of energy? If it does, it is unlikely that it will enter the market at some roughly competitive price with other sources of energy. It is more likely to wipe out the competition, to make energy as abundant as water is now. That would radically transform the prospects not only for industry and agriculture, but also for conservation and even the control of climate. It will either happen or not happen; a probablistic estimate of the event cannot, therefore, be translated into a 'scenario'. Research has been proceeding on fusion power for about forty years now; despite regular excitements, progress has been very slow. The assumption about fusion over the next twenty five years must be that it will not happen. The assumption for a hundred years can only be a naked question mark.

What sort of consideration can we take of the long run in which we are all dead, but out great-great-grandchildren are alive? The relatively precise computation of interests fades, as the time horizon increases into the very broad principles which seem to have permanent relevance. One principle still relevant is the preservation of options. We should not allow anything to happen, if we can avoid it, which irreversibly closes down possibilities for human resources and human experiences. Two applications: no species should be extinguished and no type of landscape allowed to disappear entirely.

A time-horizon has few practical consequences unless it is combined with an attitude to risk. Economists normally discuss risk in terms of degrees of aversion to it, a level of 'risk-aversion' being seen as a preference rather than as a consequence of a person's capacity for rationality. Thus, it is not irrational to risk heart disease by drinking and smoking heavily, provided one accepts the risk and likes drinking and smoking. It is necessary, but difficult, to conceive of a level of risk-aversion which is both collective and long-term. What chances should we take on behalf of the people of 2100 AD? The question cannot be ducked: a non-answer is an answer, probably a poor one.

A combination of a long time-horizon and a high aversion to risk suggests something very close to a plan to maximise stability. For a lengthy and increasingly uncertain future, we can only try to seek control. Thus it is not so surprising as it might seem at first sight to find a utilitarian (albeit, sometimes a dubious or marginal one) like J. S. Mill talking in almost millenarian terms about the 'Stationary State' in *The Principles of Political Economy*, published in 1848:

> I cannot, therefore, regard the stationary state of capital and wealth with the unaffected aversion so generally manifested towards it by political econ-

omists of the old school. I am inclined to believe that it would be, on the
whole, a very considerable improvement on our present condition . . . I
sincerely hope, for the sake of prosperity, that they will be content to be
stationary, long before necessity compels them to it.[40]

Mill's objections to continued economic and demographic growth sound
very contemporary; a long-term utilitarianism concerned with aspects of
culture generates reasoning and policy which is very close to that of
today's Greens. He fears for the spiritual consequences of over population and the loss of solitude. He argues that wild nature is under
estimated as a contribution to our well-being. He believes the benefits of
the competitive, acquisitive society to be an illusion. I find Mill's vision
of the future highly attractive and far ahead of its time.

But it does present two problems. The first, to use contemporary
managerial language, is that 'the *status quo* is not an option'. The
history of 'totalitarianism' has demonstrated that, contrary to the
fantasies of totalitarians and the nightmares of liberals, the state
effectively controls very litte. People's desires for wealth and their desires
to reproduce are not controllable. In a world of a 170 states, the sort of
direct control 'we' would need is inconceivable. Something like a
stationary state may have existed for a long time in such societies as the
Byzantine and Chinese empires, but the brute fact is that both of these
societies were destroyed by dynamic forces from outside. The Soviet
Union, left to itself, might have been a Byzantium, but the West's
capacity to undermine its ways through materialist envy and modern
communications has exceeded the expectations of all commentators. In
the contemporary world, mobility, inter-connectedness and rising expectations all militate against any possibility of a stationary state.

Yet, even if it were possible, I would now have important doubts about
whether the stationary state was desirable. Leaving aside the desirability
of stabilising population (which I concede) growth, technology and
instability seem an essential part of what we are. Remembering Butterfield's 'impossibility of history', it requires an extraordinary leap of
imagination and judgement to compare the stability of Nowhere or the
Ming dynasty or hunting/gathering with the restlessness of our own age.
This kind of utilitarian judgement cannot be made logically; we must
employ guesswork, imagery and scepticism. I do fear that much of the
appeal of the past (or the future, which is usually envisaged as a recycling of the past, rather than the present) is an irrational nostalgia. I
find it difficult to believe that any of the known candidates for 'stationary
state' was remotely as joyful as living in the West in the second half of the
twentieth century. Much of what was innovative and threatening when
Mill wrote – cobbled streets, mill chimneys, stream trains – is now the
property of Rosy Nostalgia. If he had got his stationary state we might
never have had the Football League, rock music and open-topped sports
cars. Many people might say, 'No loss, either', but that is an error, not
merely a set of tastes, as I shall try to explain in a later section.

There are considerable utilitarian dangers in either a very long time-horizon or a very low aversion to risk. We cannot stop change; we cannot plan for the long-term future in which considerable uncertainties multiply into a complete unknown. To plan for our children's children is to plan for complete strangers, whose tastes and environment we can never know and for whom we cannot really feel the kind of benevolent sympathy we feel for our own friends and children. Long-term, low-risk policies promise complete irrelevance and risk the expression of our own *Zeitgeist*, our own particular contribution to the endless human movement into the unknown.

Notes

1. Robert T. McIntosh, 'The Background and Some Current Problems of Theoretical Ecology' in Esa Saarinen (ed.), *Conceptual Issues in Ecology*, (Reidel, 1982), p. 10.
2. Martin Spray, 'Dreaming of a Green Christmas', *The Countryman* 94: 4, (1989–90), p. 142.
3. The Peppered Moth evolved from pale grey to charcoal in hue in the areas most affected by industrialisation in Britain in the nineteenth century. Since the Clean Air Act of 1956 it has become paler again. It is discussed by J. E. Lovelock, *Gaia: a new look at life on earth*, (Oxford University Press, 1979), pp. 109–10. There is also an excellent exhibition on the Peppered Moth in the Natural History Museum in Kensington.
4. Lovelock, *op. cit.*, p. 109.
5. See John Halliday, 'Darwinism, Biology and Race', Politics Working Paper, No. 49, (University of Warwick, 1990).
6. From the *Critias*, quoted by Clarence J. Glacken, 'Changing Ideas of the Habitable World' in Robert Detweiler, Jon N. Sutherland and Michael S. Werthman (eds), *Environmental Decay in Its Historical Context*, (Scott, Foresman & Co. 1973), p. 67.
7. Robin Page, 'Eyewitness to the Brutal Murder of Rural England', *The Weekend Telegraph* 11 November 1989, p. V., *The Decline of An English Village*, 2nd edition, (Ashford, 1989). See also Robin Page, *Journeys into Britain*, (Hodder and Stoughton, 1982).
8. Judith M. Brown, *Modern India, The Origins of an Asian Democracy*, (Oxford University Press, 1988), p. 32.
9. See Wilfrid Beckerman, *In Defence of Economic Growth*. (Cape, 1974), Anthony Crosland, *The Future of Socialism*, (Cape, 1956).
10. The metaphor is suggested in the Introduction to William D'Antonio (ed.), *Power and Democracy in America*, (Notre Dame University Press, 1961). The more famous examples of the genre are C. Wright Mills, *The Power Elite* (Oxford University Press, 1959) and Peter Bachrach and Morton Baratz, *Power and Poverty, Theory and Practice*, (Oxford University Press, 1970).
11. See also Lincoln Allison, 'The Nature of the Concept of Power', *European Journal of Political Research*, 2: 2, (1974), pp. 131–42 and *Right Principles, A Conservative Philosophy of Politics*, (Blackwell, 1984), pp. 136–50.
12. J. S. Mill, 'Centralisation', *The Edinburgh Review*, Vol. CXV, No. CCXXXIV, 1862, pp. 323–358. There is no 'by-line', but no doubt that Mill was the author.
13. See Lincoln Allison, 'On Dirty Public Things', *Political Geography Quarterly*, 5: 3, (1986), pp. 241–51.

14. See Allison, *Right Principles*, pp. 23–36.
15. Andrew Brennan, *Thinking about Nature, An Investigation of Nature, Value and Ecology*, (Routledge, 1988), p. 6.
16. *Ibid.*, pp. 6–7.
17. Alan Macfarlane, *The Origins of English Individualism. The Family, Property and Social Transition*, (Blackwell, 1978).
18. Richard Dawkins, *The Selfish Gene*, Second Edition, (Oxford University Press, 1989).
19. Robert Axelrod, *The Evolution of Cooperation*, (Basic Books, 1984).
20. Dawkins, *op. cit.*, p. 233.
21. See Iain MacLean, 'A Non-Zero Sum Game of Football', *British Journal of Political Science*, 10: 2, pp. 253–59.
22. Rather than merely reading Axelrod's result, I recommend that readers transfer the idea of a 'round-robin tournament' of Prisoner's Dilemma to their own families. I could not resist the temptation while preparing this section. The players consisted of:

    Woman
    Boy (12)
    Boy (9)
    Boy (6)

    The rewards were expressed in terms of a bonus on pocket money as follows:

I defect, you co-operate	+ 5p
We both co-operate	+ 3p
We both defect	0
I co-operate, you defect	– 1p

    Each pair played a number of games chosen at random and known only to me.

    Boy (12) and Boy (9) played a long series at cross-purposes. Boy (12) wanted to make as much money as possible and showed considerable willingness to co-operate, but Boy (9) only cared about beating his brother and was terrified of becoming a sucker. Naturally, the series lapsed into a long sequence of double defections in which both players did badly financially, but Boy (12) did worse. Woman exemplified the general experimental evidence by co-operating almost frantically. She did generally badly, but managed a long sequence of mutual co-operation with Boy (9) who did not manifest any of his feelings of envy towards her.

    Boy (6) was brilliantly successful and managed a better financial return than mutual co-operation. He achieved this by defecting more than 80 per cent of the time but every sixth turn he would co-operate. This encouraged opponents to believe, as he was a 'baby', that he was just on the brink of learning the benefits of co-operation. He never did and he thought it was a very good game.

    The salutary effect is in moving game theory from the purely strategic realm into relationships with pre-existing emotions; real relationships, in short.
23. J. J. Rousseau, 'Discourse on the Origins of Inequality' in G. D. H. Cole (ed.) *The Social Contract and Discourses*, (Dent, 1968), p. 192.
24. Ronald Dworkin, 'Rights as Trumps', in Jeremy Waldron (ed.) *Theories of Rights*, (Oxford University Press, 1984), pp. 153–67.
25. David Hume, 'Of Refinement in the Arts, in Eugene Miller (ed.), *Essays, Moral, Political and Literary* (Liberty Press, 1985), pp. 268–80.
26. Jonathan Porritt, *Seeing Green, The Politics of Ecology Explained*, (Blackwell, 1984), p. 196.

27. Abraham Maslow, *The Further Reaches of Human Nature*, (Viking 1971).
28. Abraham Maslow, *Towards a Psychology of Being*, (Van Nostrand Reinhold, 1962).
29. From *Principles of Penal Law*. Quoted in Raymond Carr, *English Fox Hunting*, (Weidenfeld and Nicolson, 1976), p. 197.
30. Brian Barry, *Political Argument*, (Routledge & Kegan Paul, 1965), pp. 12-13.
31. See Amartya Sen, *Choice, Welfare and Measurement*, (Oxford University Press, 1982).
32. Quoted in Richard Thomas, *The Politics of Hunting*, (Gower, 1983), p. 238.
33. Carr, *op. cit.*, p. 250.
34. S. L. Washburn and C. S. Lancaster, 'The Evolution of Hunting', in S. L. Washburn and P. C. Jay (eds), *Perspectives on Human Evolution*, (Holt, Rhinehart and Winston, 1968), pp. 213, 214, 225. See also H. D. F. Kitto, *The Greeks*, (Penguin, 1951-86), pp. 36-43.
35. Nigel Calder, *The Environment Game*, (Secker and Warburg, 1967).
36. Washburn and Lancaster, *op. cit.*, p. 217.
37. See Thomas, *op. cit.*, pp. 83-84.
38. Peter Singer, *Animal Liberation: a new ethics for our treatment of animals*, (Cape, 1976).
39. Thomas, *op. cit.*, p. 98. *Cruel Sports*, January, 1973, p. 5.
40. John Stuart Mill, *Collected Works*, (Routledge, 1965), pp. 753-4 & 765.

5 On having and eating one's environment

An important sceptical argument in this book has centred on the concept of 'ecology'. What I have argued is that 'ecology' and its associated ideas of 'harmony of nature' and 'the balance of nature' cannot be made substantive. In order to derive an environmental prescription, other, non-ecological, values must be imported.

Such scepticism implies a rejection of the normal language in which journalism and politics discuss environmental problems. This is the language of 'crisis', of easily perceptible wrongs which must be put right; the implication of such language is that environmental problems are practical rather than theoretical. We must identify past mistakes and furnish ourselves with the determination and the institutions to correct them. In its assumption of the objective basis of prescription popular environmentalism resembles Marxism or fundamentalist religion. There are 'needs' and 'tasks', the existence of which can be established objectively.

Such popular environmentalism rests on a mixed set of assumptions which, on examination, shift dramatically. One starting point is the idea of ecological collapse, of a complete breakdown of the conditions which sustain life. But this is not *literally* an issue in most environmental campaigns. Of the consequences of man's actions which we have reason to fear, only the 'nuclear winter' raises this kind of possibility. Even global warming and the erosion of the ozone layer, the most serious items on the scientific agenda, are very far from threatening life itself. The 'end of life', posited in many environmental critiques of contemporary life, is not literal, but allegorical. It does not imply the end of life, so much as 'civilised life' or 'life as we know it'. According to some criteria, these ought to have ended many years ago in certain parts of the world. Paul Ehrlich described in the 1960s the trauma of appreciating the reality of over-population in a poor part of Delhi.[1] Contemporary Bombay contains something like the population of Australia on an area the size of Manchester. In some streets, at times, one cannot move for the crush; the sea is virtually poison; at least five million people are 'homeless', by Western standards. But life goes on; not only human life, but a considerable variety of animal life. It is a life which is diverse, exciting and energetic.

More moderate predictions of disaster concern more specific effects of human activity: certain diseases will thrive, water levels will rise or current levels of consumption cannot be maintained. The view I have expressed of this kind of prediction amounts, in vulgar parlance, to asking, 'So, what's new?'. The human condition has consisted largely of adapting to medical and metereological 'disasters' and substituting products for those we have exhausted. Many of us who were brought up in older industrial areas lived with levels of pollution and bad diet which would now be considered catastrophic. In parts of northern England in the 1950s, the levels of all chest diseases were ten times a national average which was, in any case, high by international standards. Snow turned black overnight (or red if you happened to live in Consett). Eighty-five per cent of the adult population smoked cigarettes and their diet, in which beef fat and white bread were prominent, looks, in retrospect, like institutionalised self-destruction. Judged by the standards now applied by most people in the English-speaking countries, my own environment in childhood and youth was post-catastrophic. The catastrophies were local, rather than global, but utilitarians of any kind must concede Robert Goodin's observation that this hardly matters in human terms: 'London's "killer fogs" were no less lethal for being purely domestic products'.[2]

It is not my intention in making these observations to recommend complacency about environmental conditions. On the contrary, I want proper, broad comparisons between bundles of consequences of politics and institutions. These comparisons cannot be made if we assume that certain conditions simply cannot be tolerated: in some cases we may have to tolerate them; perhaps we already have experience of tolerating them; we must bear in mind that the consequences of intolerance may be even worse than those of tolerance. The final retreat of the 'ecological crisis' argument is to questions of the loss of spiritual goods, to the issues concerning industrialism raised by Mill and Wordsworth. This is a 'crisis' which can be taken seriously, but it is a very different kind of crisis. The question of whether or not our institutions and practices are serving human well-being, whether we are not going wrong in some fundamental way, is always a serious one and is to be taken even more seriously than usual when rapid change threatens many established ways of doing things. The real crisis, in short, is the question of whether technological progress, industrial advance and population growth is making life less rewarding for the people of earth.

The perception of environmental crisis, the belief that we are 'destroying the planet', is mythological in an important sense. It tends to be a belief which is held cyclically. Measured in terms of popular issue salience and media content, the issues of environmental destruction rise to the top of the urgent list, only to erode away. Their natural curve has the shape of an escarpment. There is a dramatic rise in emphasis to a peak of concern, followed by a slow decline. In 1969–70, the issues associated with 'pollution' rose from nowhere to the top of the salience league in the USA, despite the intensity of the war in Vietnam. To a slightly lesser degree this was paralleled in the other developed countries. From 1972 onwards the salience of environmental issues declined. In 1986, it rose sharply again.

The existence and shape of this cycle depends on several factors. Partly it is the 'issue-attention cycle' observed by political scientists as a general phenomenon. The steep escarpment can be associated with certain traumatic events. The Santa Barbara oil spill appears to have triggered the sharp rise in American concern with pollution in 1969. Chernobyl in 1986 gave popular credence to the critiques of nuclear power in particular, and contemporary industrialism generally, which a minority of people had held throughout. The steady decline of attention can be contributed to a general piece of psychology and also to the counter-veiling force of economic issues, which tend to force the 'environment' down the agenda. Our 'destruction of the environment' is close to being what Bertrand Russell called a 'Sunday truth'.[3] It is highly abstract in that it bears little on people's everyday objectives and spheres of control. Many people's concern with 'environment' has the same natural rhythm as their concern with God or health: there are rushes of conscience, followed by a decline into apathy as we realise how reassuringly remote death, hell and the destruction of the planet really are.

The attention cycle can be traced backwards to previous generations. In England, attention focused on 'smog' in the 1950s: the great smog of 1952 with its 6,000 'excess deaths' was the particular traumatic event.[4] In the late 1920s 'ribbon development' provided a multitude of private traumas, of individual senses of loss at the disappearance of favourite landscapes, which galvanised attention on 'the countryside'. Orwell describes a typical incident in *Coming Up For Air*.[5] The late Victorians were preoccupied with the 'slum' and the prospect of the nation being dragged down by the vice and ill-health of its inhabitants.

Such waves of attention have been effective: indeed, part of the decline of the salience of environmental issues in each case is the sense that something has been done. In the English case they gave us our planning system and our Clean Air Acts. What has now changed is that we have a global cycle. Harking back to the 1950s and earlier, events have to be explained in terms of local problems and national reactions. From Chernobyl onwards, they will always be global in perspective.

Magic and realism

For a serious utilitarian, consideration of the problems of the 'environment' must start with J. S. Mill's doubts about utilitarianism. 'Ask yourself whether you are happy, and you cease to be so', Mill warns in his *Autobiography*. The logical problem translates from individual psychology to aggregate decisions. Just as a life dedicated remorselessly to being happy would be an empty life, a society whose institutions were determindedly and precisely focused on maximising the surplus of benefit over cost for the aggregate of its citizens must fail in its own terms. The effect of measuring and comparing the benefits of everything is a form of the tyranny of small decisions. To be happy we need to know that some things are on a higher plane than the satisfaction of everyday wants; we need the security of knowing that some things will never change. A truly happy life must contain magic, wonder and reverence. The most necessary and satisfying objects of these sentiments must be aspects of the planet itself. It is the surface of the earth, in all its diversity, that inspires our deepest feelings, our senses of identity and belonging, our strivings for artistic expression. To take the broad spirit of utilitarianism seriously – to want sincerely to maximise human well-being – is to recognise these truths. J. S. Mill recognised them fully; Jeremy Bentham resolutely set his face against them. Most, though not all, of the modern tradition of utilitarianism in economics and administration has followed Bentham: the rigorous, if bogus, precision of a 'felicific calculus' rests easily on the contemporary state's bias towards technical (rather than philosophical) problems and the resulting importance of the 'expert'. It is natural to this tradition of utilitarianism to demand of, say, a mountain which might be quarried, exactly how much it is worth as a mountain, how many people climb it, what they would be prepared to pay for the experience.

A powerful defence of this narrow, rigorous form of utilitarianism is that any relaxation of the rigour must be like the thin end of a dangerous wedge. If we once stop subjecting all alternatives to the clear light of measurement, we are on a slippery slope to the thoughtless reverence for institutions and the unreasoning acceptance of principles which utilitarianism was created to destroy. The acceptance of 'higher' pleasures or of a condition of dissatisfied wisdom which might be preferable to satisfied stupidity is a large step on a retreat back to deontology. As a doctrine, utilitarianism seems to collapse which ever way it turns. Interpreted broadly, it contradicts those qualities which are distinct about itself, while interpreted narrowly it defeats its own purpose.

The solution I intend to put forward for this problem is based on the assumption that, for all its faults, broad utilitarianism is the least silly approach to policy available: its premises are the most defensible logically and the closest to contemporary western values. For its implementation it requires the recognition of two important, and apparently contradictory, principles. On the one hand, I want to put the case for *realism*, in most of the philosophical dimensions which that word might be thought to have. On the opposite hand, I want to defend and institutionalise environmental *totemism*, a prescription that some aspects of our surroundings should be treated with a reverence which places them above and beyond the precise calculation of aggregative advantages and disadvantages.

Radicalism and realism

In some of its most important aspects, the realistic component of utilitarianism can best be explained as the antithesis of radicalism. The image and etymology of radicalism are relatively clear and harmonious, at least by the standards of political theory. 'Radical' comes from the latin *radix*, a root, which is also the origin of such words as radish and radicle. Radical change means the eradication of present ways, a removal not just of visible practice and abuses, but the subterranean structures which support them. Literal radicalism, in the farm and the garden, consist of the grubbing up of the living things which are already there and starting anew.

The images of roots and eradication occur regularly throughout the Bible and furnished forms of expression beloved by early radicals. Perhaps the most popular quotation was from the book of Malachi:

> For, behold, the day cometh, that shall burn as an oven; and all the proud, yea, and all that do wickedly, shall be stubble: and the day that cometh shall burn them up, saith the Lord of Hosts, that it shall leave them neither root nor branch.[6]

Matthew has both John the Baptist and Christ using the analogy: 'Every plant, which my heavenly Father hath not planted, shall be rooted up'.[7]

At one level we can distinguish between religious and secular radicalism, between (say) economic and political radicalism and between 'green' and 'red' radicalism. But the logic of true radicalism is to dig deeper to eradicate fully and finally. It tends to face the choice between a relapse into conservative acceptance or a systematic eradication of the intertwined root systems and symbiotic relations which it finds. Thus, the view that contemporary human practices are out of harmony with nature, can draw the believer into equally radical views on pacifism, feminism and the state.

For example, according to Robert Lawler's account of the essence of contemporary disharmony between people and nature, the problem is the dominance in our culture of 'macho' and 'patriarchal' male assumptions. These are identified with the male monotheism which posits a God in the sky (*le* ciel). Patriarchy can be dated back to the Aryan invasion of India and Europe. Its norms of rape and penetration are responsible for our despoilation of the environment, our brutal exploitation of women and the weak, and our destructive aggression. They give rise to the complex syndrome of science, individualism, capitalism and industrialism. All must go, before complete self-destruction occurs. A more complete revolution than any we have previously experienced must establish the dominance of our female nature and a worship of the earth (*la* terre).[8]

Although this is an unusually and satisfyingly total account of what is wrong with human life, it is quite closely related to ideas which have been espoused by Green movements generally. The manifesto which helped *Die Grünen* effect their entry into the German Federal Parliament in 1983 incorporated a condemnation of patriarchy.[9] The typical 'fundi' package of participation, self-sufficiency, egalitarianism, 'alternative' technology, rights vested in nature, anti-racism, anti-militarism and so on, is presented as a diverse set of symptoms from the same root cause.

The radical spirit is essentially the same phenomenon, whether it is overtly religious or not, whether it is 'red' or 'green'. Emotionally, it starts with a sense of fundamental dissatisfaction with the world; intellectually its principal task is the identification of the root cause of prevailing evil. Politically it must commit itself to change in whatever is identified as the *basic* structure of society. Thus the radical spirit is often, and quite legitimately, in search of a cause, a new theory, a new project.

Where a project fails, as 'socialism' has under its applied interpretations, radicals move away to another cause; Reds become Greens because 'fundi' Greens have a project for eradicative reform which is still untried and which is based on a fundamental opposition to the *status quo*.

In clerical, authoritarian-monarchist or socialist contexts, utilitarianism has functioned as a radical doctrine. But there are tightly constrained limits to the compatibility between utilitarianism and all but the most moderate radical projects. Utilitarians can easily recommend the abolition of institutions which are functioning badly. It is difficult to sanction, though, reform which requires the eradication of habits, beliefs and practices which have lasted for centuries and which transcend our ideas of what we are. In sexual or gender relations it is one thing to recommend that women should now be allowed to do *x* or that men should now be prohibited from doing *y*. It is quite different to abolish the existing basis of male-female relations, to replace the image of nymphs and satyrs, pursuer and pursued, hard and soft which are at the very core of what desire means to us. A project for the abolition of 'macho' and 'femina' raises too many doubts about the time that it would take to pay off and the risk that it might not pay off at all, to be acceptable to utilitarians, even if you believe that it would be ultimately desirable. Sceptical utilitarianism overlaps with the arguments about organic society associated with Burkean conservatism insofar as both doubt the wisdom of growing institutions other than on existing root bases.

Of course, in contemporary western society, the distance between utilitarian and radical perspectives grows. Our institutions, particularly markets and elections, are designed and approved for utilitarian purposes. Whatever the reservations about radical reform might be in an Islamic or socialist society, the position under regimes which allow electoral and commercial competition is even more sceptical. The most common objections to radical reform are that they are 'undesirable' and 'unrealistic'. Utilitarians subsume the latter under the former. Projects are undesirable either if they can't be successfully completed or if completion would have disadvantages which outweighed its benefits.

What is it to be a 'realist' rather than an 'idealist'? I shall distinguish between four dimensions of realism.

ONTOLOGICAL REALISM

The world exists and has properties which we cannot change. It exists outside of minds, which can only conceive it coherently by positing that it is independent of ourselves. There are facts about reality, true propositions not confused by ambiguity about the terms involved or the means of observation. The distinction between reality and unreality is important, not trivial. It generates science, which is the project of systematically explaining reality. The point about science is that it aspires to be true, to represent objective reality, unlike art and in a more honest and self-correcting way than religion.

IDENTIFYING WITH REALITY

Imagine, *1*: You are a hunter-gatherer. You wander the forests and plains in an extended family group, collecting berries and spearing game. You are skilled with a spear. You obey your father, you revere the great forests and plains. You tell stories about the spirits which live in them and the fate of those who angered the spirits. When life is good, you are warm and fed, but this is not always the case.

2: You live on a commune in William Morris's 'Nowhere'. You work in the gardens, growing vegetables. At other times you make beautiful objects from leather and wood. You eat together in the great hall of what was once a 'stately home'. There is music and dancing and love-making. There are few quarrels or disagreements. Occasionally there is talk of the evils of a way of life which existed before the rural commune.

I confess that if I make serious efforts to imagine myself in these contexts, I sweat with fear. This has nothing whatsoever to do with the question of whether or not either of these two ways of life could be made available to me. An aspect of 'realism' might suggest that they never could, but the aspect which concerns me here is that which makes me, in these imaginary contexts, yearn for the urban squalor of a big match day in Manchester or Melbourne. The sense of tension, the smell of beer and cigarettes, the litter, the mass of people and the obscenity of their wit: 'I' would yearn for these things. I could not bear the thought that beyond the great plain or the rural garden there were no Jaguars burning down motorways, no chemical works, garishly lit on stormy nights, no fashionable city people drinking expensive drinks, no television comedy savagely preying on the pomposity and hypocrisy of politics.

That is because I am, and know myself to be, a creature who belongs to a particular time and place. In this, I must differ in some respect from those writers in the green and anarchist traditions who appear to assume that we can strip ourselves down to some kind of pure human essence and be fulfilled in the context appropriate to that essence. The leap of imagination seems to me to be impossibly far, much farther than the gaps of historical understanding which led Herbert Butterfield to write of 'the impossibility of history'.[10] It may be partly a question of taste, but I don't think this is an important element. I do have a taste for plains, forests and rustic gardens, as well as for deserts, moors and jungles, but these are only part of a broader taste for a variety of experience.

The realist, in this context, is the person who can identify himself with the time and place in which he lives. With W. S. Gilbert, he is likely to condemn,

The idiot who praises, in sentimental tone,
Every century but this, and every country but his own.

Realism, in this emotional context, often reveals itself in a love of detail. The person who takes great pleasure in his own times frequently loves the minute facts which decorate them, the exact specifications of diesel-electric locomotives, the batting averages of professional cricketers or the anomalies of geography and politics. His whole emotional focus is quite different from the radical or idealist, whether red, green or religious, whose vision concentrates on the unacceptable wickedness of the world he inhabits.

THE NARROWNESS OF ALTERNATIVES

Utilitarianism is necessarily realistic in that its most fundamental assumptions require approaches to policy which choose between actual options, as of now. The options which might have been, which would be in an ideal world, cannot be on the utilitarian agenda. Choice must always be constrained by the realities of what can be achieved and at what cost. We must always start from where we are.

Suppose, for instance, that we really have 'destroyed the planet', that human activity has set off causal processes which will make the planet uninhabitable within a forseeable period, say twenty years. Let us assume that the process is inexorable. This could be for either one of two different reasons. Perhaps we simply do not possess the technology to reverse the catastrophic purposes. Or the avoidance of catastrophe may require a level of institutional organisation which we cannot achieve. If catastrophe could only be avoided by the species *homo sapiens* acting as if it had a single rational will which was prepared to sacrifice parts of itself in order to survive, it would be unrealistic to plan for it.

So what should we do? For a utilitarian, breast-beating and bemoaning which are only ever of occasional use in stiffening the sinews for action, would be futile temptations. Better to be fully cognisant of the real time and resources available and to make sure that the champagne in the cellar is not left undrunk.

Realism is in obvious contradistinction to utopianism. A world much better than this one may be possible, both logically and causally, but the real constraint is that you can't get there from here. The ideal institutions cannot exist without ideal people and vice-versa: attempts to 're-educate' people, to 'transform' whole societies and to foster 'cultural' revolution, all of which are required to break through the constraints of the utopian paradox, can only create great misery without achieving their objectives. But it is important to stress that nostalgia is as clear an enemy to realism and often a more powerful one than 'utopianism'. For many people, past societies, as they imagine them, have far more appeal than the virtuous societies which utopian writers create. The past *did* exist; the questions of its logical or causal possibility do not arise. But the past may be no more attainable than the ideal. To me, as to many of my contemporaries, a society with a lower density of population, no internal combustion engines and no modernist architecture has some attractions. But it cannot be recreated. Our situation is like that of two people who drive a car into the desert. The car breaks down and they face the probability of death. There is no point in recriminations, still less in blaming the technology, without which they would never have got so far into the desert. The problem must be faced as it is, not as it might have been: only technology can solve it. It is often the case that we cannot go forward, where 'forward' is defined in terms of our chosen objectives. It is always the case, historically, that we cannot go back.

DECONSTRUCTING UNREALISM

As a philosophy, utilitarianism is peculiarly uninterested in explaining human tastes and patterns of behaviour. Unlike, say, Marxism or critical theory as broad *genres*, it allows no purpose *per se* in locating what people do in their particular social context or constructing theories as to why they do it. Utilitarianism is rational and practical. If people like hunting or climbing mountains or playing the violin, those are tastes which should be weighed and incorporated into equations about what should be done. Bentham was very specifically uninterested in the origins of tastes: it was not the sociology (less still, the psychology) of poets and pushpin players which interested him, but the numbers in each category and the extent of their pleasure. The purpose of having a hermeneutics of taste, of 'deconstructing' tastes, is very different from the purpose of utilitarian philosophy. But an excessively rigid determination to take tastes as facts without explanations has been one of the weaknesses of utilitarianism in its Benthamite and neo-classical economic forms. If our actions affect the medium- and long-term future, we must try and optimise them. Optimising into the medium-long term requires an understanding of degrees of depth and contingency in taste: we need explanations of why people make the choices that they do, which will enable us to construct probabilities about future tastes. Utilitarianism can only have a wretchedly short time-horizon and limited application unless we can predict that (say) the popularity of guitar music will prove less deeply rooted than affection for the countryside or that broadening education will increase the benefits of poetry in relation to those of pushpin.

It is important, for example, to understand the cultural factors which underlie most people's belief that 'we are destroying the planet'. It is partly radicalism in search of a cause which starts with a perception of shallowness and evil in contemporary society which is the inheritor of religious perceptions of an evil and fallen world finding expression (it is my guess) in those individuals whose own psychological conditions are based on a sense of loss or inadequacy. (By contrast, my own estimate of my own times is strongly self-congratulatory. If such comparisons make any sense at all, I cannot imagine a better context in which to live than Britain after 1950 with its vigorous popular and high cultures, its growing sense of prosperity, its effective freedoms of intellectual and sexual expression and of travel. In this respect I differ utterly from many contemporary intellectuals who express themselves in drama, cinema and social criticism and who appear to believe that we live in a particularly sad and evil society.) In white colonies (using colony according to its strict Latin root), like Australia and America, there is a degree of colonial guilt which laces the sense of ecological impropriety. Utilitarianism is, rightly, particularly hard on useless expressions of guilt, which must include almost all preoccupations with collective guilt.

Some understanding of the context of environmentalism serves to devalue or undermine its message. But some does not: I shall argue that a very important drive behind the perception of environmental decline is the loss of, and threat to, aspects of people's surroundings and conditions which I shall call 'environmental totems'. Such losses must be taken into account in utilitarian calculation. Unless we can give people a sense of security in the existence of the things that they value most and protect the meaning of the relationship between people and the planet, we will make very poor efforts to maximise human well-being.

A note on sport

A consistent, if minor, theme of the Green tradition of thought, even by the broadest definition, is a repungance for modern sport. Lymington and Massingham lined up with Kipling and Baden-Powell in condemning the world of the modern stadium, where huge crowds watch professional games' players, as an inheritantly unsatisfactory human activity, a milieu whose very existence suggests an alienated and spiritually dissatisfied population.

I can register a degree of historical agreement with this view, while adopting a wholly different emotional stance. 'Modern' sport is typified by its huge following, its bureaucratic and commercial bases of organisation and its distinction between a tiny class of professional participants and the great bulk of 'fans' who serve it as consumers and lower-level participants. It evolved out of traditional sport through a process of formalisation in education institutions and a further process of proselytising and commercialisation. The model of its evolution is now generally agreed within the growing body of social history which treats it as an important subject. Organised sport does symbolise modern life reasonably closely. It is an expression of industrialism at play. Its well-defined venues and rigorously precise treatment of time mimic and complement industrial processes. The sense of hierarchy and competition mirror and reinforce concepts of the market. The scale of competition also imitates that of industry: local markets at first, then national, followed by events on a world scale by the late-twentieth century.[11]

If you believe that there is something deeply and necessarily wrong about the life of industrial capitalism, that it is a form of life alien to the essential spiritual needs of human beings, then you are likely to find that alienation clearly symbolised by the modern stadium. Here is the urban environment, the 'mass' society, the artificial, manipulated, sense of identity and competition, a desperate extremity of taking trivial things seriously, bordering on fanaticism. Among contemporary writers

Jonathan Porritt expresses contempt and amazement at the gullibility of modern sports fans and Robert Lawler admires the aborigines for (allegedly) having a taboo against competitive games. Green radicals join a tradition of red radicals, from Leon Trotsky to Ralph Miliband, who have portrayed modern sport as the real opiate of the people, a deceit and a diversion more effective than organised religion.[12] The nature of modern sport is more reminiscent of the '*circenses*' of ancient Rome than of traditional peasant activity; it fits, almost too neatly, into John Massingham's historical model in which modern industrial society and ancient Rome are similar societies, equally spiritually bankrupt, and opposite in kind from rural Saxon society.

Thus, both sides (defined emotionally) might agree that the attitude to modern sport might serve as a touchstone of radicalism and realism. If you like the roar and push of the crowd, the sight of the full car park, the smell of beer and cigarettes and the cheerful irreverence of the obscene chants, then you may find acceptable a populist utilitarianism which extols the virtues of pushpin and is sceptical of the aggregate value of poetry. On the other hand, many intellectuals are like G. D. H. Cole: they 'shudder and turn away' at the thought of vast football crowds.[13]

My own prejudice must be already apparent. I am a creature of industrial society. To me, modern sport is one of the most exciting and rewarding of human institutions. It gives meaning to life, identity and a lasting sense of achievement to the individual. The team, and the crowd, each have a sharp, if odd, sense of community. Sport has its own sense of particularity and eternity: each act, each match, is part of the endless story of the club. The organisation of modern sport requires both an attempt at justice and an acceptance that injustice – injury, the distribution of talent, the bounce of the ball – cannot be defeated. The plot is intense; there are heroes and villains, successes and failures. Nothing is certain. It encapsulates, intensifies and prepares one for life outside the stadium. The true sports fan feels intense meaning in the arbitrariness of what happens and glories in its detail. He is the proof of the Benthamite, anti-essentialist, theory of taste and the nature of the human spirit. He, I, we could only find what gives meaning to life in a competitive industrial society: there can be no retreat to the monastery, the commune or the forest.

An Australian perspective

No understanding of contemporary environmental problems and perceptions could be complete without an appreciation of the unstudied continent.[14] Superficially, it might seem paradoxical that Australia should be at the forefront of environmental movements. The country is enormous in relation to its population. Fewer than 17 million people – the population of the New York or Bombay conurbations – inhabit an area the size of the USA. The density of population is one thirteenth that of the USA, a one hundred and fifteenth that of the UK. Yet the country has been at the forefront of environmental thinking. Tasmania produced one of the first significant votes for a Green Party. Australian philosophy (particularly at the Australian National University) has led the latest wave of philosophical attempts to query the virtues of economic growth and industrialism and to clarify contemporary ideas about nature. A number of overseas eco-philosophers have made Australia their base and spiritual home, including Richard Sylvan (New Zealand), David Suzuki (Canada) and Robert Lawler (USA). Most remarkably of all, Australia has produced the exceptional phenomenon of green trade unionism.

The phenomenon of the 'Green Ban', in which trade unionists prohibit work they believe to be environmentally harmful, emerged in the New South Wales Builders' Labourers' Federation in 1970 when a number of residents of Hunter's Hill appealed to the union for support in their opposition to the development of twelve acres of open bush. They got a positive response from a union leadership led by Jack Mundey, who was supported by Joe Owens and Bob Pringle. The peak of 'Green Bans' was from 1970–73 when the union was successful in maintaining bans on twenty-seven sites, including open spaces, historic buildings and old working-class residential areas.[15]

The immediate, case-by-case, impact of the institution of the green ban was not as great as its spiritual and ideological significance. The number and significance of bans declined as the recession deepened in 1974 and the BLF eventually went into terminal decline. But 'Mundey's one-man band' succeeded in changing the Australian outlook. Most obviously, it broke forever the image of conservation as an effete, minority interest which would never appeal to the 'masses' or the 'working class'; the image of builders' labourers standing shoulder to shoulder with upper middle-class housewives in defence of nature and beauty, in defiance of what Australians call a 'hip-pocket' view of life, was powerful and mould-breaking. In the 1990s, when everyone from members of the royal family to bishops, trade unionists and philosophers shows green concern, this seems unremarkable. But Mundey's achievements have to be seen from the world-view of the 1960s. It was almost universally assumed that real politics was about class and distributive issues and that the great mass of people would never be concerned by issues of pollution or beauty, however much they were affected by them. Absurd as this may now seem, it was a self-fulfilling prophecy which hampered conservation for a long time.

Mundey was ahead of this time in developing a new kind of radicalism. A former Communist, who had come to be vilified by the Communist Party of the Soviet Union, he rejected the traditional 'left' concern with class and ownership of the means of production in favour of a broader concern with property rights and the quality of life. David Griffin, Lord Mayor of Sydney, commented on the Green Bans that, 'What's now coming is a new type of personal property in which you have some "rights" just being in a place'.[16] This was a hostile comment, but Mundey and his supporters accepted it as fair comment. In some respects they led academic social theory. The success of David Harvey's *Social Justice and the City*, published in 1974, demonstrated that much radical thought was in search of a more complex, more flexible, debate about property rights.[17] Mundey succeeded in attracting the vilification of both the traditional left and the traditional right. The former attacked him for abandoning the working-class to pursue wealthy ladies and his own hobby horses; the latter poured scorn on the green banners setting themselves up as (unqualified) arbiters of taste. Actually, the green ban code of practice largely exonerated the unionists from this accusation: the initiative had to come from the inhabitants, not the union and no action took place until the issues had been debated and agreed at an open public meeting.

Contemporary Australia shows a high degree of environmental concern at every level of culture: eco-philosophy and green unionism are manifestations of this cultural phenomenon. But why? At a first glance one might expect Australia to have attitudes to environmental problems which fall into the pattern of 'big, new' places and thus to resemble (say) Texas which has always had a certain environmental notoriety. The answer lies in two related factors, the environmental fragility of the Australian continent and the development of an Australian nationality and self-image.

Australia is perhaps, along with California and New Zealand, the paradigm example of a colonial ecology. That is, it has been developed by a population who imported methods and habits which had evolved in completely different climatic and geomorphological circumstances. Europeans brought hoofed animals which destroyed the texture of the soil. They used ploughs, which, in a dry climate with a thin topsoil, sometimes created instant desert. They chopped down trees at a rate which might be supportable in the northern hemisphere, but which was without thought that the majority of the three hundred or so species of eucalyptus grow very slowly. With the European came the cat, the rabbit, the prickly pear, the bramble, and so on which wrought havoc when released from the constraints and competitors of the habitats in which they had developed. Some Australian farmers simply didn't know how to farm; others knew how to farm in North West Europe and the transference of techniques caused major land deterioration in Australia. This is the oldest and the newest of continents. Geologically, it is the oldest; the aborigines, now claimed to have inhabited Australia for 60,000 years, three times as long as was believed a generation ago, are among the oldest of racial types and cultures. And yet the European population is far newer, even, than those in South Africa or the Americas. Its rhythms are ecologically inappropriate to a land which interacts on a long, slow cycle, where seeds sometimes lie decades before the conditions occur which will allow germination.

The extreme low density of population in Australia creates environmental problems in itself. Like oil-slicks, people will expand to fill the area that is effectively available to them. In agriculture this has meant a history of 'opportunity cropping', of taking a crop from the land and then moving on rather than fertilising. It has encouraged the low-cost destruction of forests by ring-barking. In the urban context, the near-universal expectation of the '¼ acre block' has allowed the two largest cities to spread over thousands of square miles.[18]

It is common for Australians, for all that they constitute only the population of a large city with a whole continent – and considerable resources – at their disposal, to believe in an environmental crisis. There are good reasons why such a perception should be less ambiguous and more intense than in Western Europe. For the most part, the intensification of agriculture in Europe over the last generation has been an exchange of commercial value for aesthetic value. Woods, parks and hedges may have disappeared, but farmers have been able to say, in the spirit of Engels' Mancunian businessman, that there was a great deal of money being made. Not only has income been made, but there is no real evidence of the declining capital value of land. Conservationists have frequently alleged that the 'high input, high output' nature of modern European agriculture must ultimately be unstable and lead to a decline in the productive capacity of land. But it has been more an assertion of faith than an empirical observation. In Australia, though, as in other colonial ecologies, especially in the Americas, farming has often been a catastrophe rather than a trade-off; practices have proved to be wholly bad for the land in that they have reduced its interest and attraction *and* destroyed its productive capacity. Typically ploughing or deforestation have created soil erosion and salinity. Soil blows away, or runs away into the water catchment area and the salt level, controlled by native species, rises to ruin the productive capacity of the land. Thus, in the 'colonial' context, the perception that 'we are ruining the planet' can sometimes be much less abstract and ambiguous than in Europe.[19]

In Australia perceptions are also modified by the sheer drama of the land and its climate. The land has an elemental quality which forms a natural setting for triumph and catastrophe. A man falling off his horse in Australia might die a lonely death of thirst, but he might also discover the world's richest mineral lode, as happened at Broken Hill in 1882. As a farmer, you will dread the possibility of a drought like that of 1895–1903 which left agriculture in ruins, but you can also face the opposite possibility: in 1990 I flew over floods which covered an area equivalent to France, Germany and Italy added together. In the Australian landscape it comes naturally to accept the 'boom-bust economy' and to fear that disasters can be all-embracing.

Europeans must assume that it is natural for man to change ecology. They must also assume that ecological disasters (changes whose effects are bad by all standards) can be repaired, at least in the long term. 'Repair' does not mean that the *status quo ante* can be restored, but that the site can be made attractive, productive and habitable. In Europe we have grown up with our landscape; we have changed it over and over again. Even where we have wreaked a kind of havoc, we have turned our peat-diggings into species-rich wetlands and our slag piles into grassy hills. We have little or no conception of, or concern for, the original pre-human landscape of Europe before generations of change created the palimpsest of the contemporary landscape, like a tablet of stone with layers of writing and erosion.

Thus, from a European perspective, the standard which many eco-philosophers set for Australian attitudes to their land is one which can never be reached, if they are to live there at all. If 'nature' means the *status quo ante* 1788, then it cannot be restored. Conversely, in over-estimating the importance of environmental catastrophes the Australian eco-philosophers, professional and amateur, tend to under-estimate what can be achieved by environmental restoration. It is often quite difficult to relate what you see travelling round Australia to what is written by its ecological critics. Once the possibility of the *status quo ante* has been forgotten, it must be acknowledged that Australia has seen some excellent environmental restoration. The original mine workings of Broken Hill denuded the landscape of trees, which were needed as pit-props, for miles around, and created areas of complete desert in which wind-blown sand sometimes prevented the railways from operating. But the Broken Hill Proprietory Company (from the 1920s to 1939) and the New South Wales government have created broad restoration areas which are now maturing attractively. The circumstances for environmental restoration have never been more propitious. Our level of horticultural knowledge and capacity to furnish any area with appropriate plants has never been greater.

The Aboriginal dimension

There is a sharp and obvious contrast between the European treatment of the land in Australia and that of the aboriginal prior occupants. Among the Aborigines, according to Bolton, the '. . . pattern of life was imbued with a deeply felt sense of religious tradition which identified the people with the land and its natural features . . . The individual was subordinated to the good of the community and the community was subordinated to the environment'.[20] The Aborigines, on this account, are natural green heroes. They revered their land and maintained a stable relationship with it. Like the prior occupants (to the Europeans) of North America, they had no notion of the ownership of real estate. Their art is typically preoccupied with the 'Dreamtime', the transcendent past and future Australia inhabited by their ancestors, existing presently as a removed dimension of reality with which some mystical communication can be made. Much Aboriginal painting is about 'The ant's dreamtime', 'The possum's dreamtime' etc.

The Aborigines thus score as a model and conscience for Australian intellectuals in respect of their environment. It is almost as if England still contained 160,000 of the Anglo-Saxons so admired by Bryant and Massingham. Aborigines have a variety of social problems (like crime and alcoholism) to a wildly disproportionate extent but they have finally gained a kind of respect, though admittedly a rather abstract respect, among white Australians. In 1973 the Whitlam government recognised that they had rights by reason of their prior occupancy of Australia and in

1987 the Hawke government finally granted them all unqualified rights of citizenship.

But if green intellectuals have attributed to Aboriginal culture a capacity for living in unchanging harmony with nature, they have set a standard that is all but unattainable. For some time now, such researchers as Mirrilees and Gould have suggested the Aborigines crucially affected Australia through the practice of fire-driving and through the introduction of the dingo (possibly as 'recently' as 4,000 BC.)[21] Probably the climate has changed. The evidence suggests that Australia has become gradually more arid and that its indigenous lower-level vegetation has a diminished capacity to support life. The implication is that Aborigines changed the environment far more slowly than their colonial successors, but also that they were almost entirely incapable of restoring such 'damage' to their environment as resulted either from their own practices or from the extraneous change in climate. As Bolton has it, 'Those who would see the Aboriginal as a noble savage, better attuned than white Australians to the needs and moods of the environment, must reckon with the possibility that the Aborigines left an impoverished ecosystem behind them'.[22]

Australian totems

Many white Australians have come not only to appreciate but also to admire the totemism in Aboriginal culture. The attitude of reverence for land, which makes certain places sacred and sacrosanct, is something to which white Australians feel much closer than they did a generation ago. This is partly because they have absorbed and promulgated a kind of image of themselves which is both mythical and makes the Australian wilderness a totem. Australia is a highly urbanised country: 85 per cent of the population live in communities of more than 3000 people and 70 per cent live in the thirteen cities which have over 100,000 inhabitants. The latter is an exceptionally high figure. What is more, Australia was always an urban society. As federation approached in 1900 more than half of Australians lived in the major cities, making it the second most urban society in the world after the United Kingdom, and the colonial authorities tried in vain to get people out into the bush. But, as Russell Ward argued in *The Australian Legend*, it is the men of the bush who have disproportionately created the image of what it is to be Australian.[23] Very few Australians were emancipated convicts or itinerant rural labourers, let alone bush rangers. But it's these wild colonial boys who have set the norm for Australian attitudes, a norm popularly expressed in the film *Crocodile Dundee* and in similar television programmes and advertising campaigns. *Crocodile Dundee* was created by Paul Hogan, an urban worker (originally on the Sydney Harbour Bridge). Similarly, the Green Ban campaign drew on frontier mythology. The 'Green Ban Tabernacle Choir' sang their own version of 'Waltzing Matilda', of which the last verse was:

> Up rose the residents and said unto the government
> 'Now we have green bans and so we are free'
> Take your crazy plans and stick them up your jumpers
> All come a green ban defending with me.

One American commentator, Richard Rodewig, accepts the legend entirely. He comments, 'Push a swagman's descendant too far, and he will fight back with the ingenuity which only an environment as harsh as the Outback or the inner city can ingrain.'[24] At the literal level this is a piece of mythology: urban Australians are not the descendants of swagmen. But at the spiritual, national-cultural level, they certainly are.

Thus Australians revere a wilderness which is not in any sense home to them and which most of them experience only on rare pilgrimages. Environmentalism becomes entwined with cultural pride and the quest for national identity. As an applied ecological philosopher, Richard Sylvan develops quite a precise set of technical terms ('restitution', 'extitution', 'rehabilitation', 'reinhabitation' etc., of the general practice of restoring land). But he also writes:

> Consider what happens too often with beach sand mining on Australian coasts, both eastern and western. Those vandalistic buggers go in with their imported machinery, and knock over a rich and complex littoral rainforest growing on the dunes, which they eventually replace, after processing, with a flattened sand expanse, sparsely covered by a straggly array of schlerophyll scrubs mixed with boneseed and other imported weeds.[25]

Both the style ('bugger') and the mention of imported machinery and weeds, suggest a rugged colonial nationalism struggling against foreign exploitation, an emphasis which is popularly evident in the 'Wilderness not Woodchips' campaign that the woodchips in question are for Japanese use.

However, it is not the job of the utilitarian philosopher to subvert either totemism or nationalism. If guilt about environmental destruction is making people miserable, leading them to aspire to a return to the past which cannot be achieved, then it is a worthy target. It is worth attacking if it involves a negative reverence for objects or principles which prevents the reverential from experiencing significant pleasures. (For example a form of totemism might imply that we should never go up mountains, but only admire them from below). But if totemism and nationalism gives meaning to life, through a sense of identity and of appreciation of the world, then they are to be welcomed into the utilitarian embrace as complex systems of summary rules. Also we must accept that bad philosophy can be good propaganda. Just as we might concede (from a utilitarian standpoint) that, say, officers of the Salvation Army do good things, even though we could not possibly accept the philosophical premises of their arguments for doing those things, we can admit that Richard Sylvan has done good things for the Australian forests and has used bad philosophy to achieve this end.[26] Wilderness should prevail over woodchips for the sound utilitarian reasons that, when all aspects of pleasure are considered and a long-term assessment made, wilderness can make a much more significant contribution to human well-being than woodchips ever could. But it *may* be necessary to argue this in the theological terms of 'Let Being Be' in order that people accept the conclusion.

The general principle of totemism

J. G. Frazer, author of that classic study of man's artistic and religious beliefs, *The Golden Bough,* defined a totem as:

> . . . a class of material objects which a savage regards with superstitious respect, believing that there exists between him and every member of the class an intimate and altogether special relation . . . The connection between a man and his totem is mutually beneficient; the totem protects the man, and the man shows his respect for the totem in various ways, by not killing it if it be an animal, and not cutting or gathering it if it be a plant . . . The clan totem is reverenced by a body of men and women who call themselves by the name of the totem, believe themselves to be of one blood, descendants of a common ancestor, and are bound together by common obligations to each other and by common faith in the totem. Totemism is thus both a religious and a social system. In its religious aspect it consists of the relations of mutual respect and protection between a man and his totem; in its social aspect it consists of the relations of the clansmen to each other and to men of other clans. In the later history of totemism these two sides, the religious and the social, tend to part company . . . [27]

In an earlier work I quoted Frazer in recommending a modern, environmental form of totemism against the existing practice of utilitarianism in land-use planning.[28] The point about totemism is that people need magic, security and their own identity in order to be happy. This will be (and is being) taken from them if the institutions, whether markets, public inquiries, or whatever, operate on narrow criteria of demand and use. What people need from landscape cannot be understood if happiness is treated in a short term way and as purely rational, in the orthodox economists' sense. The questions to be asked of a 'National Park' or 'Area of Outstanding Natural Beauty' should not be 'How can we improve access?' or 'What recreational facilities should we provide?', but 'What kind of special magic does the place have and for whom?' One does not have to visit a place, or visit it very often, to appreciate its magic. Indeed, familiarity does breed contempt and easy access destroys what is special. To enjoy their environment, people should be able to believe that the country, the wilderness, even the city, is, in an extra dimension to its definable functions, something which possesses indefinable qualities, which will exist always and is worthy of our reverence.

We should, as Wordsworth put it, 'spurn a false utilitarian lure' in planning the land.[29] But I am saying this in an attempt to preserve and reconstruct a form of utilitarianism, which takes a much broader notion of human well-being, a notion which acknowledges the nature of meaning and culture in human life, and the religious and artistic impulses which they generate.

All this is now, I hope, fairly commonplace. That human beings cannot be understood, still less provided for, on the basis of a simple model of wants and want-satisfactions, the former undistinguished and unexplained, is much more commonly accepted than it was a generation ago. It is part of Robert Pois' conclusions from his study of Nazi ideas that we must be able to offer people some real magic if they are to be able to resist the dangerous magic of a Fuhrer. George Carey, the Archbishop of Canterbury, says that, 'Our world is a one-dimensional grey world bereft of mystery, awe and wonder. Western culture has been unduly influenced by the Greek tradition of knowledge rather than the Hebraic way of obedience.'[30] It is the claim of specifically *environmental* totemism that it can satisfy the need for magic by locating the object of the magic in its most natural and proper place, the earth, which raises no dangers of the magic requiring us to sacrifice our free minds in forms of obedience.

Applications of the principle of totemism

In practice, the utilitarian and 'environmental' form of totemism which I am recommending implies that a wide variety of places should be managed, not for material exploitation, nor even efficient recreation, but to fit their own images, to be or remain themselves. This concedes something to the Heideggerian slogans of the 'deep' greens. It also uses the model of man-as-tourist. But increasingly modern human beings are tourists (or quasi-tourists): we are highly mobile and see ourselves as primarily consumers, but we want our consumption to be more than the passive recycling of material objects. We are no longer obsessed with the difficulty of survival, nor are we bound within narrow, territorially based communities. Man-as-tourist is here to stay; even much of the rest of modern life – the conference, the meeting, the retraining course, the shopping expedition – must count as quasi-tourism.

Within this principle there are certain general, almost universal forms of totem corresponding to images of the earth which have ancient roots and lie deep within our cultures (or 'racial memories' as the Victorians would have put it). They represent what we seek when we travel. 'Nature' is an obvious candidate for totemisation. Mother Nature is already such a totem. We love that which is natural, a love as clearly represented in the advertising of goods as in the politics of environmental issues. But Mother Nature is a vague goddess, all but incapable of offering us anything in the way of a revealed religion and often dressed in the clothes of her cousin Rosy Nostalgia. In any context, whether natural law, natural rights or natural wheatgerm, we are incapable of distinguishing nature from the unnatural. Either everything in nature is natural, in which case being natural is a truistic property of no ethical significance, or we must draw some arbitrary line around nature which excludes homosexuality or straight lines or females who lack maternal instincts.

Nature is not beneficient nor admirable: 'she' is not rationally reprehensible; she does what she must. As Lord Tennyson wrote, at the same time that Charles Darwin was peparing the greatest and most faith-shattering product of Victorian nature study, Nature is 'red in tooth and claw' and 'shrieks' against the creed of the love of God. So it is difficult to invoke the charm of Mother Nature to define what it is we seek in landscape: the image is undiscriminating and as repulsive as it is attractive. In a colonial ecology nature has more power as an image, but little more as prescription. Should the National Parks systems of the USA or New South Wales put out their fires? Or is fire a 'natural' part of the long-term cycle? The arguments, and the fires, rage on, and 'nature' offers no resolution.

Much more precise ideas of the broad images which determine what we seek from the land are available from a number of long-established artistic and religious concepts which recur throughout written history. These include 'Paradise' and 'Arcadia'. 'Paradise' was a Persian word which passed into both Hebrew and Greek. It referred generally to a garden within the city walls and, more particularly, to the parks and gardens of the Persian emperors. The Earthly Paradise in ancient writing and religion was an area below the Equator, in size calculable as equivalent to modern Nevada or the British Isles, where souls ascended to the upper Paradise. Perfection and harmony were the attributes of Paradise: evil and discord were walled out.

The Arcadians were the stupidest of the Greeks and even in Latin *Arcadius juvenis*, a 'young Arcadian', meant a fool. But just as 'rustic' changed its implications in English from mainly 'backward' to primarily 'charming', so the image of Arcadia came to be associated with shepherds, purity and innocence. In modern terms, Arcadia would be a land without pollution and social discord, a place of ethical harmony and ecological stability where they did not even understand what a social worker, an unemployment officer or a psychologist did for a living.

A variety of landscapes somewhere between Paradise and Arcadia have naturally assumed the role of visual symbols of deep human yearnings. All our guilt and yearnings, the self-disgust which tells us that 'man is vile' (as Reginald Heber's early nineteenth-century hymn put it), our longing for purity and the ideal, the nostalgia for Golden Ages and the hope for future Millenia, take the representative form of a clean, natural, ordered landscape. It is the earthly paradise which western explorers sought among the savages, the garden into which Alice longed to pass and the 'broad, sunlit upland' to which Winston Churchill referred in his more sentimental speeches. In cinematic terms, it is the flowered meadow, backed by woods, which Edward G. Robinson was allowed to contemplate before submitting to euthanasia in the eco-nightmare, *Soylent Green*. It is what many people are hoping against hope to find when they get to the wheel of their car for a day out.

But, of course, it is not only Paradise-Arcadia we seek, any more than we want to live on a diet of puddings. Modern man follows Rousseau who confessed, 'Never does a plain, however beautiful it may be, seem so

in my eyes. I need torrents, rocks, firs, dark woods, mountains, steep roads
to climb or descend, abysses beside me to make me afraid.'[31] There have
always been the badlands and the deserts, the places beyond the pale of
civilisation, places which are too hot or too cold, too wet or too dry, too
deep and impenetrable for civilised life. We need these places to prove
ourselves, to give an extra dimension to our world, to make us appreciate
the mundane. Love Maria Willis expressed this need in her hymn
'Sussex', written in Victorian England:

> Not for ever in green pastures
> Do we ask our way to be;
> But the steep and rugged pathway
> May we tread rejoicingly.
>
> Not for ever by still waters
> Would we idly rest and stay
> But would smite the rugged fountain
> From the rocks along our way.

The map of English literature is full of badlands, from Grendel's Mere
in Beowulf to its obvious descendants like the Great Grimpen Mire in
The Hound of the Baskervilles. T. E. Lawrence followed Christ and John
the Baptist into the desert to prove himself, and I (and thousands of other
young Englishmen) followed Lawrence in the 1960s. We 'did not want
the warm clover and the play of seeding grasses; the screens of quickset,
the billowing drapery of beech and elm seemed best away . . .'. Those are
the words of Mole, pressing onwards into the Wild Wood in Kenneth
Grahame's *The Wind in the Willows*. Mole's relish is replaced by terror as
he goes deeper into the wood:

> . . . he penetrated to where the light was less and trees crouched nearer and
> nearer, and holes made ugly mouths at him on either side . . . It was over
> his shoulder, and indistinctly, that he first saw a face: a little evil wedge-
> shaped face, looking out at him from a hole. When he turned and
> confronted it, the thing had vanished . . . .[32]

Modern man follows Rousseau and Mole: every statistic suggests a
massive increase in the desire to penetrate the wilderness, to know the
land intimately, to be by the abyss. In some respects this is a very modern
instinct which has increased steadily and geometrically since industrialisation. There is scarcely any evidence for its existence among the peasantry
of rural Europe. But the images which dominate our quest to know and
experience the earth in full go back to the Bible, the classics and beyond.
Paradise, Arcadia and the Wilderness emanate from the ancient cultures
of Middle Earth and are nearly universal. But in the minds of most people
they overlap, mix and complement more particular images which relate
us to our own land and give us our sense of identity and belonging. Sir
Walter Scott asked:

> Breathes there the man, with soul so dead
> Who never to himself hath said
> This is my own, my native land?

The world is full of holy lands; most countries are God's own. Landscape is an important peg of identity, a rival and relation to language. In cultures as diverse as the Welsh, the Australian Aboriginal and the Jewish, the two come together to allocate meaning and spiritual significance to the relation between people, words and places. Less obviously, the American has his frontier, the National Parks being the 'cathedrals of America' as Daniel Boorstin saw it, the German his forest, the Englishman his 'countryside'.

'Country' is a complex bundle of images. Starting with the latin 'contrata', meaning opposite (the city), it contains in modern English sufficient mystery and contradiction to foreclose on the possibility of definition. It is not just space, or living things, or agricultural production or tradition, though all of these play a part and may be necessary conditions. 'Countryside' can only be understood in terms of the deeply-rooted meanings with which we see landscape. Perfect country would combine three images: the wholesomeness of Arcadia, edged by the threat of the Wild Wood, linked to ourselves by the particular ties of identity which make it *our* tribal totem.

So far I have talked of totems in relation to land entirely in terms of 'country' and 'wilderness'. Of course, there are also urban totems in every culture. Perhaps it is true, as a number of commentators have alleged, that English culture is perversely anti-urban. But Italian culture is heavily urban, insofar as the magic places of Italy are popularly identified with collections of buildings: *Italia in Miniatura* outside Ravenna is a portrait of a land as its architecture, just as (for example) war-time propaganda about Britain identified the country with its farms and its villages. Urban totems, and the business of urban preservation, are even more complex, conceptually and practically, than rural preservation. However, the importance of the urban in providing for human spiritual needs must be fully recognised. Cities are centres of identity, they are Meccas of belief. Just as country must vary from Arcadia to the desert, cities must be both light and elegant and deep and dark to satisfy us.

In all of these cases, rural and urban, the idea of a totem and the implication of preservation raise severe theoretical difficulties. City and country are both complex dynamic systems: we can, by considered public policy, influence the way in which they develop, but we cannot completely control them or literally preserve them. If we prevent fire in a forest, we probably change the long-term ecological balance there. We can preserve a system of farming, but not its economic place in the world or the society which it supports. If we rigorously protect an English village from all physical change, the property market turns it into a reservation for the wealthy, who are generally elderly. Young local people cannot find anywhere to live in the village, the pub and the cricket club disappear, the community declines (or is transformed: it is difficult to tell with communities). A similar process happens when you declare a *'secteur sauvegardé'* or 'conservation area' in a city. But if you start at the other end, with 'community', you only discover that community is an artificially static ideal applied to a dynamic reality.

It is possible and necessary to admit all of these theoretical problems and still to believe in environmental totemism and its preservationist implications. The narrower forms of utilitarianism also have wide conceptual ambiguities: so do the Koran, the Talmud, the Bible and the US Constitution. Utilitarianism is a philosophy in defiance of its own purpose unless it acknowledges the spiritual needs which relate people to land.

It might be thought that we already have considerable totemism in land. Since Yellowstone became a National Park in 1872, over a hundred countries have instituted systems of national parks and national monuments. In England the standard governmental response to environmental protest has been to designate some new kind of area for preservation; we have National Parks, Green Belts, Areas of Outstanding Natural Beauty, Country Parks, Conservation Areas, Nature Reserves, Sites of Special Scientific Interest, Environmentally Sensitive Areas and more. This is a gesture towards totemism, the beginnings of a development of a well-defined practical totemism. Too often we do nothing but designate: we still think that access to the areas should be maximised, that proposals to mine them should be treated 'on their merits'. A proper acknowledge-ment of the principle of totemism requires not only further rigidity of their special status to enable a sense of security in their magic, but also programmes to eliminate discordant developments, as the Australian government has shown by having motels and other modern artefacts removed from the vicinity of Ayre's Rock.

Notes

1. Paul R. Ehrlich, 'The Population Bomb' in Robert Detweiler, Jon N. Sutherland and Michael S. Werthman, *Environmental Decay in its Historical Context*, (Scott, Foresman, 1973), pp. 38–45.
2. Robert E. Goodin, 'International Ethics and the Environmental Crisis', *Ethics and International Affairs*, 4, (1990).
3. Bertrand Russell, *Power, A New Social Analysis*, (Allen & Unwin, 1938).
4. See Howard A. Scarrow, 'The Impact of British Domestic Air Pollution Legislation', *British Journal of Political Science*, 2:3, (1972).
5. See George Orwell, *Coming Up For Air*, (Secker and Warburg, 1939), p. 13.
6. Malachi, Ch. 4, V.I. *Authorised version*.
7. Matthew, Ch. 15, v. 13. *Authorised version*.
8. Robert Lawler, *Earth Harmony. The New Male Sexuality*, (Millenium, 1990).
9. See Die Grünen, *Programme of the German Green Party*, (Heretic Books, 1983).
10. Herbert Butterfield, *The Historical Novel. An Essay*. (Cambridge University Press, 1924).
11. For a fuller version of this analysis see Lincoln Allison, 'Association Football and the Urban Ethos' in John D. Wirth and Robert L. Jones (eds) *Manchester and Sao Paulo, Problems of Rabid Urban Growth*, (Stanford University Press,

1978) and Lincoln Allison, 'Batsman and Bowler: the Key Relation of Victorian England', *Journal of Sport History*, 7:2, (1980). A full-blown textbook account is Richard Holt, *Sport and the British, A Modern History*, (Oxford University Press 1989).

12. Leon Trotsky, *Where is Britain Going?* (CPGB, 1926), p. 175.
13. A reaction quoted by Hugh Dalton in *The Fateful Years, Memoirs, 1931–1945*, (Frederich Muller, 1957), p. 421.
14. During the writing of this book I visited Australia on a visiting fellowship awarded by the Sir Robert Menzies Centre for Australian Studies. I am most grateful for the opportunities afforded by the fellowship.
15. See Jack Mundey, *Green Bans and Beyond*, (Angus and Robertson (Sydney), 1981) and Richard J. Rodewig, *Green Bans, The Birth of Australian Environmental Politics: a study in public opinion and participation*, (Hale and Tremonger (Sydney) 1978). I am most grateful to Jack Mundey for talking to me at length in his characteristically frank and amusing style.
16. Quoted in Geoffrey Bolton, *Spoils and Spoilers: Australians Make Their Environment*, 1788–1980, (Allen & Unwin, 1981), p. 167.
17. See David Harvey, *Social Justice and the City*, (Edward Arnold, 1973).
18. The most general account of all this is to be found in Bolton, *op. cit.*
19. Thus the statement, absurd in itself, by David Suzuki that, 'Ecologically the occupation of Australia by Europeans was catastrophic', *The Sydney Morning Herald*, 1 May 1990, p. 15. See David Suzuki, *Inventing the Future: Reflections on Science, Technology and Nature*, (Allen & Unwin, 1990).
20. Bolton, *op. cit.*, pp. 8–9.
21. Robert D. Mirrilees, 'Man the Destroyer', *Journal of the Royal Society of Western Australia*, 51, (1958). R. A. Gould, 'Uses and effects of fire among the Western District Aborigines of Australia', *Mankind*, 8, (1971).
22. Bolton, *op. cit.*, p. 9.
23. Russell Ward, *The Australian Legend*, (Oxford University Press, 1958).
24. Rodewig, *op. cit.*, p. ix.
25. Richard Sylvan, 'Mucking with Nature', available from the Department of Philosophy, Research School of the Social Sciences, Australian National University, p. 8.
26. On the specific issue of the forests, see R. and V. Routley, *The Fight for the Forests*, 3rd edition, (ANU, 1975).
27. From J. G. Frazer, *Totemism*, 1887. Quoted in Sigmund Freud, *Totem and Taboo*, (Routledge, 1960), pp. 103–4.
28. See Lincoln Allison, *Environmental Planning: a Political and Philosophical Analysis*, (Allen & Unwin, 1975), pp. 124–30.
29. This comes from Wordsworth's sonnet protesting against the building of a railway from Kendal to Windermere which was dated October 12th, 1844 and published in the *Morning Post*. See William Wordsworth *Guide to the Lakes*, (Frowde, 1906), p. 146.
30. From *The Great God Robbery*, quoted in *The Daily Telegraph*, 26 July 1990.
31. J. J. Rousseau, *The Confessions*, (Penguin, 1966), p. 167.
32. Kenneth Grahame, *The Wind in the Willows*, (Reprint Society, 1954), pp. 57–8.

6 Principles for action

Alternative social decision mechanisms

A wide variety of intellectual tasks can be performed without a clear objective: one can remark, inform or analyse (in a number of senses of analysis) without clarifying the purpose of these exercises. But recommendation requires a further step in which objectives are defined and obstacles to the achievement of these objectives are identified; only after taking that step can we talk about problems, let alone solutions. It is anything but clear what constitutes an environmental problem, even more difficult to identify *the* problem, the existence of which is implied by the insistence of many writers in a 'green' tradition that problems must be seen systematically and holistically.

The argument maintained in this book amounts to saying that the conditions for identifying problems have not been met. Criticisms of the *status quo* on 'environmental' grounds do not have a clear notion of 'balance' or 'harmony' of nature to which to aspire and with which to compare contemporary reality. It is not demonstrable that the earth is heading for disaster by any standards. On the contrary, there is a huge menu of productive, aesthetic and hygenic standards by which performances can be judged and these can be rated within different timescales. Ecology, as I have repeatedly insisted, cannot tell us what to do. Many judgements must be imparted to produce a prescription: these include value judgements, counter-factual hypotheticals, estimates of time and risk and assessments of the worth of massive and diverse bodies of evidence. At the time of writing we rarely know which of many widely-discussed global effects of industrialism is real and are even further from agreeing how 'bad' they are, compared with real alternatives.

John Young pours a certain amount of scorn on '. . . the characteristically academic belief that the main obstacle to intelligent action is ignorance rather than conflicts of interest'.[1] I think this quite unfair as a comment on most academic writing in a wide variety of relevant fields. Most academic biologists, economists, etc., are well aware of the complexity of 'environmental' issues and of how they affect human interests and principles. But it is the simple-minded, like Paul Ehrlich, who gain prominence. What most people know about the environment comes from green propaganda in its various forms and from fairly ill-considered journalism. The result is often an idiot's mess of unstated axioms, emotive and metaphorical language and highly selective and simplified empirical evidence, all turned into practical reasoning without any serious attempt at the rational weighting of alternatives.

One of the unstated premises is usually that the nature of the status quo is morally wrong. Another, common to Marxism, Christianity and many other systems of thought, though no less questionable for that, is that wrongness must be self-destructive. 'Patriarchy', 'industrialism' or 'capitalism' must contain internal contraditions or the spores of their own decay. The equal and inverse argument is to be found in Herman Kahn's work. Free markets cannot really and seriously damage the environment. Kahn was most impressive in attacking any idea of the world exhausting its resources, but was prepared to admit doubts about the large-scale destruction of tropical forests as the major exception to his inverted Malthusianism.[2]

Two examples of the loose way in which environmental change is discussed: the health of trees and patterns of climate. German concern for 'forest-death' (*Waldsterben*) has been an important feature of politics since the 1970s. It must be understood in the context that the forest has an important totem-value for Germans, as wildnerness has for Australians and Americans. There seems to be little disagreement about the existence of the phenomenon and little agreement on its causes. The British Isles presents an even more confused picture. It is an agreed fact that the sheer amount of forest has gone up by about 50 per cent since 1945; a more dubious assertion, but one to be taken seriously, is that the amount of 'primeval' forest has gone down by about 50 per cent. Alternative reports, from different sources, suggest that the condition of the trees is either disastrously unhealthy or relatively healthy. My own experience of English forests is that many of the trees, especially the oaks and sycamores in the older forests, do look markedly unhealthy. The leaves of the oaks show a grey mould and those of the sycamores black spots.

But how is one to interpret such evidence? Oaks, taken as a whole, are the commonest of English trees, amounting to about a third of the total. They are also, ecologically, the most complex, normally playing host to over two hundred species. Virtually all of these are parasitic rather than symbiotic. They include common ivy, the polypody fern, the oak-roller moth, bracket fungus, gall wasps and acorn weevils as well as mosses and lichens. The ecological role of the oak tree involves being debilitated by parasites. The normal condition of oaks, as of human beings, is fairly unhealthy. Are they any more unhealthy now than in previous eras? We simply don't have the evidence and it would probably be very mixed and confusing if we did. Almost certainly, English oaks had to tolerate more carbon particularates and sulphur compounds in the hundred years before 1960 than they have since. At least some of the oaks' problems, as I argued earlier, are due to excessively kind conservation: we coddle them from fire, deer, use and so on and allow them to grow too old. No simple or bold statement about the state of the forests could represent reality.

The question of changing weather patterns can be taken as a touchstone of the imminence of environmental catastrophe. A dramatic change in the weather is both a necessary and sufficient condition of most predictions of global disaster. Kemp and Wall summarise many fears:

The last few years have seen changes of global weather patterns that twenty years ago we would not have imagined. Britain suffered hurricanes in 1987 and 1990 with the loss of over 15 million trees. Hurricanes Gilbert and Hugo caused horrific damage and death; whole towns and cities had to be rebuilt. Bangladesh saw its worst flooding in living memory: over 3,000 people died. Citizens died in Greece because of the searing heat and in December 1987 Arizona experienced snow at Christmas for the first time. In 1989 Ethiopia had on its hands another famine that could cause 4 million deaths. Droughts occurred in China and the Soviet Union as well as in Africa. The USA suffered crop failure because of the heat, and experts think that a 17 per cent loss of grain yield is possible over the next forty years.[3]

This passage is a travesty of partiality. *Any* period can be presented in this light if you select the evidence. The previous twenty years to the last twenty contained, in Britain alone, the deadly extremities of the 1953 floods and the 1963 freeze-up as well as such oddities as the great Wiltshire hailstones of 1967 and the tornado that turned over the caravans of Skegness in 1968, both occurring in the month of July. 'Experts' think nothing, collectively. (The subsequent paragraph even begins with that epistemological travesty, 'Scientists agree . . .'). In the case of weather there is even less agreement than in many other fields. Metereologists regard the whole process of long-term prediction as essentially unscientific. It is like predicting hands of cards which may be dealt tomorrow. Short-term weather forecasting, by comparison, is more like predicting what cards West may have when you have already seen North and South and have heard the bidding. Certainly the efforts made by the British metereological office after the government obliged it, in 1963, to produce a 'long-term' weather forecast (i.e. for one month) did prove derisory. Either a random selection of the same month in previous years or a prediction which repeated last year's weather for the period would have proved more successful than what was actually offered.[4]

Climatologists, among whom there are many enthusiastic amateurs and only a small number of professionals, do look at the broader sweep of weather changes. Until recently, the most publicised climatological theory in Britain was Professor Hubert Lamb's often repeated view that a new ice age was on the way. In its academic form the opinion related to *the next ten thousands years*, but journalists, quoting Lamb in reference to particular wintry conditions, rarely bothered to mention the timescale involved. The period in question is all-important in climatology. For example, the 'mini-ice age' of 1600–1850 is *the* event of the last millennium, but it disappears into the general cyclical 'noise' of the last ten thousand years. Climate is a complex causal phenomenon in respect of which we simply don't possess anything like the range of evidence (because 'history' is so short) that we would need to spot long-term trends. Physics and mathematics cannot predict climate; they tell us why it cannot be predicted. Climatologists are tentatively agreed that climate is becoming more (immediately) unpredictable, but insist that there could be no direct climatic evidence for 'global warming' as yet, however strong the inductive arguments that, because of the rising proportion, in particular, of carbon dioxide in the atmosphere it ought, *ceteris paribus*, to be occurring. We are far from knowing that 'global warming' is a secular trend, let alone understanding its effects, the potential for mitigation, the costs and benefits of that mitigation and the counter-vailing or complementary tendencies.

The generally low-level and confused nature of 'green' warnings about the planet should not prejudice us too greatly against the conclusions of the argument. The prophets of doom may be right for the wrong reasons. Like the billboard which proclaims that THE END IS NIGH, they will be right one day. I argued earlier that it is wholly irrational to require proof when considering warnings. There is much more to lose by ignoring warnings which turn out to be right than by reacting to those which turn out to be wrong. In this field a small stake on a 100-1, even a 1000-1, shot may be a wise move: an insurance policy, in short. The utilitarian must start his consideration of the 'environment' with the undeniable *psychological* fact, evident in the recurring cycles of concern, that vast numbers of people *feel* uneasy about their (collective) part in ecological processes. They crave stability and security, having improved those conditions already in economic fields. This utilitarian premise, combined with the uncertainties of our environmental knowledge, suggests the need for research and careful argument and for error being made to lean heavily in the direction of caution.

Given the inadequacy and complexity of evidence about envir-onmental reality, it is a relief to turn to a writer who clarifies his axioms and offers a structured theoretical argument about human institutions and ecology. John Dryzek's *Rational Ecology* takes a number of social choice mechanisms and assesses them by the standard of 'rational ecology'.[5] A social choice mechanism is a means through which a society – whether local, national, supra-national, or global – determines collec-tive outcomes (i.e. outcomes which can apply to all its members) in a given domain'.[6] Rationality is defined as 'a condition in which the organisation of human social structures' is such as to 'consistently and effectively promote or produce some value'.[7]

The models of social choice mechanisms considered include 'markets', 'administered systems', 'polyarchy', 'law', 'moral persuasion' and 'the international anarchy'. They are judged according to criteria of: 'negative feedback' (the production of responses to human-induced shortfall in life-support capability), co-ordination (across both actors and decisions), robustness (of performance across different circumstances), flexibility (in adjusting structures to cope with novel conditions) and resilience (the ability to correct severe disequilibrium)'.[8] Dryzek is extremely pessimistic about our kinds of arrangement. He establishes that, if there were severe problems with the complex interactions of ecological processes, we could not expect our institutions to be able to cope with them. He offers good reasons for pessimism and serious concern about ecological issues without having to rely on contentious and selective evidence.

This argument stands irrespective of what its author believes about ecology and ecological rationality. Which is just as well, since he makes no more progress with these elusive and deceitful concepts than do most other writers. This is partly because he shares the fashionable presumption that large-scale catastrophe is imminent and therefore that the serious problem for social theorists lies entirely in considering means of avoiding it: 'The most interesting question concerns whether or not the capacity of local, regional and global ecosystems to provide the basic needs of human (and non-human) existence is threatened. If no such stress is present or imminent, then an ecological inquiry into social choice is hardly worth pursuing.'[9] Rather than reiterate doubts about disaster, it seems reasonable to ask 'Why (on earth) not?' 'Ecology' raises complex questions of aesthetic, economic and medical values, and the relations between them, which have a profound importance for human well-being irrespective of the level of 'stress'.

Dryzek gives the conceptual game away on 'ecology' as follows:

> . . . *in the absence of human interests* (his emphasis), ecological rationality may be recognised in terms of an ecosystem's provision of life support to itself. Left to its own devices, ecological succession tends towards the production of climax ecosystems. A climax ecosystem is one in which there exists a maximum of biomass per unit of available energy flow. During succession, negative interactions between species probably tend to give way to positive, symbiotic relationships and resistance stability increases. Succession generally yields increasing homeostasis and hence increasing ecological rationality.[10]

This is an analysis grounded in the accounts of Barry Commoner and Aldo Leopold of wilderness considered as an idyll. One question about this image, as about the weather, must concern the time-scale. Homeostasis and stability are no more guaranteed in the long-term, which will include major metereological changes, in a non-human system than they are in a human one: it is merely a question of longevity. Admittedly, longevity *per se* seems to be considered a prime objective by some ecological writers. Kemp and Wall are impressed by '. . . a North American Indian asking rhetorically, "Tell me, what are the objectives of your industrial society? Can you perpetuate it for the next 6,000 years?"'[11] They sometimes talk as if longevity must be superior, as if a choice between 1000 years of collective/aboriginal life and an uncertain 100 years of urban life must be resolved in favour of the former. But, given the increasing uncertainties of the very long run and our necessary lack of sympathy with its inhabitants, it is very difficult for a utilitarian to see why we should take extreme longevity seriously as a framework, let alone as an objective. This is as true, in its way, for populations as it is for individuals. The dinosaurs and the Tasmans lasted a long time, but what good did it do them?

But what can be made of the supposed homeostasis or stability of wilderness when humans are introduced? Either we stick with the concept, in which case ecological rationality consists of mass suicide or, at best, a very non-human form of human life, confined to grazing and excreting and limited by high infant mortality, or we are left with the familiar indeterminate.

Dryzek's recommendations are dependent on his perceptions of the actual levels of stress and not merely on the force of his general theoretical warning and, therefore, will carry little conviction for anyone who accepts the major arguments of this book. His belief in decentralisation is potentially disastrous if you accept the arguments about power and human nature which I developed in Chapter 4 and his belief in Aristotelian 'practical reason' is impractically vague. It is odd that Dryzek does not direct his theoretical pessimism more specifically at 'democracy'. If you assume that the normal motivations of voters in an electoral system will be self-interested (the assumption of 'Downsian' theory and of everyday American politics), then the familiar problems of free riders, short-time horizons and the 'tyranny of small decisions' suggest extreme pessimism.[12] Even if we take the Benthamite (and normal eighteenth century) assumption that voting will be public-spirited, there are severe problems in respect of any 'ecological' objective.

The semi-official aim of world ecological awareness, endorsed by the OECD, and the Brundtlandt Commission, among others, is 'sustainable development'. Since it became current in the 1970s, this phrase has become one of the great nonsenses of the age. One does not have to be a cynic, merely a logician, to infer that any phrase so widely embraced as an objective, by institutions of 'left' and 'right', by (for example) Margaret Thatcher and many of her most virulent critics, can contain very little substantive meaning. This inference is confirmed by the myriad of definitions which are avilable. Some are honestly vague: Robert Allen refers to 'Sustainable development – development that is likely to achieve lasting satisfaction of human needs and improvement of the quality of human life.'[13] Others include their established political objectives under the heading of sustainability, as they used to do with 'justice' and 'democracy'. Typical of these is Mrs Brundtland's insistence that one dimension of sustainability must be the elimination of poverty.[14] As if poverty were not sustainable! The most commonly accepted definitions resemble that endorsed by the World Commission on Environment and Development: '. . . development that meets the needs of the present without compromising the ability of future generations to meet their own needs'.[15] But even if we could distinguish 'needs' (which I have already emphatically and entirely denied), we would have no idea, given technological innovation and substitutability, what would be required to satisfy future needs. The same kind of ambiguity applies to the Pearce Report's own definition of 'Sustainable economic growth' which 'means that real GNP per capita is increasing over time *and* the increase is not threatened by "feedback" from either biophysical impacts (pollution, resource problems) or from social impacts (social disruption)'.[16] Unless one makes the (absurd) assumption that the range of goods and services accounted in GNP will remain the same, then this definition has no practical substance. One might destroy all oak trees, pollute all air and use up all oil without *necessarily* reducing the per capita value of economic transactions: pleasure drugs, fusion power and trips to outer space might overtake them.

It is 'all very well' to pooh-pooh these definitions and pooh-poohing is one of the central tasks of conceptual analysis. But what alternative stipulation can I offer of the objectives of environmental policy? My answer comes, perhaps, more easily than some, being unconstrained by fashion or the requirments of a particular system of formal reasoning and offering no great precision, bogus or otherwise. Indeed its proper vagueness is in line with my central criterion of 'human well-being . . . broadly considered'.

The purpose of environmental reform should be to allow people a much wider range of satisfaction in their surroundings, especially in land and landscape, than is allowed by existing policies and practices. It should be to enhance the sense of magic and of boundless variety in the 'environment' and to reduce the sense of the earth being despoiled or degraded. In short, the objective is that people can get as much as possible from their existence on, and perception of, the planet. This does require giving the environment a certain (institutionalised) respect and also having careful (institutionalised) practices for avoiding damage which we would regret. It is with these objectives in mind that the following practical comments should be considered.

Markets: reviled, revived, reformed

Markets and the environment have usually been considered, by the proponents of both, to be enemies. Socialists were able to point to environmental degradation and pollution as one of the most intolerable disadvantages of the working of capitalist markets. Supporters of capitalism were wont to treat environmental regulation as just another attempt by bureaucrats, authoritarians and fools to limit the beneficence of the market. In the early 1980s there was a considerable reaction in the Republican Party against the strict forms of regulation established by the Environmental Protection Act of 1971. President Ronald Reagan and Secretary for the Interior, James Watt, were both 'sagebrush rebels', determined to reverse America's oldest and best known environmental policy by opening up the publicly owned third of the USA to commercial exploitation. Reagan remarked, 'If you've seen one redwood tree, you've seen them all'.[17] Murray Weidenbaum urged that the proper aim of Republican environmental policy should be to free wealthy entrepreneurs from the tyranny of excessive regulation.[18]

But during the 1980s both markets and the environment gained steadily in popularity, to the point at which no serious electoral politician would oppose either. Like the football star and the campus queen, their sheer popularity forced them onto the (ideological) dance floor together, irrespective of whether they were capable of dancing in step. The growing popularity of markets had both theoretical and empirical dimensions. At the theoretical level the 'public choice' theorists established that their model of the operations of states had at least as much credibility as its established rivals. This model assumed public offices and institutions are essentially channels through which individuals pursue their interests. Their target was what might be described as the *étatiste* assumption that when market failure occurred the state could always be relied on to intervene in the spirit of the long-term public interest. Rejection of that assumption casts doubt on the prescribed Keynesian role of the state as an operator of 'last resort' in all spheres of provision.[19] The empirical backing for this theoretical triumph was provided by the perception of a growing breakdown of communist and socialist methods of government, especially in the field of environmental pollution, the perception being dramatised and made irreversible by the trauma of Chernobyl.

There remain, then, two ideas which have popular support: markets must be freed, but environments must be protected. Academic debate contains sharp divisions on the compatibility of markets and successful environmental management. Dryzek dismisses markets at least as forcefully as he dismisses any social choice mechanism. Markets are peculiarly 'myopic':

> Private enterprise, consumer sovereignty markets may have their good points, but it should be clear by now that ecological rationality is not one of them. Markets of this sort merit unequivocable condemnation for their failure to achieve negative feed-back and coordination in their interaction with ecosystems. Further, none of the reforms to market systems . . . offers any significant promise of improvement.[20]

Converseley, the Pearce team start with an assumption of the enormous potential of markets for providing satisfactory outcomes:

> The most desirable feature of the price mechanism is that it signals to consumers what the cost of producing a particular product is, and to producers what consumers' relative valuations are. In a nutshell this is the elegance and virtue of free markets which economists have (generally) found so attractive since the time of Adam Smith.[21]

From this point of view the environmental problem is that many goods have zero prices and most are not priced at full cost; including external costs. The price we pay for sewage removal and treatment should include a factor for the effect on waterways, including fishing and swimming, but it usually doesn't. Green consumerism is a very inefficient mechanism for correcting the market. What is required is either a 'full privatisation' in which all goods (including breathing fresh air or walking in the hills) have a price which will affect productive decisions such as whether to pollute or to 'develop' mountain areas, or a modification of markets to ensure that prices represent true and full marginal costs.[22] It is the latter which Pearce *et. al.* favour. Thus an equation:

$$P = MC + MEC = MSC^{23}$$

where P = price
      MC = marginal cost of production
      MEC = marginal external cost of production
      MSC = marginal social cost.

There are alternative formulations, but this encapsulates the essence. It is principally operated through tax incentives (and disincentives). The practical application is commonly called the 'Polluter Pays Principle', which, in its OECD formulation, reads:

> The principle to be used for allocating costs of pollution prevention and control measures to encourage rational use of scarce environmental resources and to avoid distortions in international trade and investment is the so-called 'Polluter Pays Principle'. This principle means that the environment is in an acceptable state. In other words, the cost of these measures should be reflected in the cost of goods and services which cause pollution in production and/or consumption. Such measures should not be accompanied by subsidies that would create significant distortions in international trade and investment.[24]

A typical example is of a carbon tax on fuels (it might also be a sulphur tax). Tax is levied in relation to the cost of repairing the damage caused by the taxed ingredient: the more carbon (or sulphur) in a fuel, the more it is taxed. There will be an incentive to develop carbon-free and sulphur-free fuels and a proportional disincentive to burn those which are 'dirty'.

In itself, so far as it goes, *ceteris paribus*, and all that, the principle of market modification is a good thing. The suspicion must be that it is something of an ideological convenience which allows free market writers like Samual Brittan and politicians like Margaret Thatcher to take account of environmental problems and claim that their philosophy always took account of them.[25] Such market language is perhaps good and necessary rhetoric to persuade people of the importance of environmental considerations. When the Automobile Association or the British Road Federation demand a better deal for the motorist, and specifically that all of the Road Fund Licence fee be spent on roads, it is important to get a proper account of motor car use which includes pollution, health care, double glazing and the need to travel far to find peace, security and variety. But beyond a few limited examples like the carbon tax, it is difficult to image many market modifications actually being implemented. Dryzek lists a number including taxing pollution and the use of 'commons' like the sea and subsidising tree-planting and ecological research. He questions why 'most governments make no serious moves in the direction of any of them'.[26] Most of them hurt in an electoral system. Consider the total reluctance of US governments to increase substantially the price of gasoline to something like world levels when its economists, ecologists, state department and treasury officials are *all* telling it to do so! Many examples which fit the principle would be difficult and costly to implement: take the fate of dog licences as an example.

The real danger of market modification is that it is likely to be taken to be a comprehensive or adequate approach to environmental problems. If it is, then there will be the same kinds of risible over-formality and under-emphais of spirital values in re-structuring the market as there has been in direct environmental decison-making where cost-benefit analysis has been used. (The assessment of the value of a Norman church by reference to its fire insurance policy by the Roskill Commission remains the most notorious.)

It follows from the argument I put earlier about external diseconomies, that the idea of 'marginal external cost' is artibrary and open-ended. Only a clear moral principle (not included in the Pearce report and alien to most economic thinking) can limit the idea of who can be considered responsible for which effects in the world and, conversely, who can be considered affected by an act of production or consumption. People who drive motor cars pollute my atmosphere, wake me up, endanger my life and the lives of my family and friends, clutter the landscape and slaughter wildlife. They also ruin the peace of rural areas and cause profound social changes including the undermining of community spirit and regional character. Which of these counts under MEC? Economic writing offers considerable variety. Pearce, reporting to a Conservative government, treats 'pollution', carefully defined, as his paradigm case. E. J. Mishan, further removed from the locus of social decisions, wants a much broader definition which would enable thim to tax or sue aeroplanes out of the sky.[27]

A crucial admission in the Pearce report concerns 'option' and 'existence' values. In broad utilitarian, rather than narrowly economic, terms these are the benefits of having goods and services available irrespective of whether we ever use them and the pleasure of knowing that something exists without (otherwise) using it in any way. Existence value is defined by Pearce as 'a value placed on an environmental good and which is unrelated to any actual or potential use of the good'.[28] Pearce, as an economist, tends to scratch his head a bit when faced with existence values. They '. . . are certainly fuzzy values. It is not very clear how they are best defined'.[29] Indeed the attempts he quotes, by Brookshire, Eubanks and Randall, to measure the existence value of grizzly bears and bighorn sheep reach the limits of risibility.[30]

Just as external diseconomies can be translated, as utilitarian argument, into a much broader ethical idea, so can existence values. Existence values are the essence of the good life. The pleasure of being of the earth and knowing its richness and variety is on a different scale from any use values. Our hightest expressions of thankfulness concern existence value:

> For the beauty of each hour
> Of the day and of the night
> Hill and vale, and tree and flower,
> Sun and moon and stars of light.[31]

Folliott Pierpoint thanked his Maker.

Our deepest environmental worries concern existence value. As a distinguished botanist put it recently, in unashamedly aesthetic terms:

> To one who, for nearly 80 years has found our natural world fascinating and beautiful, it has become more and more distressing and emotionally painful to see it made increasingly and often shockingly homogenised and drab. The incredible diversity that makes Nature so interesting and satisfying to observe and investigate is disappearing at an exponentially increasing rate. The beauty that makes life so pleasant and worth living fades almost daily before our eyes, mainly in the names of 'progress' and profit.!

He ends:

> At present it seems to us that, if there is something particularly beautiful or interesting in the world, there is always someone ready and waiting, for profit or power, to destroy or anyway change it – a jaundiced view some may say, but one which we have become insreasingly forced to adopt.[32]

The person who could alleviate that kind of fear, rather than the one who can make two ears of corn grow where one grew before, would be the greatest imaginable benefactor of the current age. The mere knowledge that what lies beyond the horizon is inconceivably complex and varied and that some of it is beautiful and some eternal is the greatest party of environmental joy.

Market modification, conceived as the only necessary environmental reform, can go in two directions. It can allow open-ended concepts like 'existence value' to broaden it to an almost impossibly vague set of considerations. Or it can stick to rigorous, narrowly assimilable components of marginal external cost, in which case it will create a legislative argument in which the genies of broad utilitarian ideas have to be fitted in to the small and narrow bottles of the economist's framework, as political argument has had to fit itself into the categories of theology in many societies.

These arguments do not imply an attack on market mechanisms. I have argued previously that only the prosperity created by markets can create the resources and the will which are required to improve the environment. Nor is it an attack on market modification which has a minor, but useful, role to play in environmental improvement, that area being mainly limited to well-defined pollution. It is an attack on market modification presented as a panacea, to the exclusion of other forms of protection of the environment. Markets are resilient and adaptable: they can survive much incursion and still produce their benefits. Modification is not the only way of using them without being dominated by them. They can stand excluded totems and authoritarian regulation. To put it simply, we would be better off on a planet which was half devoted to parks administered by a world state to enhance beauty and variety and half devoted to the working of the market than on a planet wholly run by a modified market, however well the modification had been made.

Is there an optimal system of ownership?

In the history of environmental movements, including the planning movement, relatively little attention has been given to the advantages and disadvantages of markets *per se*. Questions of what sort of goods should be distributed by markets and what kinds of regulative constraints should be put on those markets have been dwarfed by and subsumed under questions of property rights. How should land be owned, in what size of units and by whom? Insofar as land is not simply 'owned', according to the 'full liberal model' of ownership, how are property rights divided? What are the effects of different kinds of division?[33]

These questions descend from traditional debates about good husbandry. In contemporary terms the argument about husbandry has always been about sustainability, about maintaining the condition of land rather than the maximising of production or income. Good husbandry can be a complex concept: the condition of land can be judged by its beauty, its productive potential or its range of species. They are not necessarily the same thing. Husbandry is, in principle, also complex, but more often bad husbandry can be treated simply: salinity and soil depletion are bad from all points of view.

In the abstract, good husbandry can be related to the security of tenure and the scale of operations. If a person is certain that the land will remain his and is transferable to his children, if it is large enough to provide a good living and can be managed heterogenously, but small enough for an individual to know intimately and to control, then we can expect good husbandry. Thus, under certain assumptions, consideration of the concept of husbandry translates itself into prescriptions for ownership. It suggests that land is likely to be best managed if it is fully privately owned and of a size range which avoids the diseconomies of large- and small-scale.[34]

But these considerations represent only one dimension of the argument. The other dimension concerns feelings about land – love of it, pride in it, understanding of it – which are not necessarily functions of the system of ownership. If a place is one's home, then maximising current profit from it is not rational, but lunatic. The family estate is no more susceptible to this sort of rationality than is the family; neither can be assessed and rejected as if they were a piece of machinery.

Any survey of the relationship between systems of property rights and the quality of husbandry must report confusion and complexity. In a colonial context private ownership has often (though not always) proved disastrous. In Australia, Oklahoma and Brazil, for example, private owners with no real feeling of identity with their land and no understanding of its workings have taken off opportunity crops for immediate profit and left run-off, salinity and dust-bowls behind them. In the realm of public ownership, there is a similarly mixed picture. Some East European and Soviet collective farms have demonstrated very bad husbandry, but the West could learn from the better examples of management of Soviet mountains and forests. In Britain it was the assumption of conservationists in the debate over water privatisation that the regional water authorities had managed much of their lands very well. British Rail and the Forestry Commission have a much poorer reputation, the latter largely (in my view) undeserved. In all of these cases the bodies concerned were not supposed to be profit-maximisers, but to manage on a broad set of utilitarian criteria which included 'having due regard to the interests of amenity', a clause applied to them all under the Countryside Act of 1968.

The debate about privatisation has been largely about whether this mix of criteria can work effectively or whether it is not preferable to have a profit-maximising institution operating within strict constraints set by a regulatory body which is independent and prepared for legal confrontation. It is not a debate which can be resolved generally. In the field of land-use planning and architecture, public regulation of private activity has usually worked better than self-regulation by public bodies. But privatisation has also put an end to some established practices of good husbandry.

In the 1980s the Church of England and Oxford and Cambridge colleges frequently proved to be 'environmentally unfriendly' as landowners. This is hardly surprising, as their spokesman often pointed out, for these institutions land-ownership must be subordinated to their duties to provide clerical livings and education respectively. In the same period many cereal farmers also proved bad husbandmen; as subsidies declined and interest rates rose, many tried to squeeze more and more income from their land, with a diminishing concern for its long-term condition. Converseley, as Marion Shoard concedes, major financial institutions and wealthy foreign owners often proved to be environmentally good owners, because they were far more concerned with capital value and prestige than with income.

The two general necessary conditions of good husbandry can be said to be a high degree of practical knowledge of the land and a high degree of identification with it. What these conditions imply for any prescription or reform of systems of ownership depends on the context. People can be alienated from their land and manage it badly as owners, tenants, private employees or public employees. In an earlier section I defended aristocratic economics, as both complement and contrast to Schumacher's recommendation of Buddhist economics. Perhaps the greatest of aristocratic landowners in recent years was Hugh Algernon Percy, 10th Duke of Northumberland, England's largest landowner. In a House of Lords debate on capital taxation the late duke attacked the general assumption that it was good to undermine aristocratic estates by high levels of capital taxation. Death duties, he said, did more harm to the countryside than they did good to the exchequer:

> Those who glibly talk of relieving the owners of land of their burdens are remarkably reticent about whose shoulders those burdens are to be laid upon.
> Those who wash their hands and say it doesn't matter who owns the land as

long as it is efficiently farmed ... should consider whether a distant boardroom, or perhaps some form of not very efficient agricultural executive committee, would prove satisfactory substitutes for the personal care and loyalty which owners, great and small, tenant farmers, owner-occupiers and those who tend the stock and plough the land have often for generations devoted to the soil and to the countryside.[35]

In the aristocratic model there are two classes, committed to the land on different scales. The aristocrat sees the needs of his estate as a whole, lowland and upland farms, moors, forests and coasts. His tenant farmer knows and works his smaller patch and has, barring vicious levels of mismanagement, security of tenure. The two roles, the two forms of knowledge, are symbiotic.

This aristocratic model is worth bearing in mind when considering land management, but in many circumstances it cannot be copied. The environmentalist should look on aristocracy with a sympathetic eye where it does exist, but aristocracies cannot be created. Even among aristocrats, 'Hughie' Northumberland would be difficult to imitate. The size of his estate and the age of his lineage were extreme as were his commitment to his land and his knowledge of it. He eschewed a political career to tend his estates and was (among many other offices) chairman of the Agricultural Research Council, president of the Royal Agricultural Society of England and chairman of the Medical Research Council. He is generally considered to have done more to eliminate foot-and-mouth disease from Great Britain than any other person. Much as I have sympathy for the current efforts of the Prussian aristocracy to reclaim their estates in Poland and (the former) East Germany, their link with their lands is a broken one and their ability to win the sort of respect among those who work the land that the 'King of Northumberland' possessed must be very limited.

My admiration for the aristocratic model is relatively rare. More influential in modern England (and, in a broader interpretation, in modern Europe) has been the admiration of John Massingham, Sir Arthur Bryant and their circle, for the virtues of the sturdy Anglo-Saxon 'yeoman', tending and loving his modest patch, treating larger issues through democratic co-operation with his neighbours, eschewing greed, debt and grand ambition, knowing his land, suspicious of change and of theory. Indirectly this image has been influential; it has helped mould tax and subsidy arrangements which have allowed the proportion of land which is farmed by owner-occupiers in Britain to rise from 20 per cent to 60 per cent since 1918. It, too, despite the current lack of mutual respect between farmers and conservationists, is exemplified in reality (and in unreality by Dan, chiefly among the Archers) and must remain part of any consideration of good land management.

But it is also important to accept that public employees can have a highly developed sense of stewardship (in John Passmore's sense of that term). Many park-keepers and groundsmen do; an *esprit de corps* of stewardship on a larger scale exists in the administration of the National Parks and Forestry services of the USA, even though they have quite different ideas of their own role. Such a sense requires an inculcation of pride and responsibility as well as knowledge. It will be easier to nurture a sense of stewardship in the public service in ordered and prosperous societies where a lifetime career can be offered.[36]

One does not have to own land to have the right attitude for good husbandry. Ownership and property rights matter to the encouragement of good husbandry. They affect the crucial factors of understanding a place and identifying with it. The relationship depends on all the complexities of context. There can be no question of defining an optimal relationship nor of constructing a general appraisal of the worth and appropriateness of alternative systems of property rights from the point of view of the stewardship of nature.

Applying the principle of environmental totemism

The principle of environmental totemism acknowledges a relationship between people and land which cannot be contained within concepts of use and production. The contribution of 'the environment' to human well-being through people's generalised feelings for nature and beauty and their particular senses of identity and history, is huge and immeasurable. It acknowledges deep and ineradicable human desires for solitude, grandeur and intimacy with the natural world. It prescribes a system of strict conservation for certain areas. These will be set aside under appropriate conditions of ownership, often public ownership with a highly paid and trained ranger force. Totem is compatible with, indeed usually requires, *tapu* (or 'taboo' in its old form of anglicisation): conservation requires exclusive regulation of activities and artefacts incompatible with the *genius loci*. Areas must be protected in this way irrespective of their productive potential and the particular interests of their inhabitants.

Philosophically, conservation should be seen as a utilitarian 'summary rule', in John Rawls' sense.[37] The maintenance of the rule, the security derived from its existence, overrides the particular judgement of issues except in extreme cases where a strong case has to be made. It is analogous to the need, in nearly all cases, for utilitarians to avoid punishing the innocent and to be seen to be avoiding it. Theologically, it draws on the tradition of Christian 'stewardship' of the earth which modifies and undermines the right of exploitation of Genesis I :26 out of existence. On the other side, it is incompatible with a deference to nature or an acknowledgement of non-human rights *per se*. The principle rejects ethical mysticism about nature, but acknowledges the importance of artistic mysticism.

Acceptance of the principle envisages that the two types of place will, increasingly, diverge, that the 'holy places' are deliberately meant to operate on a separate basis. They will not be perceived as 'normal' or 'ordinary', but as more 'natural', 'historical', 'wild' or 'permanent'. For example, where normal life is dominated by motor vehicles and aeroplanes, it may often be appropriate that conserved areas largely exclude these. There should also be a practice of *restoration*, as is already established in the French *secteurs sauvegardés* and in some of the Australian states' national parks. That is, the thing conserved is not necessarily defined by the status quo at the instigation of the conservation policy. Inappropriate artefacts can be removed with the aim of getting areas back to a more natural state or to its condition in a 'classic' historical period. It is particularly important to maintain the variety of the world. We are, and will remain for the indefinite future, in an age of tourism. The amount of leisure people have (largely because of the decline of domestic drudgery rather than of paid work) has gone up and the real cost of travel has gone down. These were exclusive 'western' phenomena, but Japan now dominates international tourism and a much wider variety of countries have rapidly rising numbers of people who travel abroad. This is also a period of productive homogenisation where, for example, the same toys and cars are found throughout the world. There is a danger of increasing numbers of blasé, world-weary travellers, pathetically seeking novelty and 'reality'. We must preserve the diversity of the world and it cuts no ice with utilitarians to say that this can only be done 'artificially'.

The holy and unholy places should exist in a kind of spiritual symbiosis. The protected places increasingly gain in charm and excitement from their comparison with the mundane. The ordinary world gains in freedom and confidence: it is more able to enjoy the benefits of the market and the particular fashions and flavours of the age because they are no longer so threatening. We will be secure in the knowledge that the homogenised, efficient world is only part of reality. The variety of holy ground should be absolute. Very substantial parts, on a global scale, will be wilderness. (About a third of the world's land surface is currently classified as wilderness by most sources, meaning that human activity has had no substantial impact on its eco-system.)[38] Much would be countryside, ranging from near-wilderness systems of rough grazing to intimate garden environments. There should be the maximum variety of urban areas. The local significance of areas must be taken into account in designation which should extend downwards in size to include small parks and the kinds of places which might be called a 'child's wilderness' or which in Australia are called 'urban bush'.

The attitude to the market presupposed by such arrangements is both admiring and fearful. Markets have a high capacity for providing goods and services, for solving problems, for innovating, adapting and substituting. They are quite capable of living with stern regulations. Forbid the use of a practice, a substance or an area and the market learns to substitute for it: that is its strength. But where they not only fail, but can have enormous destructive potential, is in dealing with the cultural and spiritual dimensions of human well-being, with the arts, the community and the environment. Totems cannot be substituted.

In putting this argument I risk the accusation that I am merely prescribing what is already occurring, like Saint-Exupery's 'King of the

Asteroids' commanding the planets to go round the sun. After all, policies of 'island' or 'reservation', as they are sometimes stigmatised by planners and conservationists, are an extremely common feature of government policies all over the world. Since the first 'National Park' was designated at Yellowstone in 1872 (followed in 1877 by the Royal National Park in New South Wales) the idea has spread to over 100 countries. In the USA, the area of National Parks, National Forests, state parks or state forests, each taken separately, is bigger than the entire area of many European countries. In England and Wales the range of designations includes National Parks, Areas of Outstanding Natural Beauty, Green Belts, Forest Parks, Nature Reserves, sites of Special Scientific Interest, Conservation Areas, Environmentally Sensitive Areas and is equivalent to over half the land surface.

Many designations excite opposition from conservationists as well as local people: this is true of current proposals to introduce a system of national parks in Scotland as it has been for virtually every proposed extension to the system of national parks in England Wales since the first designations of the 1950s. Many people fear that designation brings publicity, followed by tourist and recreational development, which is ultimately destructive of the character of the area. Sadly, in many parts of the world, the whole business of designation has misfired. The popularity of such policies demonstrates a sense of the importance of totemism. But it is generally a limited, poorly formed sense. What is lacking is a rigorous theory of the justification of totemism. The policy is often constrained by a fear of exposing the incompatibility between totemism and prevailing interests and principles and, therefore, lacks clarity and determination. In Africa and South America the problem has usually been lack of resources to combat the squatters and the poachers. In the USA the system has endured sniping from different generations of 'sagebrush rebels', pointing out the incompatibility of the system with 'the American way'. But is has gained from the extreme contrast with the absence of suitable totems on most of the land of the U.S.A., justifying Boorstin's comparison between American National Parks and European cathedrals.

In England and Wales the system has suffered from what is often said to be a typically English reluctance to define basic principles and objectives. This has been complicated by three separate ministerial establishments being involved in designation: the planning establishment is responsible for most, but the scientific establishment has the Nature Reserves and Sites of Special Scientific Interest, and the agricultural establishment has introduced its own Environmentally Sensitive Areas. The last is a clear case of pre-emptive designation, introducing a system of compensation for farmers to refrain from certain kinds of environmental disruption in order to undermine the case for stricter planning controls on farming. But the core problem of most designations is philosophical woolliness. Are such areas special because their existence contributes to our culture and spiritual resources? Or can they be justified only as supplying a specific demand? On the one hand,

English national parks ban such sports as water-skiing and refuse (in sharp contrast to the Alps) to allow the provision of any mechanical means of ascending mountains. They compromise with motor vehicles, rarely restricting them or providing alternative transport, but quietly avoiding road improvements. On the other hand, they often justify themselves as satisfiers of demand as if walking were no more a legitimate demand than cross-country motor-cycling, and their role was primarily as an arena and arbiter for conflicting recreational demands. Thus LARA, the Land Access and Rights Association, which speaks for the interests of nine motor-sport organisations, primarily with respect to green lanes, is to be treated as just another interest to be compromised with that of the Ramblers Association.

National parks, in many countries, and similar designations, exist to enshrine some of the most deep-seated human values: beauty, tradition, local identity and affection for nature. If they existed merely to satisfy 'recreational' demand they should be abolished and replaced by Professor Pearce's rejected option, a 'full privatisation' in which rights to motorcycle over the mountain, to fish, to water-ski and to watch the sunset from the highest point, would be sold on the market at their full marginal cost.

The recommendation that considerable investment should be made in preserving the character of places is made notwithstanding the extreme difficulty of the concept of character. The concept is difficult enough when used in relation to wilderness; as I suggested earlier, some arguments about preserving wilderness, like the US National Parks Service's dilemmas about forest fires, reveal the core weaknesses of the concepts of 'nature' and 'ecology'. But these problems look relatively straightforward when compared with those of either urban or pastoral human eco-systems. Very often in these cases policy faces the disjunction that you cannot preserve both the human system and the physical appearance. I have always argued that since the former must change, preservation should focus on the latter, but, remembering that architecture and pastoral landscape were largely the product of human skills and aspirations which are now defunct, it is often the case that only a semblance of the original can be preserved.

However, semblances matter. That we don't know exactly what 'art', 'sport' or 'knowledge' are does not prevent us from treating them as vastly important objectives which cannot be fully achieved by market mechanisms. The last resort criterion for the conservationist must be variety. There must remain jungles, deserts, cathedrals, ancient M'dinas, wild moors, fertile plains and pastoral uplands and they must fit our deeply-rooted images of these things.

Liberty and authority in environmentalism

The main thrust of conservation policy must contain a great deal of preventative regulation. In terms of a distinction which is clearer in United States law than in other contexts, the environmental role of the state must employ, for many purposes, 'police power', rather than civil litigation, taxation or 'eminent domain' (the recognition of the state's interest in land and its occasional necessity to purchase compulsorily, subject to due process and fair compensation). If people discharge chemicals into rivers or drive vehicles where they should not go, they should not be taxed, sued, or subsidised for abstention, but punished.

The major advantages of criminalisation over other methods of achieving public objectives are that it maximises the sense of clarity and security about arrangements and, to a much greater extent, carries moral implications. But one disadvantage is that it requires the expense of policing. This implication has often been shirked. Much of the *existing* range of environmental crime in Great Britain is virtually unpoliced. A Pollution Inspectorate was finally unified in 1987 from a variety of Victorian bureaucracies, but it employs only 48 qualified staff at the time of writing. Where county police forces have environmental responsibilities as, for example, in the cases of litter, 'fouling', dumping, graffiti, vandalism, or stubble-burning, they have proved very reluctant to fulfil their prescribed role. This is partly because the norms of existing police forces give them little concern for environmental crime, but also because they perceive it as an area with very low detection rates. Outside of existing police responsibilities, the smokeless zone system set up by the Clean Air Act of 1956 is virtually unenforced (though reasonably effective, even so) and there is no regular, let alone comprehensive, system of surveillance in respect of development control.

What is needed is a new environmental police force, a kind of national ranger service, which can take over and co-ordinate all of these roles and operate a variety of preventative and repair services. It should include traffic wardens and the traffic police. Its underlying general purpose should be to establish that environmental crime has serious consequences for the general well-being and is being treated accordingly. Perhaps its uniformed branches should wear green!

The policies recommended here are undeniably authoritarian: they require a great authoratitive regulation of individual activity by state officials than is currently the case, at least in practice. They are not paternalist and clearly do not breach J. S. Mill's 'one very simple principle . . . that the sole end for which mankind are warranted, individually or collectively, in interfering with the liberty of action of any of their number, is self-protection'.[39] It is generally agreed that the principle is fraught with ambiguity, but also clear that environmental regulation falls under the heading of self-protection. This kind of authoritarianism is entirely compatible with a libertarian view on regulations which can only be justified by primary reference to the good of the persons regulated, like drugs or tobacco. (Of course these do raise some public questions, like 'secondary smoking' but they are quite different from (say) issues involving motor cars, which can never be even predominately private.)

In justifying his practical principles, Mill says, 'I regard utility as the ultimate appeal on all ethical questions; but it must be utility in the largest sense, grounded on the permanent interests of a man as a progressive being',[40] I accept this statement as a description of my own basis for policy. 'Utility' needs much qualification and explication, of course, and one would now say 'person' rather than 'man', Mill's contribution to feminism allowing us to treat this as a semantic issue. The major excision must be of the word 'progressive' which can only be understood in terms of Victorian assumptions of the necessity and possibility of a general moral improvement of mankind. It is now both tainted and outmoded because, during this century, 'progress' has justified too much wickedness and offered derisory compensation. It should be replaced by 'spiritual' or 'cultural'. The main thrust of this book is that the 'environment' is central to the spiritual or cultural interests of human beings.

But even if they are not paternalistic, the principles for action being expounded here are authoritarian and involve the removal of certain liberties. The reduction of liberty requires justification; there is a *prima facie* assumption (often held as an unconsidered prejudice) that authoritarianism is a bad thing. Of course, one could hide behind the complexity of the concept of freedom. It is difficult to distinguish unfreedoms from inabilities. Most constraints on freedom can be construed as internal to people: they consist of fears, norms, beliefs or ignorance. Thus it is difficult to distinguish constraints on a person's freedom from other aspects of that person's mental condition and, thus, the person himself. One can always slip into the assumption that freedom is an overriding good, that anything we think is good on balance must necessarily maximise freedom, an assumption which quickly leads to calling regulation liberation.[41]

But a utilitarian, especially one of Mill's leanings, does not need to hide behind the petticoats of arguments like these. Freedom is not an overriding good, but it does have a special status. 'Freedom' is too vague to serve as a summary rule, but certain forms of freedom, enshrined as summary rules, contribute enormously to human well-being. These must start with freedom of intellectual expression and with Mill's classic argument that no good can come from restricting ideas. It is quite different from the vulgar 'free speech', is applied in practice to the printed word and is compatible with the regulation of expression in many media. Intellectual expression is the most important summary rule of freedom, but there are others of comparable value, including sexual freedom and the freedom to travel which also contribute immensely to human well-being. But the importance of freedom is mocked if these arguments are extended to pushpin, to dog dirt and to four-wheel drive, off-road vehicles. There are denials of freedom which are hugely harmful, those which are wrong, but trivial (like banning pushpin), and those which are beneficial.

There is neither *a priori* reasoning nor empirical evidence to suggest that freedom is a house of cards, that if you pull one freedom away, you threaten all freedoms. Governments do not threaten the freedom of ideas when they make people wear seat belts in motor vehicles. The spirit of respect for privacy and individuality is not undermined by restricting the sale of guns or aerosols. The United Kingdom has forms of gun control and development control which would be considered intolerably authoritarian (and unconstitutional) in the United States. Sweden and Iceland have far more repressive regulations covering alcohol and dogs, respectively, but those regulations do not undermine the rationale of the sexual tolerance and freedom of movement which exists in those countries.

There are, admittedly, some troubling marginal cases. Certain kinds of environmental regulation might be thought to threaten freedom of expression in a fairly serious sense. Some strict development control, which involves design guides, might be thought to fall under rules covering the freedom of expression. If you believe (to take one notorious example) that you are making an important 'statement' by having the rear end of a large plastic shark appearing from the roof of your house, then you will see conservation area regulations as a serious assault on freedom. I confess to some doubts on this score, but my prescribed arrangements are, after all, intended to enhace options in *some* areas. I am not impressed, either, by the claims that the visual arts are central to the importance of a free interplay of ideas. In any case, the visual arts must always operate primarily on smaller canvasses which can be treated as entirely private.

Another problem might concern children. The freedom to have and bring up children is surely a serious one, whose protection is important to human well-being. I accept that the best of arrangements is that in which people (meaning particularly, but not exclusively, women) have the maximum freedom to choose whether or not to have children. I believe that if this freedom is truly maximised, in all its respects, there will not be a 'population problem'. My underlying assumption has been that, although I can imagine circumstances in which 'human numbers are destructive of fundamental human values' (to use Ehrlich's formulation), these circumstances are far from real or inevitable at the time of writing. Thus I find these two important marginal cases throw some, but not much, doubt on my assertion that the freedoms breeched by implementation of a justifiable environmental authoritarianism are not important freedoms.

The international anarchy

The state is often discussed in terms of what can be called the 'sub-Hegelian we'. Faults are discovered in the status quo and reforms are proposed. In the discussion of reform, the state appears as an ideal, a rational actor which intervenes to solve problems. 'We' can have more national parks, increase the tax on packaging or ban aerosols. It is idealistic and sometimes misplaced to think of the state in this way, but it can be sufficiently realistic as to be constructive. States do possess enormous authority which they sometimes use to implement an over-whelming public will.

But we cannot talk about the *world* like that. International society is an anarchy, as Dryzek points out. It has laws, but in terms of Herbert Hart's model of law as a system of rules, it has only primary rules which allocate rights.[42] These rules are (surprisingly) often obeyed, but there are no effective secondary rules, which are required to support the maintenance and reform of primary rules, and only the occasional flickerings of a 'rule of recognition' which determines the source and definition of legality. These flickerings are beginning to look more like a constant flame in the case of the acceptance of European Community countries of European Court decisions, but they have developed little at world level.

In the absence of law and sovereignty, there is war and bargaining. Utilitarianism can justify war only against extreme malice. Bargaining has potentially catastrophic limitations. Suppose the prevailing wind blows across Urbania and into Ruritania. It is alleged that the Urbanians are releasing chemicals into the air which carry into Ruritania, causing damage to human health and to wildlife. If Urbania and Ruritania are part of a strong federal system, then the machinery of Centralian government will referee disputes between the two. There will be federal civil courts, in which individuals can put claims, and a supreme court to adjudicate relations between the two state governments. Pressure for a fair resolution of the dispute will come through the electoral system, if there is one. These mechanisms are not optimal; there is a tendency within states to dump dirty public things on poor, underpopulated or peripheral regions which don't vote for the governing party.[43] But they do exist.

If Ruritania and Urbania are sovereign states, Urbania is a classic 'free rider'. It has no incentive to reduce its pollution. Unless Ruritania is also polluting Urbania, the potential for bagaining is limited and probably inequitable; the Ruritania government's bargaining can only consist of bribery or moral persuasion. Ruritanians are likely to have nationalistic responses to the allegations. They may instinctively believe even the strongest versions of what the Urbanians are doing to them and regard it as typical of the way Urbanians have treated people over the centuries. Urbanians are likely to reciprocate and their response will be exacerbated by their offence at the Ruritanians opening old wounds. Negotiations are likely to begin in an atmosphere of accusation. The best defensive move for the Urbanians is to bog the whole thing down at the stage of scientific assessment: they should demand proof and precision about Ruritanian damage and the attribution to Urbanian pollution.

Of course, this model can be further complicated. More countries can be introduced, on the polluter and recipient side. There are far more complex issues than pollution, including the destruction of tropical forests. But no more complex example is required to demonstrate that the international anarchy is an extremely inefficient mechanism for max-imising global well-being and that this inefficiency becomes steadily more important as economic activity and its ecological effects occur on a global scale. As Dryzek puts it, 'From the perspective of ecological rationality, the international system is clearly in bad shape'.[44]

These worries are founded in the theory of social decision-making, but the practice reinforces them thoroughly. Even the relatively favourable circumstances of negotiations about acid rain between the United States and Canada look depressingly like the model. These two countries have only a minimal history of antipathy and have a successful tradition of institutional co-operation. Even so, discussions quickly stagnated at the technical 'proof' stage and their main lesson, according to their principal researcher, is that, 'Negotiations break down when the actions of one country are perceived as causing the problem'.[45] Across the Atlantic, the tactics of US government and industry were duplicated by the British Central Electricity Generating Board, whose dogged refusal to accept any consequences of their activities as proven was often matched by hysterically pessimistic and xenophobic responses from the Scandinavian recipients.

John Carroll's general account of 'transfrontier' environmental politics ends by positing a treaty grap. It is certainly not that nothing is being done: more conventions, agreements and treaties on environmental questions have been ratified since 1970 than in the whole of history up to that date. It is that there is a growing shortfall of arrangements in relation to problems. However many measures are agreed, they never catch up with the problems. He writes that:

> ... there is a very large gap between the *direction* of our efforts in international environmental diplomacy, namely toward *more* treaties and other diplomatic instruments and certainly toward more publicity and more awareness surrounding them, and the *direction* of the environmental course of events in our modern world today, namely toward increased rapidity of environmental decay and degradation, even into crisis proportions.[46]

He concludes, almost as an afterthought, that as existing institutions cannot cope, perhaps 'deep' green thinking ought to be taken seriously and we should look to a global change in our philosophical outlook.

But the arguments of committed 'fundi' greens are particularly weak on questions of the practical inadequacies of the international system. They tend to blame the western industrialised nations for the destruction of ecologically sound, Third World ways. But even if one accepts both those judgements (that there were such sound practices and western industrialisation has destroyed them), what kind of prescription do they generate? The process is irreversible; the dynamic of industrialism and nationalism in the 'developing' countries cannot be turned back by decree. Sentimentalising those few Third World movements which do wish to reject industry, like the Bougainville Revolutionary Army and its agrarian socialist objectives, is an irrelevance which takes no cognisance of the kind of arguments about growth, power and the dynamics of human nature which I put in Chapter 4. This is one respect in which it is impossible to reverse time; hoping the world will become a grand

Bougainville (without the RTZ copper mine) is like preaching into a hurricane.[47] One might as well recommend, more conservatively, that the world be returned to the empires of 1914. From the point of view of environmental management, and economics and freedom (especially in the developing world) this might well be a good thing. But it is irrelevant to a serious discussion of policy. To put it brutally, if the world is doomed unless a 'deep' green philosophy is adopted on a global scale, then the world is doomed. We might as well stop bemoaning the fact and plan on an appropriate timescale.

But is it really that bad? I have argued throughout this book that most environmental critiques of the status quo are axiomatically biased towards pessimism and, crucially, that they fail to distinguish success-fully between environmental change and catastrophe. There is no realistic theoretical solution to the international problem, the 'world state' of H. G. Wells' vision being (arguably) even more irrelevant than when he conceived it. But there are some contextual grounds for optimism. The development of European Community environmental policy does offer a model for improvement. The agreed broad picture is of a leader, West Germany, responding to internal political pressures to improve its own regulations and then using the 'level playing field' argument to press for uniformity of regulation as an aspect of fair international competition. Thus a good deal of 'levelling up' has occurred and the European corner of the planet has reversed Carroll's treaty 'gap'. It is also the case that national pride is affected by international surveys of (say) dirty beaches and rivers and national politics is influenced by the authority of European comparisons and recommendations.

On a global level we can put some faith in the age of the tourist. Just as 'Europa Nostra' has come to symbolise a common sense of heritage which means that many Germans and Englishmen care just as much about saving Venice as any Italian, there is a growing identification with the world environment. Swedes regard the rainforest, Frenchmen the desert, as part of their expectations of a lifetime's experience, as Amer-icans and Australians have regarded the cities of Europe for generations. These perceptions provide the context in which governments operate internationally and are prepared to use resources. This global conscious-ness first began to find formal recognition in the 1970s with such events as World and European Heritage Years. It is symbolised by the sites on the World Heritage List, which was crucial (in alliance with the Australian federal government) in saving the forests of central Tasmania from hydro-electric development in the 1980s.

It must be recognised that rich Western nations must heavily influence, finance and, even, coerce the co-operation of poor countries in envir-onmental matters. As John Young says, attacking the myth that left to themselves developing countries will prove effectively friendly to global ecological stability, '. . . the reforms required for the establishment of a sustainable world will have to begin in the wealthy countries which dominate the world economy and either directly or indirectly determine the direction of economic development in the rest of the planet'.[48]

On 'Greenness' in ideology

It has not been an objective of this section to recommend precise policies. To pluck one issue from an indefinitely large number, the question of whether Scotland should have national parks and, if so, whether they should be based on the English model or the French or even the American, is beyond the scope of this book. Totemism does not necessarily imply national parks: in many cases, their recreational emphasis may be inappropriate to particular areas. Precise policy recommendations require consideration of local detail. I have been dealing here with principles for action, which exclude certain reasons from policy argument, suggest general objectives and clarify the constraints and limitations on policies.

These principles are drawn from the main theme of the book as a whole, which has been a defence of a form of broad, sceptical utiltarianism. The philosophical position from which I have worked is very close to that of John Stuart Mill; it is not the same philosophy, but the same sort of philosophy, conceiving problems in a very similar way, but making different judgements. The position I have expounded might be typified by various writers as 'light green' (as the Australian historian Geoffrey Blainey would put it) or 'shallowly ecological' (in Arne Naess's terms) or one of 'social ecology' or, in more old fashioned terms, environmentalist or conservationist. There are good reasons for ignoring these taxonomies. Not only are the positions they name vague and overlapping, but they often fail to distinguish the two potentially independent dimensions of policy and philosophy. There are good reasons for rejecting, as spurious and obfuscating essentialism, any attempt to construct clear categories of 'high Tory', 'low Tory', 'conservative', 'liberal', 'libertarian' etc. Similarly, one must be very sceptical of any attempt at drawing lines between types of greenness. But three elements in green philosophical movements are so disparate in kind that they must be distinguished, even if they have to be given arbitrary names.

First, there is environmentalism, which wants to reform the management of the non-human context of human life and the relationship between people and the earth. Typically, it sees the aspects of human life as being very important to well-being and as being inadequately, perhaps badly, served by existing methods of social decision-making. Environmentalism is fully compatible with utilitarianism, broadly defined, and is usually an application of utilitarianism.

Second, there is the religion of nature which seeks to replace established judgements by reverential attitude to nature. Typically, this philosophy harks back to the virtues of earlier (pre-industrial, pre-utilitarian) stages of human development and evokes the concept of 'ecology' as a modernisation of the values of nature. The religion of nature is made coherent by a deontological ethics which rejects utilitarianism and attributes rights to nature. Aspects of the religion of nature occur in many forms, ranging from nudism to animal rights to reformulations of orthodox theology. Politically, it finds very diverse expression, in Nazism, anarchism and many nationalities.

Finally, there are the green radicals. I don't mean radicals in the vulgar sense of people who want a lot of changes (I may even be radical in this sense), but in the etymological correct and more provocative sense that I analysed in Chapter 5. Radicals start with an overriding belief in the wrongness of the world; they seek to eradicate its fundamental structures and assumptions. Typically, because wrongness rather than a particular wrong is their base assumption, they are radicals before they are greens. Many green radicals are former red radicals or refugees from other failed radicalisms. These include André Gorz in France, Rudolf Bahro in Germany, Murray Bookchin in the USA and Jeremy Seabrook in England. Although there is much supposedly green thinking in these writers, there is remarkably little environmentalism in the sense of a concern for policies for nature reserves, national parks or urban conservation, for example. The same is true of the *Green Manifesto*, which contains radical policies for defence, health, education and animal liberation, but almost nothing about how to preserve what is best in the environment. There is a rejection of 'preserving the social and economic arrangements of Thatcher's Britain by protecting middle-class views from the intrusion of lower-class housing in green belt areas and the maintenance of green fields for the gentry to pursue sports such as fox hunting and game shooting'.[49]

Justice is the typical radical value. The *Manifesto* says that, . . . talk about the politics of ecology that does not embrace social justice is meaningless. They are inseparable, just as feminism, anti-racism and anti-sexism are an integral part of green politics.'[50] To the sceptical utilitarian justice is the most suspect of values, an arbitrary predicate, often used as an emotive dressing for values antithetical to the general well-being. For example, at least as good an 'ecological' argument can be made for a return to 'macho' values and well-defined, subsidiary role for women in society as can be made for its opposite.

The utilitarian environmentalist thus has three kinds of enemy. There are the narrow economic utilitarians, who (since they are in power) he has spent most of his energy on attacking. There are the religious naturists, whose mysticism can be taken to diverse practical conclusions; their philosophical premises are unacceptable, but their policies can be quite sympathetic. Totemism moves quite close to 'letting being be'. And there are the moral radicals, who start with a distaste for life as it is lived now.

Which of these is the greater enemy? Undoubtedly, it is the radical, who seeks to divert concern for the environment to his own separate moral purposes. It is the spirit of this radicalism which is so telling from a utilitarian point of view. It is not just that they are like the doctor who tells you that you have cancer; they are like the doctor who implies that you deserve cancer and delights in the implication. In the *Green Manifesto* are reasonable statements like '. . . it is wrong to keep social animals in solitary confinement'[51], but also much, much hand-rubbing consignment of existing human culture to the flames: 'The English meat-and-two-veg diet . . . has to go'[51], and no regrets for the lost joy of the family gathered round roast beef, Yorkshire puddings and (in our case) seven vegetables.

Meat must go because it obviously means so much to people. So must motor cars and competitive sport and national pride, irrespective of any calculaton of well-being. This has not got much to do with the environment, but it is in the tradition of the fanatical radical throughout the ages, of the Inquisition, the Puritans, the *Cheka*, the Ayatollahs and the Red Guards. Such radicalism is the revenge of the unhappy: it is premised on a hatred of life and driven by malice. Uniquely, from a utilitarian standpoint, it deserves the name *evil*.

Notes

1. John Young, *Post Environmentalism*, (Belhaven, 1990), p. 4.
2. See, especially, Julian L. Simon and Herman Kahn (eds), *The Resourceful Earth, A Response to 'Global 2000'*, (Blackwell, 1984).
3. Penny Kemp and Derek Wall, *A Green Manifesto for the 1990s*, (Penguin, 1990), p. 37.
4. See Richard Petrie, 'The Alternative Weather Forecast', *The Countryman*, 92: 3 (1987). (Richard Petrie is a pseudonym used by Lincoln Allison).
5. John Dryzek, *Rational Ecology, Environment and Political Economy*, (Blackwell, 1987).
6. *Ibid.*, p. 7.
7. *Ibid.*, p. 25.
8. *Ibid.*, pp. 11–12.
9. *Ibid.*, p. 10.
10. *Ibid.*, p. 44.
11. Kemp and Wall, *op. cit.*, p. 38.
12. See Anthony Downs, *An Economic Theory of Democracy*, (Harper and Row, 1957).
13. Robert Allen, *How to Save the World*, (Kogan Page, 1980) p. 23.
14. Gro Harlem Brundtland in the Sir Peter Scott Lecture, Bristol, 18th October 1986. Quoted in David Pearce, Anil Markandya, Edward B. Barbier, *Blueprint for a Green Economy*, (Earthscan, 1989) pp. 174–75.
15. World Commission on Environment and Development, *Our Common Future*, (Oxford University Press, 1987).
16. Pearce *et. al.*, *op. cit.*, p. 33.
17. Quoted in Young, *op. cit.*, p. 63.
18. Murray L. Weidenbaum, 'Free the Fortune 500', in Theodore D. Goldfarb (ed.), *Taking Sides: Clashing Views on Controversial Environmental Issues*, (Dushkin, 1983).
19. For general accounts of the theory see Dennis C. Mueller, *Public Choice*, (Cambridge University Press, 1979), or Iain McLean, *Public Choice, an Introduction*, (Blackwell, 1987).

20. Dryzek, *op. cit.*, pp. 86–87.
21. Pearce *et. al.*, *op. cit.*, p. 154.
22. *Ibid.*, p. 155.
23. *Ibid.*, p. 156.
24. OECD, *The Polluter Pays Principle: Definition, Analysis Implementation*, (OECD, 1975).
25. See Samuel Brittan, 'The Green Power of Market Forces', *The Financial Times*, 4 May, 1989.
26. Dryzek, *op. cit.*, p. 84.
27. See E. J. Mishan, *The Costs of Economic Growth*, (Staples 1967 and Penguin, 1969) or 'The Spillover Enemy', *Encounter*, 33: 6, (1969).
28. Pearce *et. al.*, *op. cit.*, p. 75.
29. *Ibid.*, p. 61.
30. D. Brookshire, L. Eubanks and A. Randall, 'Estimating option prices and existence values for wildlife resources', *Land Economics*, 9: 1, (1983).
31. This is the second verse of the hymn, 'For the beauty of the earth' by Folliott Sandford Pierpoint (1834–1917), normally sung to the old English tune 'Goodfellow'.
32. F. Raymond Fosberg, Botanist Emeritus of the National Museum of Natural History in Washington 'Editorial Comment', *Environmental Conservation*, 16: 1, (1989) p. 4.
33. For an account of the 'full liberal model' of ownership, see A. M. Honoré, 'Ownership', in A. G. Guest (ed.), *Oxford Essays in Jurisprudence*, (Oxford University Press, 1961).
34. A fuller version of this argument can be found in Lincoln Allison, *Right Principles, A Conservative Philosophy of Politics*, (Blackwell, 1986), pp. 99–113.
35. Quoted in the (anonymous) obituary in *The Daily Telegraph*, 12 October 1988, p. 25.
36. A classic account of individual responsibility and collective norms in the federal forestry service of the USA is Herbert Kaufman, *The Forest Ranger, A Study in Administrative Behaviour*, (Johns Hopkins University Press, 1960).
37. See Chapter 1 above, and John Rawls, 'Two Concepts of Rules', *Philosophical Review*, Vol LXIV, no. 1, (1955).
38. See J. Michael McCloskey and Heather Spalding, 'The World's Remaining Wilderness', *Geographical*, Vol. LXII, no. 8, (1990). Professor McCloskey is Chairman of the Sierra Club. The definition of wilderness is 'land without permanent human settlements or roads and is land that is not regularly cultivated or heavily and continuously grazed' (p. 17). This definition is interpreted strictly: even tyre tracks dis-qualify and only blocks of a million acres (1500 square miles, 4000 kilometres) are considered.
The publication of this research was generally considered as a piece of good news by conservationists, but it does reveal that the overwhelming majority of the world's wilderness is under ice for most of the time. It is concentrated in the Antartic and the polar and tundra regions of Canada, Greenland and the Soviet Union. Most of the rest is in the Sahara Desert.
I confess to being sceptical about the usefulness of defining wilderness, or about the part played in human well-being by (say) the remote Outback as opposed to the Blue Mountains National Park of New South Wales, which can easily be visited on a day trip from Sydney. But I am convinced by the arguments of many West Coast and Antipodean academics that wilderness ought to be protected from use and development.

39. John Stuart Mill, 'On Liberty', in John Stuart Mill, *Utilitarianism, Liberty and Representative Government*, (Dent, Everyman, 1971), pp. 72–73.
40. *Ibid.*, p. 74.
41. For a full account of these arguments see Allison, *op. cit.*, pp. 114–35 and Lincoln Allison, 'Liberty: A Correct and Authoritarian Account', *Political Studies*, Vol. XXXIX, no. 3, (1981).
42. See Herbert Hart, *The Concept of Law*, (Oxford University Press, 1961).
43. See Lincoln Allison, 'On Dirty Public Things' *Political Geography Quarterly*, 5: 3, (1986).
44. Dryzek, *op. cit.*, p. 178.
45. Jurgen Schmandt in Jurgen Schmandt and Hilliard Roderick, *Acid Rain and Friendly Neighbours, The Policy Dispute between Canada and the United States*, (Duke University Press, 1985), p. 251.
46. John E. Carroll (ed.), *International Environmental Diplomacy: The Management and Resolution of Transfrontier Environmental Problems*, (Cambridge University Press, 1988), pp. 277–8.
47. Bougainville is much disused by Australian and New Zealand Greens. See also Kemp and Wall, *op. cit.*, p. 17.
48. Young, *op. cit.*, p. 170.
49. Kemp and Wall, *op. cit.*, p. 87.
50. *Ibid.*
51. *Ibid.*, p. 125.
52. *Ibid.*, p. 127.

Index